Reviews

"You have an amazing story."
          -Heidi Mitchell, Literary Agent, D.C. Jacobson & Assoc. LLC

"This is a totally absorbing read and an honest one."
          - Dr. Sam Lowry, Publisher, Ambassador International

Wow! What a great trip for me to the past that never gets old. Whether you know a little of the story, a lot of the story, or none of the story at all, this book is a must read.

While it's a story about two people who came from two completely different backgrounds, you can't help but get totally encapsulated in how God brought Ben and Anita together. They shared their lives with each other in ways most people can't or maybe won't, living their dreams along the way, used by God to touch thousands of others, including myself, with their undying love for those around them whether in the USA or Liberia. Do you want to read a true love story? A story of intrigue and surprises? A story of how difficult it is to live in another culture and the problems a black man and a white woman face when they fall in love? Finally, do you want to read a story about how God's Love can sustain someone through the good times and the bad times? Then read this book!
I, for one, have become a better person over my lifetime because of my friendship with Ben and Anita Dennis and their boys! This book has helped me to love them even more!

Rev. Dr. Robert M. Roegner
LCMS World Mission, Missionary to Liberia, West Africa 1981-90
LCMS World Mission, Area Secretary for Africa 1990-96
Lutheran Bible Translators, Executive Director 1996-99
LCMS World Mission, Executive Director 2001-2008

Beyond Myself: The Farm Girl and The African Chief is an honest and enthralling true story about a cross-cultural and interracial love that develops between a farm girl and an African chief in the midsixties and spans nearly five decades. It's about love, loyalty, forgiveness, and the adventures that can unfold when one chooses to walk the path less traveled, which often winds outside of our comfort zone and straight into uncertainty.

When Anita enrolls in Anthropology 101 as a sophomore in college, the last thing she expects is to strike up a friendship and eventually fall in love with her professor, who is not only many years her senior but who also bears the marks of an African chief in star-shaped scars on his cheeks. In an era far less accepting of interracial relationships than today, the notion of a relationship between a black man and white woman has "scandalous" written all over it. Anita navigates the conflicting emotions of a budding love toward the end of the civil rights movement with parents who oppose it strongly.

I thought I had experienced pushback when I married a South African man in the twenty-first century, and I assumed I'd experienced Africa in my two and a half years living in South Africa. However, as I read her story, I found myself continually in awe of her ability to surrender to all that was placed before her. I loved her honesty and rawness as she shared her experiences and treasured her ability to forgive.

—Holly Mthethwa, author of *Hot Chocolate in June*

I love your prose. It is only you that would narrate the intricacies of Gbandi and Mende life and culture in such a fascinating manner. With your commanding knowledge of your husband's people, you weave together an intriguing account of your lives together. Even readers who are not familiar with Gbandi and Mende culture will have little problem in understanding your story. I learned a lot about Dr. Dennis in your book about slavery and racism, but I got a clearer knowledge of him from *Beyond Myself*.

—Losay Lalugba, son of the late chief Lalugba of Vahun

Beyond Myself

THE FARM GIRL AND THE AFRICAN CHIEF

God bless you, Carol ! Love, Anita

ANITA KATHERINE DENNIS

WESTBOW®
PRESS
A DIVISION OF THOMAS NELSON
& ZONDERVAN

WestBow Press books may be ordered through booksellers or by contacting:

WestBow Press
A Division of Thomas Nelson & Zondervan
1663 Liberty Drive
Bloomington, IN 47403
www.westbowpress.com
1 (866) 928-1240

Scripture taken from the Holy Bible, NEW INTERNATIONAL VERSION®. Copyright © 1973, 1978, 1984 by Biblica, Inc. All rights reserved worldwide. Used by permission. NEW INTERNATIONAL VERSION® and NIV® are registered trademarks of Biblica, Inc. Use of either trademark for the offering of goods or services requires the prior written consent of Biblica US, Inc.

ISBN: 978-1-4908-5955-2 (sc)
ISBN: 978-1-4908-5957-6 (hc)
ISBN: 978-1-4908-5956-9 (e)

Library of Congress Control Number: 2014920138

Printed in the United States of America.

WestBow Press rev. date: 11/20/2014

CONTENTS

I will sing of the Lord's great love forever;
with my mouth I will make your faithfulness known
through all generations.
—Psalm 89:1

Guinea

Sierra
Leone

Voinjama

Lofa County

Ivory
Coast

Monrovia

AFRICA

LIBERIA

LIBERIA   Atlantic Ocean

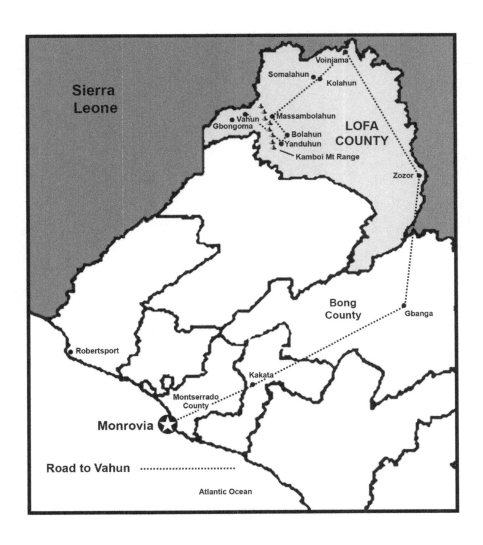

Sierra
Leone

Voinjama

Somalahun
Kolahun

Vahun
Gbongoma
Massambolahun
LOFA
COUNTY
Bolahun
Yanduhun
Kamboi Mt Range

Zozor

Bong
County
Gbanga

Robertsport

Kakata

Montserrado
County

Monrovia

Road to Vahun

Atlantic Ocean

Cast of Characters in Alphabetical Order

Some names have been changed
in a spirit of Christian love.

Allen and Mary Lou—first team of missionaries in Vahun
Angie Brooks Randolph—Ben's sister
Ben Jr.—my oldest son
Benii—major masked being of the Mende tribe
C. C. Dennis—Ben's America-Liberian uncle; Jimmy Dennis' father
Carol and George—second set of missionaries in Vahun
Chief Ngombu Tejjeh—powerful Mende chief in Guma District, Lofa
    County, during the 1800s
Dennis and Chris—third set of missionaries in Vahun
Doris—Jimmy Dennis' wife
Edgar—black community leader in Flint
Ellen Johnson Sirleaf—president of Liberia, 2006–present
Etna and Elliott Acolatse—Ben's America-Liberian friends
Gary, Eddie, Mary, Ophelia, Ken, Karen, Phil, Julie, Donna, and Becky—
    summer study abroad students, 1973
Hattie—my friend in New York City
Harry—Ben's Gbandi nephew
Hawah—widow of Gbandi chief Boaki Kovah
J. Rud & Gladys—Ben's Gbandi relatives
Jim—my older brother
Jimmy Dennis—Ben's America-Liberian cousin
Joanna—my baby sister
Joe—my middle son
Kpanah—Momoh's wife

Kpanah Mali—Ben's Gbandi mother
Miriam—my cook in Vahun
Morlu—Ben's Gbandi brother in Somalahun
Momoh—our next-door neighbor in Vahun
Moses, Timbeh, and Salia—my houseboys
Nancy—my sister-in-law, Patrick's wife
Ngombu Tejjeh Dennis—Ben's Mende father
Old Man Brima—Ben's oldest Mende brother in Vahun
Pastor Danielson—Mende lay pastor in Vahun
Patrick—Ben's Mende brother in Vahun
Peter—youngest son
Richie—Hattie's son
Rev. Strickland—pastor of Mt. Zion Baptist Church, Athens, Ohio
Samuel Doe—head of the 1980 coup and president of Liberia 1985–90
Sandy—my older sister
Solomah—Ben's Gbandi nephew
Thomas—Ben's Mende nephew
William R. Tolbert Jr.—president of Liberia 1971–1980
William V. S. Tubman—president of Liberia 1944–1971
Winona—Ben's daughter from his first marriage

INTRODUCTION

No one is born naturally or spiritually with
character; it must be developed.
—Oswald Chambers, *My Utmost for His Highest*

Massambolahun, Upcountry Liberia, West Africa, summer, 1973

It was 9 p.m. and pitch black. I was a 27-year-old, red-headed white woman sitting in the chief's chair at the front of an open meeting house. My husband, Ben, was with grateful elders, so I was taking his place of honor. In my lap was our 4-year-old son, Bengie, kept awake by the rapid-fire drumming and the roar of rain on the corrugated zinc roof. By the light of kerosene lanterns, Gbandi dancers gyrated acrobatically up the center aisle. Men and women on crowded wooden benches stared at me.

#

Scenes from my past remind me of 1950s Tarzan movies I watched as a child. The minute our Land Rover stopped, crowds enveloped us with drums booming and women playing *sassas* (beaded gourds). The jeeps carrying our traveling party zipped around us. As if on cue, lightning lit up the sky and it poured. The crowd ran to the meeting house. I was swept up with it, carrying Bengie in my arms.

We began our journey that morning in Monrovia, the capital of Liberia. Our intention was to reach Vahun—Ben's father's village—by nightfall. However, as we progressed toward it, successive Gbandi villages delayed us with their outpourings of gratitude. We were traveling on a new road, bulldozed by a Swedish company, at the request of the Liberian president, William R. Tolbert Jr., as a favor to Ben.

At midnight, a tall Gbandi man summoned me away from the meeting house, a break in the rain giving Ben the opportunity to push on. The rudimentary road over the Kamboi mountain range looked like the mighty hand of God Himself had clawed a path through the forest; felled trees lay scattered on both sides. The thunderstorm transformed the road's red clay surface into greasy ooze. Gullies were beginning to cross it in various places. Even when dry, Kamboi's steepest incline was navigable only by a 4-wheel-drive vehicle. During the height of rainy season, the road was impassible.

As we drove away, a soft rain began, the headlights barely piercing the night. The rain and fog on the windshield made it hard for me to see from the front passenger seat. On both sides of the road, the remaining cotton trees stood as eerie sentinels. The only sound in the vehicle was the wipers knocking back and forth. Thankfully, Bengie was asleep in my lap.

We edged down a slope and onto a two-log bridge—one log for each set of wheels. I held my breath. Just past the bridge, we were mired in clay. The driver stopped, grinding into 4-wheel drive for the steepest incline; the men's musty, nervous sweat revealed their palpable anxiety.

I looked up, fear fueling my imagination. I wanted to see the world, but this was beyond anything I had dreamed of. Only God could get us through this. I was terrified. Closing my eyes, I willed myself to sleep. I didn't want to witness our deaths. Exhaustion took over.

That ride over Kamboi wasn't the only time I desperately needed to trust God. Marrying Ben had been a challenge in itself—another step in my journey of faith. In the many steps to follow, I learned that stereotypes contain elements of truth but are never the whole picture. To get that, you must let my memory snapshots unfold as they happened. The account of Ben's life has been told. This is my story.

CHAPTER 1

Anthropology 101

◇◇◇◇◇◇◇◇◇◇◇◇◇◇◇

We are our choices.
—Jean-Paul Sartre

Ohio University, my sophomore fall term, 1964

I was careful to be early quickly grabbing an aisle seat in the second row. The other students scrambling for seats instantly quieted down as Dr. Dennis strode into the room and plunked his large briefcase down on the small table in front. He fit the image of a professor in his dark suit, white shirt, pencil-thin tie, '60s glasses, and side-part "college boy" haircut. If not for the star markings on his cheeks, he could easily have passed for a black American.

Four campus jocks sauntered in as he emptied his briefcase. Since all the seats were taken, they stood along the back wall. My hope to remain in this class was dashed.

Dr. Dennis announced, "My name is Benjamin Dennis. I'm serious about anthropology. I expect the same from you. I want you here for every class because, in addition to the readings, the lecture material will be on the exams."

I looked over the syllabus—3 books to read and a term paper, as well as the exam dates and grading scale. I'd never seen anything so organized or daunting.

He continued. "Sit in the same seat because I'll be taking attendance. If your score is between 2 grades, I'll check your record. Those who have been here regularly will get the higher grade. You must have your term-paper outline approved by me. Make an appointment with my secretary to see me in my office. For anyone who thinks this class is a 'Mickey,' I'll sign you out right now."

The guys standing in the back quietly came forward and took him up on his offer. As they left, I breathed a sigh of relief. I was sure this class would prove interesting. I had no idea how right I would be about that.

#

Getting into the class had been difficult. As soon as I arrived on campus after the summer of my freshman year, I decided to broaden my education and change my social studies elective in journalism. "Anthropology, the Study of Man" caught my eye as I pored over the schedule of course offerings. I loved people. I was eager to learn about other cultures. What could be more perfect? When I saw that Dr. Dennis taught it, I thought, *I may have a chance to get in at the last minute.* Unlike most other professors, he had been approachable and friendly when I met him during the spring semester of my freshman year.

That afternoon, I was scanning the ground for pebbles on the hill near the art building when I noticed someone out of the corner of my eye coming up the incline toward me, carrying a large briefcase with a golden clasp. Seeing me bent over, he offered, "May I help you?"

I continued with my task, saying, "No, I'm just collecting some stones for a potted plant."

His unusual accent made me curious, though, and I looked up, shielding my eyes from the sun behind him.

He smiled broadly and said, "My name is Benjamin Dennis. I'm a professor here. What's your major?"

"Journalism. Where are you from?"

"Liberia."

"What's that?"

"It's a small country on the west coast of Africa. In fact, my uncle's a newspaper publisher there."

"Do they have newspapers in Africa?"

"Oh, yes! Our capital, Monrovia, is a modern city. I actually grew up in Berlin, Germany. My governess and our servants were German."

Back at Bryan Hall, I told my roommates, "I just met a professor here, and he's very nice."

High school graduation picture, 1963

I had graduated from high school in the spring of 1963, and that fall I headed off to Ohio University, a fresh slate waiting to be written upon. I loved living in Bryan Hall, meeting and discovering girls from very different backgrounds. Since the university was virtually isolated within Appalachia, it offered cultural opportunities, and I took advantage of the foreign films, plays, musicals, and chamber music concerts, as well as the Kennedy lecture series. I reveled in interesting introductory classes, dorm life, new ideas, and a broad spectrum of people. I enjoyed walking around the campus and the town of Athens.

Several weeks after our first encounter, I became curious about who he was when I ran into him again. I attended the Lutheran campus services at Galbraith Chapel, having grown up Lutheran in a German rural community in Ohio. I went to the pastor's Bible studies at the Lutheran campus house during the week. At the same time, I wanted to learn what other denominations taught about God. Each Sunday, after the chapel service, I walked to Baptist, Catholic, Christian Science, Methodist, or Presbyterian churches around town.

That Sunday, I noticed a white clapboard church at the north end of Main Street. The sign under the stained-glass window, which showed "The Good Shepherd," read, "Mt. Zion Baptist Church." From the small entryway, I scanned the sanctuary. The curved walnut pews were empty. I heard a bass voice coming from the back corner. It belonged to a tall, bald black man with a mustache who stood, a Bible in his hands, before a small group of black men and women.

He smiled and said, "I'm Reverend Strickland. Please come and join us."

I sat down, and no sooner did the pastor resume his Bible class than Dr. Dennis walked in and sat down in the pew behind me. I assumed he was a church member. He later told me he thought I was a member. We were both first-time visitors.

When the class finished, he and I stayed for the service—he in one pew, I in another. Afterward he spoke with me briefly in the entryway, his broad smile and white teeth lighting up his face. We returned to the campus walking down Main Street on opposite sidewalks. I glanced over and noticed he was nicely dressed, but his shoes looked too big for him. As he strode along, he used his large black umbrella like a walking stick.

In the fall of my sophomore year, when I met with him in his office to get a change order into his class, he said, "I'm sorry, but it's already full. The sociology building is old, and the fire marshals will no longer let students stand along the back wall. Besides, I don't want people in my class that I like."

"But I really want to take this class! Isn't there *any* way I can get in?"

"Not unless someone drops it. I'll sign your change order for now, but you'll be the first to go. I must give preference to those who already signed up."

Walking back to my dorm, I puzzled over his remark about not wanting people in his class that he liked. I didn't know what to make of it. In high school, I received good grades, but I was never part of the social scene, since Dad never let me use the car to go to evening activities in Deshler, ten miles away. This professor was nothing like the local high school farm boys I grew up with, who hardly stirred my interest. As with everyone else in the sixth grade, I passed love notes to my first, second, and third boyfriends. In the eighth grade, I kissed several boys while playing spin the bottle at a friend's party. I had crushes on several intellectual boys in high school, but I never had much to put in "Dear Diary." In college, during my freshman year, I was briefly interested in a guy who lived at the Lutheran campus house, but nothing came of it.

That night, as I lay in my top bunk, I pondered what happened that day and my ignorance concerning black people—including my childhood racial baggage. As a 5-year-old in St. Louis, Missouri, I listened with my family to *Amos and Andy* on the large cabinet radio in the living room. We laughed at the jokes and assumed all Negroes were that way—funny, but lazy rascals. At bedtime, Mom read me "Little Black Sambo," complete with details about his black face, sad eyes, and grotesque mouth. Poor Sambo; he melted away in a syrupy dark-brown puddle.

In the 7th grade at Westhope School in our farm community, fifteen of us performed as pickaninies in ragged clothes for the spring festival performance. The makeup crew made us "darkies" with huge white lips. We sat in a semicircle of hay bales on the stage; our parents in folding chairs on the gym floor. A World War II veteran in the community objected, but our music teacher insisted that the Negro minstrel was a legitimate art form. I thought nothing of it.

Dressed as a little black boy, I said, "When ah takes a shower, ah sings just as loud as ah kin!"

The girl across from me said, "Why's that, Rastus?"

I said, "Cause de ain't no lock on the bafroom doh!"

In high school, I leafed through the "coon song" sheet music on Grandma Meyer's piano, wondering how that had all come about, but I said nothing. The only Negroes I ever saw were those I glimpsed out of the car window when we visited Grandma and Grandpa Reuter in Columbus.

In 1959, when I was in the 8th grade, I read about the civil rights movement in *LIFE* magazine. I scorned the injustice to Negroes and spoke to my mom about it. She said, "It's a big problem because colored people don't have the same capacity." I bristled and argued with her, even though I had no evidence to the contrary. At the same time, the movement didn't touch my life. I was focused on my own little world with its petty problems. During my freshman year at OU, for the first time, I spoke face-to-face with black people—3 roommates in a corner room at Bryan Hall. They were attractive and friendly, but they kept to themselves. I had no personal connection to blacks and couldn't imagine how much that would change.

CHAPTER 2

Friends with a Professor

◇◇◇◇◇◇◇◇◇◇◇◇◇◇

Each new friend gives the possibility of anything!
—Stephen Richards

Dr. Dennis's office, Sociology Building, Ohio University, sophomore fall term, 1964

As Dr. Dennis and I sat in his office, we pored over my term paper outline. He asked me for my ideas and gave me some of his. The hour flew by. Suddenly he looked at his watch and said, "I've got another student coming in five minutes. You need to get started on this. Why not drop by my apartment this Saturday and we'll finish our discussion? I live right on campus." Although I was surprised, I agreed and was somewhat intrigued.

\#

During his class, I was fascinated not only by anthropology but also by his depth of knowledge and confidence as a professor. Here was a man I admired, opening a world I longed to explore. He compensated for his strong accent, which often made it hard to follow his lecture, by writing anthropological terms on the blackboard. His personal interest in students was unusual. One day he announced, "I don't want any of you to throw

away an opportunity to learn. In fact, I hate stupidity as God hates sin."
Not only that, but he also gave freely of his time after class.

It turned out his tree-shaded apartment wasn't far from Bryan Hall. As
I stepped up on the wooden stoop at the front door, I noticed that the place
looked like nondescript temporary housing for graduate students, which
it was. He greeted me at the door, and I noticed his starched white shirt
had frayed cuffs. The place was small but immaculately kept. The truth is
that it looked as though he lived in poverty; the spare furniture screamed
"Appalachian second-hand store." The living room's most imposing feature
was a large mission-style desk under the window, piled high with books
and papers. The adjoining kitchen had a simple dinette.

I took a seat on the small couch, and he settled into a well-worn
rocking chair with a Naugahyde seat cover. He took out a pack of cigarettes
and offered it to me. When I declined, he lit one for himself. As we
discussed possible topics for my paper, I noticed his distinctive way of
holding the cigarette to his lips between his thumb and index finger, using
it to punctuate his points. I was eager to begin my paper after our lengthy
conversation, as I walked back to the dorm.

One day after class he said, "How's your paper coming? This is my last
class for the day. How about we discuss it while walking across campus?"
OU's lovely hilly setting was enhanced by the wooded Hocking River
skirting its buildings. During this and subsequent walks, it was heady
becoming friends with a professor. He was such an interesting person; we
never ran out of things to talk about.

From the very beginning, our shared faith was central to our relationship.
I invited him to the Bible study at the Lutheran campus house. He came
regularly, contributing to the discussion. He also accompanied me to the
campus services, explaining that he had attended a Lutheran church in
Berlin as a boy.

Along with exploring all that college had to offer, I sought to grow in
my faith. In fact, God was always part of my life—a steady rock of love I
went to in prayer to forgive my sins, allay my fears, and solve my problems.
Peace Lutheran Church, of German heritage, was the center of my family's
social life—especially the potluck dinners in the church basement. Tables
of meatloaf, potato salad, pork and sauerkraut, apple and cherry pies, and,
of course, Jell-O salad, were a delight to everyone's taste buds. The women
visited while cleaning up the kitchen. The men played cards, their cigars

generating smoke haze. We kids amused ourselves playing gossip in the infant cry room upstairs.

My childhood revolved around the seasons and our faith. Winters were time for school; summers, the farm; and every weekend, church. We attended church every Sunday unless we were ill. The highlight of Christmas was the Christmas Eve service, in which we children sang carols and each said our "piece"—a memorized Bible verse. Our excitement was enhanced by knowing we'd open our gifts under the tree when we got home.

I grew up attending Sunday school and also Saturday school, where we learned Bible history. I was confirmed in the eighth grade, after two years of classes in the church basement. On the bus ride after school, I memorized my Bible verses before the driver dropped me off at the church. I took God seriously, and my confirmation verse was "Be faithful, even to the point of death, and I will give you the crown of life."

Still, there were significant differences in our faith history. In contrast to my experience, Dr. Dennis was exposed to numerous religious influences from infancy because his father was Baptist and his mother, Muslim. As a member of an African tribe, he was familiar with animism and ancestor worship. Besides the church in Berlin, he joined the Baptist church in Monrovia as a teenager in Liberia. He knew the superstitions of the tribal people as well as the Americo-Liberians—those descendants of free Negroes and slaves that founded Liberia before the American Civil War. In America, several dynamic pastors of Negro Baptist churches had mentored him during his college days. His global perspective was evident, as he often prayed for Christian endeavors worldwide; meanwhile, I concentrated on local and personal needs.

I was attracted not only by his faith but also by his charm—his warmth and dazzling smile. What drew me as well was his underlying vulnerability. Despite his accomplishments and friendly manner, he bore an aura of loneliness. While commanding in the classroom, he was simple and humble when one-on-one.

I should have been apprehensive about where this would lead, but I wasn't.

Pals at Bryan Hall, freshman year

CHAPTER 3

Love on a College Campus

◇◇◇◇◇◇◇◇◇◇◇◇◇◇◇◇

I've blessed the day I found you.
I want to stay around you.

Without your sweet love,
What would life be?

—Jerry Butler, *Let It Be Me*

Ohio University, sophomore spring term, 1965

During the spring semester of Anthropology 102, Ben and I became good friends. I occasionally visited his apartment, and I knew he was separated from his wife and 4-year-old daughter, Winona, whom he missed very much. When I asked him why he was separated, he said in measured words, "I took this job so we could make a fresh start, but she refused to come." I would later learn the ways in which their marriage was irretrievably broken, but he didn't elaborate then.

One Sunday morning, I went to his apartment so we could walk together to the chapel. As he opened the door, he said, "My wife paid me a surprise visit."

I stood in the living room and watched a tall, attractive black woman with a nice figure come out of the door of the spare bedroom, the back zipper of her dress open.

She ignored me and ordered, "Ben, zip me up."

Ben awkwardly introduced us. "This is Anita, one of my students. She'll be going with us to church." His jaw tightened as he added, "You have to hurry up. We're going to be late."

She acknowledged me perfunctorily and returned to the bedroom. We arrived at the service twenty minutes late. Feeling uncomfortable, I was relieved to part ways with the couple at the chapel steps. On the walk back to Bryan Hall, my mind swirled with disappointment and unanswered questions. If Ben and she were on such dreadful terms as he had led me to believe, why had she come to visit?

#

After class the following Monday, I went to his office and said to him, "This doesn't look good. You're still a married man. I think we should cool our friendship."

His voice grew quietly sad but determined. "Even if our friendship ends, I'll *never* go back to her."

Having witnessed their brief exchanges and the tension between them, I believed him. He went on to tell me about the final straw, after which he moved into the spare bedroom and focused on taking care of Winona, then 2 years old and in a crib. However, he didn't separate from his wife until 2 years later, when he came to OU. I simply listened, knowing nothing of separation or divorce among my relatives.

With a look of resignation, he concluded by saying, "I'll honor your wishes."

In the classes that followed, he was distant and distracted in his lectures. I sensed he missed our friendship as much as I did. In fact, the idea of ending it made me realize how much I cared for him. I was able to stay away for only 3 weeks. One Saturday, I stopped by his apartment. His voice sounded forlorn as he answered my knock. "Come in. It's open."

As I walked in, I was surprised to see him sitting on the living room floor, clipping his toenails, wearing a bright green terry cloth bathrobe two sizes too big. His glum expression made him look as lonely and despondent as he sounded. When I said "Hello," he stared at me so intently that I realized how much I meant to him. And so our friendship deepened.

Over the Easter spring break, I told my parents I had become good friends with one of my professors—a man from Africa. They looked puzzled, but when I asked Mom if I could take him a small Easter basket, she readily agreed. We filled it with candy and a colored boiled egg. Ben was pleased and displayed it on the little shelf in his kitchen.

One day, I told him after class, "I want to take you to one of my favorite places." It was a picturesque graveyard of old tombstones that reminded me of reading Edgar Lee Masters' *Spoon River Anthology*. We sat on the grass in the shade of a large tree on top of a hill overlooking rows of graves, quietly contemplating death and the passage of time.

After a while, I said, "I know we're good friends, but do you think of me as a girl?"

He smiled and said with his usual easygoing charm, "Of course! Why wouldn't I?"

"Are you interested in me that way?"

"Yes, I am."

I was excited but tried not to show it. As if by arrangement, a light rain began. We rushed back to campus, and he offered to cook supper for me. That simple meal of baked chicken breasts covered with tomato paste, a pot of rice, and canned green beans was the best I ever ate. We sat and talked in our "five-star" restaurant as though we were the only two people in the whole wide world.

After dinner, his eyes lingered on me as he said, "Nya lo ngo a bie."

"What's that?"

"It's my mother's Gbandi language. It means 'You are my friend. I love you.'"

That evening, he kissed me for the first time. It was awkward— certainly not a movie-screen kiss—and I was repelled by the cigarette smoke on his breath.

Afterward, he said, "Kissing is a Western thing. The Mendes don't do it. At least, I never saw them."

I said, "If you want to keep kissing me, that smoking has to go."

While he smoked two packs a day, the air in his apartment never bothered me since he kept the windows open. The following week, he quit cold turkey. We commenced to do "the Western thing," and it took my breath away.

Our relationship grew through simple activities: taking walks, visiting in his apartment, eating meals together. We were perfectly content with everyday activities. Nothing elaborate was needed.

Spring in southern Ohio was a wonderful time to fall in love; the Appalachian Mountains covered with budding green trees made an ideal backdrop. One afternoon, we explored the extensive grounds of the nearby state mental hospital with its quiet ponds and gracefully drooping elm trees. We walked up a grassy hill and lay on our backs. No one could see us as we watched puffy white clouds float by in a gloriously blue sky. We were alone in the world; in love and deliciously happy. I wanted to stay there forever where nothing could touch us.

I asked him, "What are those markings on your cheeks?"

He said, "They were put on my face when I was 8 days old to identify me as royalty. I'm descended from a very powerful Mende chief named Ngombu Tejjeh. This process began during the days of slavery to keep Africans of other tribes from capturing leaders of the society. After the cuts were made, ashes were rubbed into them to ensure a lasting scar."

As poster children for "opposites attract," we joked about our obvious differences. He was shorter than I was, and I discovered his large shoes were "elevators" that made him an inch and a half taller. Since he was 16 years older than me, I called him "Old Man."

He loved my red hair, which came from my Scotch-Irish great-grandmother, and he called me "White Girl." He admired my erect shoulders, saying his were rounded because he had slept in the same bassinet with his twin brother. I called his wide feet with short toes "elephant feet." He countered by saying my narrow feet had "finger toes."

On one of our walks by the river, I teased, "You're so old, I bet I can beat you in a race." We were running neck and neck when he suddenly took off as if I were standing still.

Catching my breath, I said, "Where'd you learn to run like that?"

Flashing his famous smile, he said, "Soccer."

His love of animals endeared him to me. He left peanuts on the ledge outside his office window for a squirrel he named Suzie. At his apartment, a calico cat he named Tiger, "adopted" him and had one litter after another. One night, the neighbors complained about the howling tomcats by his window. When he discovered a raccoon eating Tiger's food, he splashed boiling water on it to kill it. Several days later, he was relieved to see it back again because he felt guilty.

He was everything I wasn't—highly educated with a dual doctorate degree in anthropology and sociology, teaching classes in both disciplines. He intrigued me with his British expressions, such as "step up" and "buck up," from his days at Queens College, Oxford University. He had lived in Africa and Europe and had visited India and Japan. As a foreign student during the 1950s, he saw a lot of the United States—something I never did.

In contrast, enrolling at Ohio University was, in many ways, the beginning of my life, having come from a secure but isolated childhood on a farm in northwestern Ohio. Even then we weren't a typical farm family. When I was 5 years old, we moved from a brick home in the suburbs of St. Louis, Missouri, where Dad worked for the Monsanto Chemical Company as a chemical engineer. Life changed drastically when he decided to work one of the farms Grandpa Meyer acquired during the Great Depression. Sandwiched between two sisters, I felt that nothing special was done for me. I just got along and tried to do my part.

In terms of politics, my parents were staunch Republicans. When Mom said, "Harry Truman was a good president," it was significant because it meant a Democrat could do something right. In 1960, when I asked her if she was going to vote for Richard Nixon, she said, "Everyone's vote is *private*. That's why you go into a booth." During the campaign when I was in high school, my brother, Jim, took my older sister, Sandy, and me to Deshler, a whistle stop for Nixon on the B&O railroad. The crowd, which screamed and cheered, was sure that the country was headed for a disaster if John Kennedy was elected.

My mailing address was the village of Malinta, 5 miles away. Mom bought groceries in Hamler, 5 miles in another direction. When I described Malinta as "one stoplight, a grocery store, a hardware store, a post office, and 2 churches," Ben kidded me with a Bible reference: "Can anything good come out of Nazareth? Indeed it has!" The only traveling I did prior to college was a visit to Biloxi, Mississippi, when Jim was in the air force, and a senior high school class trip to Washington, DC.

Ben's English accent—a mixture of Mende, Gbandi, and German sounds—made communication a challenge. He had his own unique way of pronouncing words. Like everyone else, I had trouble deciphering what he meant.

One afternoon, we were buying groceries at the local Kroger store. Ben discovered I liked caramel syrup over ice cream. Determined to please me, he told the clerk, "I want to buy some cameral syrup."

She said, "What's that, sir?"

"Cameral syrup."

"What?"

"Stuff you put on ice cream."

"Oh, you mean *caramel* syrup."

"That's right."

She yelled to the back, "Mike, would you check if we have caramel syrup?"

Mike shouted back, "What kind of syrup?"

Ben yelled, "Cameral syrup!"

"*What?*"

The clerk, who knew Ben, said, "Wait a minute, sir, let *me* tell him."

We laughed about it on the way back to his apartment.

One day, he told me, "I'm going to call you Nita. That will be my pet name for you."

Another time, he gave me *The Prophet* by Kahlil Gibran, inscribing it, "It's not the size of a gift that matters, but the love with which it's given." When he said, "Knowing you is like falling in love for the first time; you'll always be loved," I thought, *Wow. This guy is romantic.*

Near the end of the spring semester, he said, "I've found my love song for you. I chaperoned one of the sorority dances last Saturday night, and they played it. I just bought the record." On his cheap record player, we listened to "Let It Be Me" on an album by Jerry Butler. It became his love song to me.

I was concerned about our future together. Instead of visiting a foreign country, I "fell in love with one." We were the most unlikely marriage candidates—the classic odd couple. He was a 35-year-old black professor. I was a 19-year-old white college student. I grew up on an Ohio farm. He came from an African village. My view of the world was naive and narrow. His mindset was global and sophisticated.

We were taking a great risk. Firstly, we were in a forbidden professor/student liaison, and secondly, interracial marriages were uncommon and against the law in 17 states in the 1960s. In 1955, a decade earlier, Emmett Till, a 14-year-old black teenager was murdered while visiting relatives in Mississippi for supposedly flirting with a white woman. Even in Ohio, we couldn't ignore the realities of an interracial relationship. On top of that, the cultural differences seemed overwhelming. He was descended from a powerful chief. How could I be a chief's wife?

A girl in the dorm warned me, "If you go with a black man, no white man will have you." It was one thing to walk along the Hocking River or visit cemeteries in Athens, where we were deliriously in love and "nothing could touch us." It was quite another thing each time we reached the campus and had to "return to earth," Ben heading to his apartment and I to my dorm. He wanted marriage, not an affair, and he used all his charm to break down my reservations, explaining that it wasn't as big a deal in Europe as it was in America.

When I voiced objections to marrying an older man, he told me about Clyde and Florence Kluckhohn, the famous anthropology team in which professor and student became partners in more ways than one, coauthoring several books.

When I insisted, "We can never marry. I can't live in Africa" (my dreams of going to Australia were one thing; this was quite another), he said, "I'm living here now. My career is here."

"Well, I can never leave my church," I protested.

He replied calmly, "I'm Baptist now, but I'll consider joining your faith. As you know, I'm familiar with the Lutheran church. I'll examine its teachings further. If I agree, I'll join."

"I don't think we should have biracial children. Look at all the problems they'd face. We could just adopt."

He said firmly, "I want my own children."

For the time being, I was head over heels in love with him and wanted to spend the rest of my life at his side. I could give him the stability he craved; he would provide me the adventure I longed for. While he opened the world to me, I'd give him the personal love he needed.

Ben and I in the early days

Going home that summer, I knew I'd somehow have to tell my parents that my friendship with the African professor had graduated into something much more serious. I was named "Anita" after my mother, and I was always close to her. During high school, Dad gave me the same nickname Mom's father gave her—"Neetsie." We became close during the spring of my college freshman year when I invited him to Father's Weekend. As he strode across the campus on his long legs, he looked younger than his 50 years. He opened up about his own college days as we attended the welcome tea and went on the college tour. His parting words were, "When you left for college, you were the apple of my eye." I didn't realize how drastically our relationship would change.

CHAPTER 4

The Price I Paid

◇◇◇◇◇◇◇◇◇◇◇◇◇

Out of the blue, she brings this man home,
and you expect me to accept this?
—Spencer Tracy in *Guess Who's Coming to Dinner*

Ohio University, junior fall semester, 1965

I was walking with Mom and Dad across campus to the School of Journalism. We passed the sociology building. I looked up at Ben's office window. Suddenly I darted away and ran up the stairs to the second floor, desperate to at least say good-bye.

Rushing into his office, I saw his broad smile as he rose from his chair and said, "You're back! Have a seat. I'm glad to see you! How was your Thanksgiving?"

I blurted out, "I had to come and say farewell. My parents are taking me out of school."

With anguish in his voice, he said, "Oh, Nita, how can they do this to you? I can't believe it. It's so unfair. You're almost at the end of the semester. I'm the one to blame. I never wanted this to happen to you!" He stood there, his arms motionless by his side, tears streaming down his cheeks.

I longed to put my arms around him. Instead I steeled myself and quickly said, "I can't stay. They're waiting for me," and I ran out.

Mom and Dad said nothing as I joined them on the sidewalk. At the School of Journalism, the director said, "Wouldn't you like to rethink this? She's doing so well." It was no use. Dad was adamant and would give no explanation.

At Bryan Hall, as I packed my clothes, my roommate said, "You don't have to go. You're of age, you know." Some girls from down the hall came into my room and chimed in, but I couldn't heed their advice. Although I was nineteen, I thought my father knew best.

#

Recently a white woman asked me, "Just because you don't want your daughter to marry a black man because of the trouble she'll face, does that make you a racist?" Her question startled me, revealing the realities of racism lingering in the twenty-first century, despite the changes since the 1960s. I can only describe the price I paid.

The summer after my sophomore year, when I told my parents I had fallen in love with Ben, their primary objection was that he was married. They never mentioned race—the elephant in the room. Even for myself, I couldn't justify the fact that Ben was black and African, not to mention 16 years older than me and still married. I knew it would be hard for them to accept that Ben was separated but not yet divorced, but I told them anyway because I trusted them. They had never let me down.

My announcement destroyed my father's dream of a normal life for me. The shock on his face quickly turned to anger. With all the determination he could muster, he demanded, "This can't continue. If you want to go back to school this fall, you have to promise *never* to see him again. That's all there is to it." He got up from the kitchen table and left the room. There was no doubt he meant it. From that point on, he was relentless in trying to save me from "the error of my ways."

That summer, Dad's ultimatum hung over my head like a sword of Damocles. From every angle, any future with Ben looked like an impossible dream. We were from two different worlds. Everyone and everything was against us.

Ironically, that summer was also filled with success. I continued pursuing a journalism degree despite my growing interest in anthropology and sociology and had secured a 3-month internship at a local paper in Napoleon, 20 miles away. It was exciting to work in a newspaper office. The publisher and I came up with a plan for me to write a series of articles about local historical figures as well as our local claim to fame—Girty's Island in the Maumee River, once inhabited by Simon Girty, a liaison between the British and their Indian allies during the American Revolution. I also had the opportunity to sample news reporting and advertising.

The city news reporter was my age, and we became good friends. She comforted me when the sports writer called me "Virginia," with an emphasis on "virgin" that made me blush. I shared my relationship dilemma with her, and we commiserated since she didn't have a boyfriend and I was losing mine. It was exhilarating to try my wings in journalism. I met many people and was pleased to see my name in a byline. The series of historical articles was a great success, prompting more subscriptions. Mom and Dad shared my fifteen minutes of local fame when people from church said the articles were interesting.

At the same time, I was haunted and in mourning because I could see no way out of my predicament. My parents didn't harp on the issue, but I was well aware they would never relent, especially Dad. I knew I should obey them, but I couldn't bear the thought of losing Ben. I was determined to return to college that fall. Our love seemed hopeless, a big mistake after all. I finally bowed to my parents' wisdom and will – without hope. Worn down, I reluctantly agreed to never see Ben again, sincerely intending to keep my promise.

That fall of my junior year, when I arrived back on campus, all the wonderful memories from the previous spring flooded my mind. Nothing was the same without Ben. Three weeks after classes began, I stopped by his apartment, rationalizing to myself that I simply wanted to see if he was okay. As soon as I saw him, I melted, knowing how much I still loved him. During that fall semester of my junior year, we resumed our relationship until the Thanksgiving break.

When I arrived home for the break, Dad wasted no time as we sat at the kitchen table for supper. With Mom watching, he asked directly, "Are you seeing Ben?"

I meekly answered, "Yes."

He said, "Well, then, I warned you. That's it. We're taking you out of school."

After they took me out of school, dead silence ruled on the drive home from OU. I sat in back, lost and in shock.

The next morning at breakfast, Dad said, "You have to meet with the pastor." I didn't look forward to it, knowing what he'd say, but I had no choice. In the pastor's office at the parsonage, he sat behind his desk in a black suit, his dark hair slicked with Brylcreem. He fiddled with his tie clasp. I knew instantly that Dad had filled him in when he began by saying firmly, "This relationship is *sin* because he's a married man. When you take what doesn't belong to you and you repent, you give it back. There can *never* be any future relationship with him, because of how it began. The only way to be right with God is to have *nothing* more to do with him."

He never addressed race. Since Ben was still married, I had no counter argument. Deep down inside, I agreed that everything with Ben had started out wrong. I left feeling forlorn. A week later, a letter from Ben arrived. Excited, I ripped it open, only to read how devastated he was. I hardly had time to digest it before Dad walked into the living room and demanded, "Hand it to me. No more letters." I became more dejected.

That winter on our remote, all-too-quiet farm, I was a zombie, snatched from the life I loved. The Ohio skies were gray; my life was grayer. I moved into Jim's empty front bedroom and sunk into a deep depression. Long hours of sleep were my only escape. I went through the motions, taking one step after another with no idea what came next. Solemn politeness ruled the home atmosphere. I wanted to escape my life that had no future. I didn't even *want* a future. There was no hope, no promise of anything.

My parents' drastic action took its toll on them as well. Their world was turned upside down, just like mine. People at church wondered why I hadn't gone back to school after the Thanksgiving break. In February, Dad was hospitalized with a bleeding ulcer; ¾ of his stomach was removed.

Mom and I were getting ready to visit him in the hospital. She was hardly a typical farm wife—fashion conscious and never without makeup. We were using the mirror together when I bumped my watch off the counter and into the toilet. Fishing it out, I sobbed, "It's ruined! It's the watch Ben gave me." She said nothing, but she looked at me intently with pity in her eyes, and I loved her for it. She had no choice but to agree with Dad. However, she never lectured me.

In March I helped Mom spruce up the house, tackling her to-do list. I sewed bedspreads, hung pictures, and selected accent pieces for the living room. It was good, at least, to be doing *something*. I bought Dad farm pictures to hang on his office wall.

One afternoon, I walked into his office and he abruptly quit typing. He turned and asked me, tight-lipped, "How far have you and Ben gone? Are you still a virgin?"

I felt humiliated and meekly whispered, "Yes."

I never hated or blamed my parents, because I had no answer for their reasonable objections.

In April, Dad said, "It's time for you to join the real world. I want you to get a job and pay rent."

I applied at the Campbell's Soup Company in Napoleon since I had no spirit or credentials for anything else. In fact, I had worked there the summer after my freshman year of college to earn spending money. The "tomato pack" was hardly glamorous. I sat on a stool in a blasting hot factory, sorting tomatoes rolling by on screeching metal rollers as the foreman screamed instructions in my ear. Each afternoon, I left work with ringing ears and damp hair plastered under my hairnet. I needed the money, and I knew it was temporary.

When I began my new job, the only opening was the 3 p.m. to midnight shift. I worked on the top floor of the factory with four other women. We used large metal forks to fit soup cans on a conveyor belt when they were needed, or to stack them in a bin when they weren't. The noise was so loud that the foreman banged his steel pole on the concrete floor to get our attention. Working in a coal mine was the only thing that seemed worse.

One night, I made the mistake of telling one of the women why I was there. After that, factory gossip guaranteed that I ate alone in the cafeteria. Sometime after I left, I ran into a man who worked there, and he said to me, "We couldn't figure how a pretty girl like you could fall for a colored man."

Me, pretty? I was in jeans and a shirt with a hairnet! Those night hours ensured I had no social life. Besides, I was a misfit in my farming community. I slept until late, ate lunch, and got ready for work. It was pitch black when I pulled into our gravel driveway after work, the house dark and quiet. I went straight to bed. Somehow I made it through another day. I paid rent.

July came and Dad didn't know what to do with me. Sandy was teaching in a parochial school in Baltimore, Maryland. She invited me to spend the rest of the summer with her. Dad allowed me to leave home on one condition—I'd never contact Ben again. Figuring all was hopeless, I agreed.

Baltimore was my "escape from jail." I had to support myself if I wanted to stay. I scoured newspaper offices, but the reply was always the same: "You've only completed a high school degree. Sorry, we can't hire you."

My options were limited.

CHAPTER 5

Fork in the Road

◇◇◇◇◇◇◇◇◇◇◇◇◇◇

God never gives us strength for tomorrow, or for the next hour,
but only for the strain of the moment.
—Oswald Chambers, *My Utmost for His Highest*

Sandy's apartment in Baltimore, July 1966

In the small living room, my hands shook as I opened the letter from United Airlines. It said, "Congratulations. This is to inform you that you have been selected for training in the United Airlines Stewardess Program. Please report to our office next week." I was thrilled to know I'd been accepted, but the letter arrived a day too late—all in God's plan.

\#

Journalism looked like a dead end, so I mulled over two other options. I would either become an airline stewardess or join a new church program I had heard about called the Prince of Peace Volunteers, where young people spread Christianity among the urban poor while living alongside them.

When I applied at United Airlines, the woman in charge said, "You'll get a letter in a week if we're interested."

Back at Sandy's apartment, I prayed, "Lord, if You want me to be a stewardess, let me hear in seven days. If not, I'll go into the Prince of Peace Program."

A week went by—no letter. I signed up for the church program. A day later, the United Airlines acceptance letter arrived, but the decision was made. I took my sign from God seriously. That September, I boarded a bus for New Haven, Connecticut, to be trained to work in the slums.

We 10 young people came from different backgrounds—some dropouts from college, others interested in missionary work—all of us searching to find ourselves. We were driven to an old house in a blighted area not far from the Yale University campus. The pastor leading our 6-week training resided in the parsonage down the street. We lived like the poor to identify and empathize with them. The policy was that we would receive living expenses only, our limited communal food budget guaranteeing we ate like the destitute—few vegetables, little meat, and lots of starch.

At one point, we participated in a demonstration against the demolition of our neighborhood to clear the way for upscale townhouses, virtually eliminating the poor from that area of town. We were part of a sit-in at the mayor's office along with local organizers and a handful of college students. It wasn't long before a police officer announced, "If you don't leave immediately, we'll arrest you." I was afraid of having a prison record, so I left, as did most of our group. The pastor bailed out the two guys who stayed.

A day later, I wrote to a blind friend who lived in Bryan Hall. I had introduced her to Ben, and she took a sociology class from him. After I left the campus, she continued her friendship with him. On one level, I realized that any relationship with him was impossible. At the same time, I wondered whatever happened to him. I wrote her about my adventures and then added, "By the way, how's Ben?"

A week later, a letter arrived—with Ben's return address. I held my breath while tearing open the envelope. The minute I read his scrawled handwriting, I knew I never stopped loving him. Ten minutes later, I called him on our one telephone in the living room. I poured out my heart to him with the entire group listening—much to my chagrin.

We wrote each other often. When I had an abscessed tooth, the church paid to have it pulled. Ben covered the expense to replace it with a permanent bridge.

In October, we were sent by twos to different cities. My partner was Beth, a high school graduate who limped as a result of childhood polio. We were assigned to the Bronx in New York City—an even greater culture shock than New Haven; so unlike anything I'd ever known. Under the direction of a Lutheran church, we were to help with outreach into the changing neighborhood. The influx of black and Hispanic families triggered "white flight," and the German immigrant congregation dwindled.

Each morning, we reported to the church and were given various duties supervised by the vicar, such as teaching weekday religious classes to public schoolchildren or tutoring black kids in reading. Beth concentrated on that area. My focus was the Hispanic congregation, which worshipped in the adjacent chapel; I attended services and visited families to foster fellowship within the group.

Steve, the church social worker, arranged for Beth and me to stay in a rented room at a nearby house owned by a Hispanic family. The double bed, which the two of us shared, had seen better days. Whenever we laid in it, we quickly sank down and rolled into each other. The refrigerator froze everything, giving a new meaning to the term "crisp lettuce."

A week later we moved into a large apartment building within walking distance of the church. Some of the units were very nice. Our place, with its secondhand furniture, was not one of them. Each time we opened a kitchen cupboard, a swarm of cockroaches scrambled every which way. The management sprayed if we called them, but it was a hopeless battle.

On Christmas Eve, Ben called to wish me a Merry Christmas. We were keeping in touch by phone, and I later found out that during those months his phone bills were over $300—in the '60s! I received a letter from him every day except Sunday—two on Mondays. He professed his undying love as he wrote, "White Girl, you are really living inside of me." He knew the obstacles I was facing. He couldn't promise they would end, but he said, "No one will love you the way I do—ever." Each letter described his loneliness and longing for me. I was the most important thing in his life. Without me, his apartment was empty and nothing would ever be the same. The highlight of his day was to sit down in the evening and write me before he went to bed.

At the same time, he lamented that his divorce was taking forever. He suspected his lawyer wasn't on his side since he was a family friend, but he refused to change attorneys because he thought it would make the case drag on longer. I began to wonder if he would ever be free.

I wrote a former roommate at Bryan Hall, hoping she'd sympathize. She answered with a scathing reply, "You should be *ashamed* of yourself. You've shamed and alienated your parents. Absolutely nothing good can ever come from this! Come to your senses."

No one held any hope for our relationship. I never heard, "Marry him; he's worth it," or received any suggestion that our union would last. Around that time, I received news of 2 cousins my age marrying perfectly matched men. I was envious until I heard that one of them divorced after having 2 babies and the other ended up living in one state, her husband in another.

In January of 1967, I wrote my parents with the truth. After Dad learned that Ben and I were in contact again, he sent a steady stream of typed letters, each telling me that I betrayed Mom and him; he said my soul was in grave danger and I was headed straight for hell. A few weeks later, four boxes arrived at my apartment containing the possessions I had left at home.

I loved Ben, but he was nowhere around. The perpetual delay in his divorce seemed like an eternity to me. With things looking impossible, I distracted myself with my work.

My other church assignment was to visit German shut-ins from the congregation. When I knocked, Hattie, blind, groped her way to the door in a wheelchair, one leg amputated at the knee from diabetes. She had worked at Macy's in Herald Square, and she explained, "My reward each day when I got off work was a banana split heaped with toppings." She looked older than her 60s, her housedress rumpled and her straight white hair in a careless side part. She was eager to talk. Her 21-year-old son, Richie, was hardly home, working long hours in his brother-in-law's print shop on Long Island.

In mid-February, the pastor in charge of the Prince of Peace program requested a meeting. From behind his desk, his dark brown eyes studied me as he said, "Anita, you're doing well in our program. The people like you, and you're getting into stride. However, your father's informed us that you're involved with a married man. Is this true?"

I was stunned, but I said meekly, "I'll drop out of the program if you want me to."

He held up his hand, "Let's talk about it first. I find it helps to make a list of pros and cons. Let's do the cons first. He's still married, right?"

"Yes."

"He's considerably older than you."

"Yes."

"He's from another country." (He, too, never addressed race.)

"Yes."

"Your parents are opposed to this relationship."

"Yes."

Although the litany of negatives seemed overwhelming, to his credit, he didn't stop there.

"Okay, let's list the pros," he said.

"I know it looks impossible. The only pros I can think of are that we love each other and we're both Christians. If you only knew him ..."

Despite his sympathy for me, the expression on his face told me he doubted Ben was a Christian. I loved him as a pastor and suggested, "I understand that I'll have to drop out of the program. I'll write a letter to the congregation, but I won't tell them exactly why I'm leaving. I just hope they'll understand that I love them and this has nothing to do with them."

I left feeling abandoned by everyone. When I told Ben, he was angry with my father. "How can your parents force the program to dismiss you? You're a young, single girl. New York City is a rough place."

I stopped by to see Hattie and told her I needed a job. She suggested, "Why not try Macy's?" There was one opening—taking phone orders for a carpet-cleaning concession in an obscure, windowless office on the seventh floor. I took it.

I rented a room on the second story of an elderly church member's large house. Each night, when I came home from work, I ate supper with her as she watched her favorite TV program—the 1960s version of *Tarzan*.

I became friends with my boss at Macy's, a Jamaican woman who wore bright red lipstick. When I told her about Ben, she said, "Black American women are going to hate you. You're taking one of their good men."

One evening, I stopped to see Hattie after work. While we were talking, she momentarily passed out and was groggy as she regained consciousness. I heard a key in the lock, and Richie walked in the door. He looked like Elvis—tall and slim, with coal-black hair and grey-blue eyes. I told him what had happened, and he said, "We'd better take her to the hospital."

It was a freezing winter night. We struggled to fit her into the front seat of his black VW. At the city hospital, the auditorium was filled with beds side by side, separated by white curtains. The doctor wanted to keep her overnight, but there was nothing available. We managed to get her back into the car and take her to a private hospital. There, patients on gurneys lined the hall. That doctor couldn't admit her either. It was 2 a.m. Hattie was exhausted, and so were we. At her apartment, the two of us could barely lift her into bed.

The next day, I stopped by again after work. With panic in her voice, she said, "My body's falling apart. I've got stuff coming out of both ends. I think I'm dying. I'm scared."

I reassured her as best I knew, "Jesus said He was going to prepare a place for us in heaven. You'll be with Him."

The following morning, the church secretary called. "I'm sorry to tell you … Hattie slumped over while she was talking on the phone. She died from a brain aneurysm." The family invited me to her funeral as a special guest because they knew how much I had brightened her final year.

Richie and I had grown close through the ordeal of his mother's last days and the funeral. When he brought me home afterward, he said, "How about I show you the city?" I accepted.

I told Richie about Ben and tried to keep a certain distance. At the same time, that spring in New York was wonderful. Richie shared his city, and it became ours. We scanned the sights in all directions from the top of the Empire State Building. We sat watching the city lights from a bluff—a well-known romantic area—with cars parked around us. One Saturday, he took me to the end of Long Island. At Montauk Point, we watched the crashing waves slap the lighthouse.

Another weekend, we visited a monastery in upstate New York. I'd never seen one and was captivated by the artwork on the stone walls and the monks solemnly strolling by under the arches. It was a balmy afternoon as we ate our picnic lunch on the idyllic grounds.

In time, Richie became more than a welcome distraction. He was funny, willing to take me anywhere, and his voice softened each time he looked intently at me. When my phone calls to Ben became infrequent, Ben wondered why. My excuse of being too busy rang hollow. I told him the truth, and he insisted I choose—his love or Richie's. There was no middle ground. Deep in my heart, I was glad for his ultimatum, but it posed a dilemma. I had two very different men who adored me, but what did I want in life?

If I wanted an everyday marriage in a white community, Richie was the ideal German Lutheran candidate. In fact, in personality, he was the male version of me. As two peas in a pod, we were well matched in values.

Our birthdays were three days apart. A life with him would be a walk in the park, compared to a roller-coaster ride with Ben.

In comparison, Ben offered more promise of intellect and income as a college professor, and yet more challenge as a black man and African chief. Richie offered me a comfortable community; Ben would lead me into a whole *new* world. In the final analysis, nothing compared to Ben in my heart. During our next phone call, I told him, "I'm all yours."

I was Richie's first love. He didn't want to lose me. Each time I broke up with him, he did something dramatically romantic. The first time, he brought me a plastic jumping frog that had made me laugh hysterically when we played a game at his sister's house. The second, he managed to get tickets to *You're a Good Man, Charlie Brown*, playing in a Greenwich Village theatre since he knew I really wanted to see it. The third time, he watched for me outside the subway terminal at Macy's and insisted on driving me home, pleading his case along the way.

Finally, I made a clean break and he accepted it. Meanwhile, Ben was taking classes from the OU campus pastor and was confirmed as a Lutheran. I knew he was serious and unwavering.

That June, he invited me for a weekend visit in Columbus, 50 miles north of Athens. We hadn't seen each other for 2 years. When we first fell in love, I asked him to let his woolly hair grow. The first thing I noticed as I stepped off the Greyhound bus was his bushy hair. He reminded me of Kwame Nkrumah, who had been president of Ghana.

It took me a while to get used to being with him. We were both nervous, not knowing what to say, engaging in small talk: "How are you? How was your trip?" There was so much ground to cover. We didn't kiss until we were in the motel room, and even then, it was awkward at first.

He told me, "I'm ashamed to tell you this. While you were on the farm, I was so despondent that I wanted to kill your father for taking you away from me. I was in such a trance of rage, I reached Toledo before I realized I didn't know how to get to your farm. It brought me to my senses, and I drove home. The only way I kept my sanity while you were gone was to write a book about my mother's tribe."

Columbus was in the midst of a heat wave, but it was freezing in the room; the air conditioner setting was stuck at 60 degrees. To keep things simple, I asked Ben, "Can you see if they can bring us some blankets?"

The clerk came to the door, wiping his brow. "Sir, did you ask for *blankets?*"

Ben said sheepishly, "Yes, I did."

The clerk knitted his eyebrows. "Well, I guess you can have whatever you want, but this is sure *hard* to understand."

As soon as the door closed, we burst out laughing.

We took a day trip to Athens on Saturday so I could see the campus and the house he was renting. It was immaculate, as usual. In the kitchen, he handed me a large packet of letters addressed to me, stamped "Return to Sender"—the ones my father never showed me. He brought over the little pastel Easter basket I gave him when we first became friends. It was falling apart, the eggshell cracked and the egg dried up. How sentimental he was!

Back in Columbus, he took me to the Lazarus department store, an impressive, 9-story building downtown. In the exclusive dress department, he bought me a very expensive dress and coat ensemble—high fashion at that time. I never had anything like it.

I hated to say good-bye. I wanted to stay there with him. I watched him from the window as the bus pulled away. He stood there, waving the whole time, until he was out of sight.

The return to New York City was depressing. I was alone again and unhappy. Our time in Columbus and Athens was wonderful, but there were still uncertainties. Ben wasn't free. I somehow managed to get up on Monday and go back to work.

Three weeks later, I was in my bedroom when the landlady called from the kitchen, "There's someone at the door for you!"

I ran down the stairs to see a delivery man at the back door, holding a long box under his arm and a small package in his hand. He smiled and said, "Please sign for these." I tore open the box, which held a dozen long-stemmed red roses with a card from Ben saying, "I love you. Will you marry me?" My hands quivered as I scratched open the small box he handed me, and I gasped upon seeing a diamond engagement ring. I rushed to the phone.

He said, "I knew my case was coming up for the 6th time, so I drove to Lansing. My lawyer never even showed up. I told the judge I'd agree to any terms."

It turned out Ben's lawyer had done very well—for his wife. The settlement included $5,000 in cash, the house and the car, as well as $250 per month in child support until Winona reached 18 or graduated from high school.

The important thing was that Ben was free at last. We wasted no time. At the beginning of August, my Jamaican boss and her husband picked up the 4 boxes of my earthly possessions and took them to the shipping office. I bought a bus ticket to Athens and was on my way back to Ohio University and the love of my life.

CHAPTER 6

Do You Take This Man?

◇◇◇◇◇◇◇◇◇◇◇◇◇◇◇

No other human relationship impacts us
at the very core of our being as does marriage.
—Bill Crowder

Athens, Ohio, March 9, 1968

Our wedding day was unusually warm and sunny even for southern Ohio. Rev. Strickland, the pastor of Mt. Zion Baptist church, where we met the 2nd time, officiated. His living room was dark, the heavy drapes slightly open, softening the frayed edges of the couch's floral slipcover.

There were no fancy preliminaries. In fact, that morning I had bought a vacuum and cleaned his apartment. A 50-year-old Liberian graduate student at OU was Ben's best man. Just before the ceremony, I was introduced to the pastor's friend, a member of the church. She signed as the second witness on our marriage certificate.

Ben was in his best black suit. I wore a sleeveless white satin brocade sheath I had purchased for 12 dollars—a sample in the sewing department at Macy's—never dreaming it would one day serve as my wedding dress. Ben had offered to buy the matching wedding ring. I didn't have the heart for it since I was pregnant and this wasn't a "perfect" wedding. Instead I used a friendship ring a high school friend gave me.

#

That previous August of 1967, when I returned to the Ohio University campus, Ben told me he had been on his knees twice a day, praying that God would bring me back to him. With the future uncertain, the only thing I was sure of was his love for me and mine for him. His poignant daily love letters while I was in New York City demonstrated his faithfulness, devotion, and commitment. I knew he needed me, and I loved and trusted him with all my heart. He wouldn't betray or hurt me. I never questioned his faith or Christian commitment. I intended to make a difference in his life. He had already made a huge difference in mine.

He arranged for me to stay with an ambitious black graduate student in her apartment near the campus. I worked as a secretary for two professors in the linguistics department, spending mornings with one on the second floor of the speech building and afternoons with the other on the third floor. I wanted to get married quickly with no fanfare. However, Ben hesitated, insisting, "If we marry without your father's consent, it'll close the door for any reconciliation."

I knew my father well enough to know his feelings weren't any different, but Ben encouraged me to write my folks and ask if we could visit them for Thanksgiving so they and the pastor could meet Ben. I mentioned that Ben was divorced, and I had moved back to Athens. We were engaged and wanted their blessing.

As Thanksgiving and Christmas came and went, I checked the mail each day—nothing. The New Year arrived, but still no news from home. I trudged to work in the light snow, shivering even though I was bundled in my coat.

When I became nauseated in February, I thought it was the stomach flu. Ben said, "I want you to see my doctor." After the doctor examined me, he called me into his office. He sat at his desk, his white hair matching his lab coat. Touching his fingertips together, he cheerfully announced, "Congratulations! You're six weeks pregnant." I felt as if he had hit me in the face. My first thought was, *No matter what happens, I won't kill this baby. I'll have it and I'll raise it.*

I was the fallen woman—Hester Prynne with the scarlet letter. Ben was waiting in the car. When I gave him the news, he said soberly, "I didn't want this to happen."

We were both stunned.

Back at his apartment, I sobbed. My plan for returning to school was dashed. He tried to encourage me. "I'm happy. This is my baby. We'll get married right away. I'll tell the campus pastor." He told me later it was one of the hardest things he ever did.

My pregnancy meant the die was cast. In a way, I was relieved. After waiting almost 3 years, we were finally going to be man and wife. The next day, running errands on Main Street in Athens, I felt so ashamed walking into Woolworth's that I wondered, *If these people knew I'm an unwed mother, what would they think of me?* I hurried and finished my shopping so I could return to the privacy of my apartment.

On the day of our wedding, Ben was noticeably tense as he stood beside me. His first marriage had been a disaster, and our union wasn't taking place under the most auspicious circumstances. I, on the other hand, was naive, idealistic, and without hesitation, ignoring any uncertainty about marrying someone of another race and culture.

When the pastor intoned in his rich bass voice, "Do you take this man to be your lawfully wedded husband; to honor and obey him as long as you both shall live?" I said quietly, but firmly, "I do."

After our vows, Ben kissed me and whispered in my ear, "God gave you to me."

And so Anita Katherine Meyer became Anita Katherine Dennis.

Following the brief ceremony, we posed at a local portrait studio for a wedding picture. I can't help smiling when I look at it.

Wedding Portrait created by F. Darrel Tom, master
photographer, owner of Lamborn Studios, Athens, Ohio

We dined afterward with Ben's best man at a steak house in town, and
then Ben and I went back to our apartment. Flowers soon arrived from
the graduate student I had lived with. Six months later, I received my one
and only wedding gift—a dutch oven from my godmother, Dad's younger
sister.

That night, perhaps the enormity of my marriage affected me after all.
I spent the first evening of my "honeymoon" heaving my wedding dinner
into the toilet. Things went downhill from there. I couldn't keep ice chips
down, retching on an empty stomach. Two weeks after we married, Ben
called an ambulance at 2 a.m. As the attendants slid me in, I heard one
of them say, "She's so still, she looks dead." I was dehydrated, so I was
given IVs.

Eight days later, I was sent home with suppositories to calm my nerves.
I lay there all day, half asleep, half awake. The medication made me so
dizzy that I barely managed to totter to the bathroom, much less dare to
walk down the hall to the kitchen.

I was alone in the world except for Ben. In my guilt and depression,
I prayed, "Lord, as a sign to confirm that You've forgiven me, please let
me have a boy." I surmised that sons were important for an African chief.

Ben did what he could before he left for the office in the morning, but
my weakness and helplessness came at the worst possible time. He was
then chairman of the sociology department, overseeing its expansion into
anthropology and social work—incredibly busy hiring faculty to staff the

new departments. He came home in the afternoon as soon as he could, eager to prepare anything I might desire.

One afternoon, I said, "Strawberries sound good." He rushed out and bought some. By the time he returned, I had lost my appetite for them or anything else. Years later, he told me he wondered if he had gotten a lemon for a wife.

One night, he hosted a party for a visiting African dignitary at our apartment. I lay in the dark bedroom, listening to the loud African music. He rushed in from time to time to check on me and bring me something to eat. At one point, he walked in with a purple vase filled with gorgeous red and yellow tulips, and said, "One of the guests heard you were sick and brought these for you." How that touched my heart!

I cycled in and out of the hospital. During one of my stays, I shared a room with a 16-year-old Appalachian girl who had given birth to a big baby girl. The father was a withered 90-year-old man.

I saw them as a caricature of Ben and me and strangely identified with the girl. In my pity and concern for her, I thought, *What did she get herself into? What did I get myself into? She'll have to raise that child alone. Will I?*

During one of the father's visits, I asked them about their relationship. She looked at him and said, "Well, he was the only man around."

He retorted, "She just wouldn't leave me alone. What was I to do?"

The man and his cronies stayed every afternoon, smoking up a storm. I gasped in the smoke haze, but when I complained to the nurse, she said, "I'm sorry, but they have the right to smoke."

I persisted. "Can't you open this window by my head?"

"I don't think so." After she left, I managed to crack it open myself and survived by drawing in the fresh, cool air pouring over my face.

By the 4th month of pregnancy, my nausea had gradually disappeared. Food tasted good again. I put on weight and regained my strength. I had to get ready for this baby! I attended childbirth classes at the hospital. We bought baby clothes and a used crib for the small bedroom.

My aunt Renata, Dad's older sister, came for a visit. She had been an army nurse in New Guinea during World War II and was eager to meet Ben. She loaned us a small bassinet to put beside our bed.

Ben was very protective of me during pregnancy. When I was 8 months along and hanging new curtains I made, he put his arm by my leg so I wouldn't fall from the chair while reaching for the rod on top. He told me pregnant women became more beautiful each day.

One day I asked him, "If it's a boy, what should we name him?"

"I want him named after me. He'll have my tribal names—Benjamin Ngombu Tejjeh Gongoli Guyanh Dennis."

I was intrigued and puzzled. "How do you spell all that? What do they mean?"

"Ngombu means 'fire.' Tejjeh means 'leader.' Gongoli means 'a hard nut to crack' or 'someone who's stubborn.' Guyanh means 'chief.' I'm not sure how to spell them. I'll think of something."

As a teenage medic in Liberia, Ben had delivered a baby and was well aware of the dangers of childbirth. When I had my first contraction and exclaimed, "Oooh ...," he immediately said, "Let's get going."

We arrived at the hospital that evening in plenty of time. In fact, the nurse gave me a sleeping pill. My contractions awakened me around 4 a.m. and 4 hours later, on the morning of October 25, 1968, Benjamin Jr., nicknamed "Bengie," was born. I was exhausted but content as Ben walked into my room, exulting, "The doctor showed him to me before he was even cleaned up. I have a son!" I breathed a prayer of thanks to the Lord for assuring me I was forgiven through giving me a son.

It was Halloween the night after I came home from the hospital. I was tired and told Ben to ignore the trick-or-treaters at our door. He couldn't, since he loved kids; he gave away our candy and scrambled for all the change in the house.

We attended the campus church, and the pastor baptized Bengie at our apartment. My brother, Jim, and his wife, and my sister, Sandy, were there, but the ones who mattered most weren't.

We spent Thanksgiving by ourselves, and our first Christmas together was bleak without family. Our tree sat in the corner of the dining room, but something was missing—relatives around it. The campus pastor saved the situation by inviting us to join his family for a Christmas Day dinner at his home in Lancaster, a town 40 miles away. Their 6 children bustling around the house and the warm conversation at the table soothed my dejection.

That morning before we left for Lancaster, Ben surprised me by handing me a box, and said, "Open this."

It was a classic black dress in my size, although not my style. I said, "How'd you know my measurements?"

He said, "I told the clerk you were her size."

Ben liked to give presents, but he had a hard time picking out gifts for me on his own. More often than not, before Christmas and my birthday, he said, "Be sure and get yourself something you like." He searched for the perfect card, sometimes asking the drugstore clerk's advice. As a result, it had a mushy printed message, and he added to it with his usual scrawl, saying how much he loved me and how much I meant to him. He kept the card under his pillow until he saw me open my eyes. Then he pulled it out and gave it to me.

Everything was new to me as a wife and mother, while Ben had experienced marriage and raising Winona. Mom wasn't there to help me, so I consulted *Baby and Child Care* by Dr. Benjamin Spock. It was a lifesaver since I knew nothing about babies and Ben was usually at work.

After Christmas, I wrote a letter to my parents, enclosing pictures of Bengie. I hoped that seeing their first grandchild might soften their resolve.

Ten days later, there was a letter from them in the mailbox. I eagerly opened it, and Bengie's baby pictures fell to the floor. I felt as if they slapped me in the face. They weren't simply turning their backs on Ben and me; they were rejecting their grandson. Holding back my tears, I grabbed the pictures and stumbled to the couch to read the letter. Dad said Mom was very sick, hinting it was my fault. He ended with his usual mantra—if I loved them, I'd repent and come home. Through my enormous hurt and disappointment, I realized I'd have to make a new home for myself.

We made our first trip as a family in January when Bengie was 3 months old. Ben had a speaking engagement at the Toledo Sisters of Notre Dame convent. On our way there, Bengie slept in a small baby bed wedged in the backseat of our blue VW bug. The nuns enjoyed Ben's talk and cooed over Bengie.

The following summer, we rented a house. I was busy with our son and sprucing things up. Soon after we married, we had purchased our own furniture. Since the house had an enclosed back porch, we bought a Sears washer and dryer. I no longer had to trudge to the Laundromat with a 6-month-old.

Although I wanted to earn my degree, I was content as a young homemaker and mother for the time being. I grew up in a rural 1950s setting where career aspirations for women were the exception. My greatest role model was my mom, who took pride in canning, upholstering furniture, and sewing tailored clothes. My goal was to be a good wife and mother, albeit an educated one, with my focus primarily on family and home. Since

Ben's ex-wife's main interests had been outside the home, he appreciated that I kept a nicely decorated and orderly house—despite a child who loved to explore. I had seen pictures of Winona but had never met her. And yet she was a reminder of Ben's first marriage. I knew that while he was separated from her, he had voluntarily and regularly sent child support.

One morning, the local sheriff knocked on our door. "Sir, I have an order from the Friend of the Court in Michigan. You missed your last payment."

Looking down, Ben replied tersely, "It'll be in the mail today." I felt sorry for him because of the embarrassment. I knew how faithful he had been for all those years.

In the spring of 1969, I took a sociology class from another professor, but it was a considerable strain. I received an A but opted out of signing up for more classes. Instead, while Bengie napped, I sat at our electric typewriter in the dining room, editing Ben's book on his mother's Gbandi tribe, first deciphering his German syntax and scrawled handwriting on yellow legal tablets. It was no easy task, but I kept up with it, fascinated by the material.

Ben was advisor to the African Student Association, and through him I met many African students, as well as faculty members from other countries. Anthony, a Liberian graduate student, was a regular visitor. He was charming and made Bengie laugh by saying, "I'm going to marry a bea-*U*-ti-ful girl!"

Although my parents remained distant and silent, several of Dad's relatives had visited us at our first apartment. At our rental house, I was happy to reconnect with 2 cousins in Columbus on Mom's side of the family. One of them told me my aunt said, "Anita never knew what hit her."

When Winona was 10-years-old, she paid us a visit. She was quiet, and I was nervous, wanting her to like me. Her hair needed washing, and I offered to do it. She told me to use Vaseline to moisturize it and handed me her wide-tooth comb. Her clothes needed washing, and I did that too. One night, she said her stomach hurt. Ben took her to the emergency room, but she was fine—more scared than anything. He tried to make her feel welcome by talking about things they shared. When I kissed her good-bye, I felt very inadequate as her "mother." A week later, Ben petitioned for custody, but he received only visitation rights. In a sense, I was relieved.

I was inexperienced and living life as a white woman. What did I know about the racial realities she would face?

Secure in the deepening love of our marriage, I was willing to go anywhere with Ben. I just never knew we'd leave our sheltered academic community so soon.

CHAPTER 7

Faculty Wife? Student?

◇◇◇◇◇◇◇◇◇◇◇◇◇◇

The only constant in life is change.
—Heraclitus

Ballroom, University of Michigan, Ann Arbor, fall 1970

At the reception for new faculty, I cringed as I realized how underdressed I was. My simple powder-blue dress looked ridiculously pathetic next to another faculty wife from the University of Michigan–Flint in her stunning black sheath with diamond earrings and a mink stole. I glanced over at the stylish and sophisticated women in the line.

Slinking down into myself, I hoped Ben wouldn't notice that I looked like a country bumpkin. If I embarrassed him, thankfully he didn't show it. He was his usual charming self as he greeted President Roben Fleming. I felt out of place, ill-equipped for this role. On top of that, I hadn't even graduated from college. Would I end up making Ben ashamed of me? Could I ever fit into this lifestyle?

\#

In Athens, in the spring of 1969, the phone rang late one night. We were both sound asleep. Ben fumbled to reach the phone on the dresser across the room. It was a call from his good friend Edgar, who had befriended a number of African students, including Ben, at Michigan State University. As a black community leader in Flint, Michigan, he worked in a General Motors assembly plant to "stay close to the people," despite his college degree. Edgar got right to the point. "I want you up here. There are no black professors and only five or six black students at the U of M–Flint. We've got to change that. I'll talk to the dean if you'll agree to come."

Ben asked a dean at Ohio University for advice about the offer, and he said, "Ben, we'll miss you, but I think it's a good move. You're going there as a couple. Anita can fully begin her life as a faculty wife."

In the summer of 1970, we headed to the urban branch campus of the University of Michigan in Flint. Unlike OU, nestled in the rural Appalachian Mountains, this was a college setting where students lived off campus. General Motors was the great equalizer, guaranteeing good salaries in the shop for both whites and blacks, right out of high school. Charles Stewart Mott was the local GM benefactor, and the Flint public schools were integrated through the school magnet program.

We rented a house for a month until Edgar came by one day and said, "Ben, I've found you a place. It needs work, but it's in Evergreen Valley, not far from the college." The neighborhood was lily-white at the time, so we essentially integrated it.

To say the house needed work was an understatement. I painfully discovered my husband wasn't a handyman when he tried to fix the plumbing and failed at other simple home repairs. I was surprised. I thought it came with the marriage territory since Dad could fix anything.

Ben warned me he was a lousy painter. He joked, "When I lived in married student housing at Michigan State, they gave me four gallons of paint for the apartment. I think all four of them ended up on me and the carpet. I went back for more paint, and the man in charge took one look at me and said, 'No more painting for you! We'll finish it up.'"

We hired one of Edgar's friends to finish off the basement. It worked out well for him since GM was on strike that summer. Ben focused on cleanup and the yard, spreading grass seed and fertilizer the Mende way— scattering it methodically by hand. He planted flowers along the front of the house.

It took 3 months to finish painting and decorating, but I was pleased to use my imagination in a house we owned. With white walls throughout, I chose green shag carpeting in the living room, pink tulip wallpaper in the bathroom, and black-and-white checkerboard vinyl floor tiles in the kitchen and dining area.

While I was busy settling in, that fall I joined the university wives' book club, where I quickly noticed that the women were older than me and lived in large, beautiful homes. I enjoyed the discussions and contributed, but I left the group after I went back to school a year later. To be honest, I didn't regret missing their teas and fashion shows, which seemed trivial compared to serious events in the world.

We found a Lutheran Church on the north side that had one black member whose wife was Baptist. During our time there, the German congregation dwindled as the neighborhood became black. This church became our primary social group, despite our other academic associations. At first, it was a typical, reserved congregation, but Ben gradually charmed the members by greeting them with his African hug. A year after we joined, everyone was hugging each other. White women asked Ben for their "holy kiss" on the cheek.

Ben kept disappearing with Edgar. I resented it because I needed him at home, especially during the renovations. He explained, "I've got to go. Edgar wants me to meet people in the NAACP and become acquainted with the local black community. That's one of the reasons he brought me here."

Edgar made good use of Ben. He had him speak at black community events. Ben encouraged black students on campus. He visited schools on the north side, recruiting black students to attend the university. My main contacts with the black community were through Edgar, as well as his wife and her sister—all college graduates. While their home reflected an upper-middle-class lifestyle, they were dedicated to helping their less-fortunate fellow blacks.

Flint was racially calm. Schools were integrated, but blacks wanted more. "Fights for rights" groups popped up. Despite GM's investment in the community, the black north side lagged behind in economic development. Social and political equity were far from becoming reality. Racism was alive and well in Flint.

White students came into the sociology office to see "Dr. Dennis." They sat waiting as Ben went into his door marked, "Sociology, Dr. Dennis." Invariably, the secretary had to ask them, "Weren't you waiting for Dr. Dennis? He just walked into his office."

Ben told me, "What really hurt was when the black students did the same thing."

At several university functions, I met famous blacks, including Gwendolyn Brooks, the Pulitzer Prize–winning poet; Wallace Terry, the author of *Bloods*; and Mamie Till-Mobley, the mother of Emmet Till, who became a champion for civil rights after her son's death. I shivered thinking about what she went through and admired her bravery for speaking out.

As a professor, Ben was driven to excellence. At night he was home but not home since he was reading and writing lectures. I said, "Why don't you do that during the day?"

He explained, "This is an urban campus. Students are always dropping by. On top of that, the other faculty members give me their 'problem' students."

He was ambitious, but he wanted others to succeed as well. He refused the chairmanship but was kept busy developing new courses in sociology and anthropology. At faculty meetings, he waited while others gave their input. When he finally weighed in on the topic, they listened since he had a way of getting to the heart of the issue.

He made a gracious entrance and exit at faculty events, circulating effortlessly, telling his famous stories and making everyone laugh. I embarrassed him, at times, when I latched onto someone for a lengthy conversation, being more comfortable one-on-one. At home he scolded, "These affairs aren't for deep conversations. You're there to meet lots of people."

Since he was the "new kid on the block," established faculty frequently invited us to dinner in their homes. I reciprocated by hosting a few dinners at our place—nervous, since I wasn't a gourmet cook. I perfected some dishes, which became my regulars, and they were well received.

I once served my pork specialty to a Jewish couple. Ben didn't know till the last minute. He was livid. "What were you *thinking!*"

I said, "I can't change it now. It's the only meat I fixed!"

Thankfully they were very gracious about it, complimenting me on the meal.

From my days in New York City, I had regularly received letters from Dad, but I hadn't seen my parents in four years. I dreaded opening each letter, but I read every word. For some strange reason, I saved them in a folder in the file cabinet in the basement. The message was always the same:

"Your soul is in grave danger." Ben could tell when he came home from the office that I received another letter because I was in a funk.

Being shut out of my parents' house meant that I lost my close relationship with my baby sister, Joanna, as well. During those years, she finished high school and went away to college. She was the only one at home and out of contact with us siblings since Dad was on the outs with all of us for different reasons. Joanna essentially agreed with Dad. Jim, Sandy, and I forged a kinship out of our estrangement and supported each other.

During the summer of 1970, when we moved to Flint, Aunt Renata was diagnosed with esophageal cancer in a hospital in Indiana. She was the first relative on Dad's side of the family to visit us, and she had befriended Sandy as well. Ben's classes hadn't begun, so he suggested Sandy and I visit her while he took care of things at home.

In late August, when she died, Ben said, "We've got to go to the funeral."

During the service, we kept a distance from my parents. At the gravesite, as I watched Renata's casket being lowered into the grave, I was struck by the stark reality of the brevity of life. I realized I couldn't waste this rare opportunity to reconnect, so I walked over, put my arms around Mom, and said, "I've missed you."

We both started crying as Dad stood watching. Jim and Sandy came over too. We all walked into the adjacent field where the cars were parked in order to have some privacy. It was fruitless. The shouting match between Dad and Jim was clearly heard by the entire Meyer clan, embarrassing all of us, especially Dad. Jim championed our cause. "Dad! You've got to give them a *chance!* Ben's *really* a nice guy." There was more to it than Jim simply defending me. He and his wife had hosted Ben and me in Detroit when I was five months pregnant. I've always loved him for his support.

While we were arguing, Bengie, in his blue corduroy parka, ran around on the beaten grass between the parked cars, oblivious to the tears and heated discussion. Mom couldn't take her eyes off of him. Finally she relented and said, "Can I hold him?"

I said, "Sure, Mom!" and picked him up and handed him to her. She melted as she held him and stroked his soft, curly brown hair. Thereafter, he held a special place in her heart as the first grandchild. Years later, Jim told me, "Mom and Dad reconciled with you because you had kids." There was probably more than a grain of truth in that.

As tempers cooled, it was agreed that Ben and I could visit Mom and Dad for Thanksgiving. Back home in my kitchen, I cried and prayed, "Lord, You know I can't forgive them for all they've done to me. I want to, but I can't on my own strength. I need Your help." As a guarantee of faithfulness on my part, I walked down to the basement, took out the file folder of Dad's letters, and threw them in the trash. I knew I had to let the past be past.

We pulled into the lane of the new ranch house Dad had built when I was in the 6th grade, a quarter mile from the old farmstead. With its central heat, painted walls, and modern bathroom, it was a palace compared to the old farmhouse we lived in when we first moved to Ohio. However, the yard's trees, which were just twigs, couldn't compare with the stately elms at the old place. Even so, our tabletop farmland at the new house teemed with wildlife—crayfish in the creek, iridescent pheasants in the fields, crickets serenading the summer nights, and an occasional deer hopping out of the line fence, a row of shrubs and trees that separated the fields. I loved sitting in our swing at the end of the day, looking over the summer fields and peaceful sunset in the broad sky, the air sweet with hay, wheat, or corn.

Driving up to the garage door, I noticed Mom and Dad had landscaped the place while I was gone and the trees had filled out. At the kitchen table, you could have reached out and grabbed the tension in the air. Dad wouldn't look directly at us; his eyes remained focused on his plate. His body was stiff, his jaw tight, his words brief. Mom tried to soften things by making small talk.

That Thanksgiving weekend was unusually cold. It was late when Ben and I settled into bed in my old bedroom, relieved to be by ourselves. We didn't want to talk. We needed sleep.

It was not to be. From the bathroom, I heard Mom yell to Dad, "Honey! I think the pump's frozen!"

Immediately Ben got up and started putting on his clothes.

Puzzled, I said, "What are you doing? You don't know anything about pumps."

He answered quietly but firmly, "If I can help, I will. If not, I'll keep him company in the barn."

The next morning, we asked my parents for their forgiveness. Dad said, "It's not up to us. You've got to meet with the pastor. Call for an appointment." We drove to the church to face the music in silence. The pastor sat behind his desk, just as he had done 4 years earlier when he insisted I give Ben up. After an awkward pause, he told us, "It's up to you and your parents. If they forgive you, the church has no argument."

We went back to the house feeling like a hot potato. Maybe *no one* wanted to forgive us. However, that Sunday, we were allowed to take communion. During church, the congregation realized that reconciliation had taken place, not only with Mom and Dad but also with the body of Christ. After the service, everyone stood in the center aisle as usual, quietly waiting to shake the pastor's hand as they filed out. When we reached the narthex and later the church steps, no one spoke to us, although they visited with each other. They probably didn't know what to make of us. Still, reentering my home church was a big milestone.

If Thanksgiving was breaking the ice, Christmas was like a spring thaw. The joy of being together again began to ease the pain all around. My parents had suffered some bleak holidays as well. Mom reveled in spending time with her grandchild. I bought Dad an expensive clock radio and Mom a mirror and set of candle holders for her dining room buffet. Both gifts were a hit.

That following spring of 1971, they visited us in Flint in our newly renovated home. Ben took them to the campus and showed them his office. They knew I was a faculty wife and I would eventually go back to school. Several of Dad's relatives had earned college degrees—some, masters and even doctorates—but none could boast a dual doctorate like Ben, teaching at the university level in both anthropology and sociology. They attended church with us and saw how the congregation accepted us. It was evident that Ben and I were happy together.

Ben fought prejudice his entire life with simple love and sincere charm. He brought its full force to establish a relationship with my parents. Whatever Dad said, Ben listened meekly and accepted, never arguing about anything. He was willing to eat the biggest slice of humble pie for my sake. He once told me, "You gave up so much for me," and years later, he commented, "I was the package your parents had to accept to have you back."

During visits to the farm, Ben was determined to win my parents over by pitching in on any chore possible, no matter how nasty or risky. As soon as we arrived and he unloaded the car, he emptied wastebaskets and took out the garbage. He and I gathered eggs together from my parents' five thousand chickens. He wore Mom's coveralls since Dad was tall and his coveralls would have swallowed him. One day, Dad hoisted Ben in the front loader on his tractor to trim a tree. When I saw him precariously balanced up in the air, I exclaimed to Mom, "Dad's going to kill my husband trying that stuff."

Ben's helpfulness and charm especially melted Mom's heart. I believe he became her favorite son-in-law. Every Christmas, when she baked her nine varieties of German cookies, she invariably brought a sample of each to Ben, fresh out of the oven, and said, "Try *this* one, Ben."

He later told me, "I was full before we ate supper."

I think Ben enjoyed being absorbed into my family. When he was married to his ex-wife for 11 years, helping her large family financially, he felt they were manipulating him for their advantage. At that time, he was an integral part of Negro life in America—fully established in the black community with some white contacts, mostly through the university. Marrying me meant he "belonged" to a white American family with German roots. He knew my parents were honest, despite their early treatment. He continued to have black American friends, but he was no longer completely enveloped in black life.

In the fall of 1971, when Bengie was 2 and a half, I enrolled as a junior majoring in sociology with a minor in anthropology. I wanted to major in anthropology, but there weren't enough courses since Ben was the only anthropologist at the time. During my last 2 years of college, I took 3 sociology and 3 anthropology classes from Ben. My favorite subject was social psychology (how society determines behavior), and my favorite course was "Culture and Personality" (how culture shapes personality).

My "Religion in America" sociology class, taught by another professor, turned me into a Lutheran rebel. I discovered that churches had white congregations with white pastors, and black congregations with white and black pastors, but there were no integrated churches or white congregations with black pastors. I decided to write my term paper on how well the membership of local churches reflected the makeup of their surrounding neighborhoods. Some didn't. The district president refused to give me access to any membership statistics. He said, "What would be the point?" I said nothing but thought, *He knows exactly the point.*

A few students complained to the administration that I spoke too much in Ben's classes, asked too many questions, and received favorable treatment regarding grades. I got As in his classes, but I did the same in my other subjects. The university dismissed the complaint.

On school days, I dropped Bengie off at the campus child care center at the adjacent church. I enjoyed my classes, relishing being back in the intellectual atmosphere of college life. At 26, I was older than most of the other students, but I identified more with them than the faculty. I related well to the other faculty wives who were taking classes since we shared that dual identity.

However, I quickly realized that my carefree college days were gone forever. I had a husband and child to care for and a house to maintain. After I picked up Bengie, there were no extracurricular campus activities for me, and going to school full-time with a toddler didn't leave much time or energy for socializing.

One reason we moved to Flint was to be closer to Winona, since her mother lived an hour away in Lansing. That Thanksgiving, I went to pick her up for a holiday visit while Ben was still in class. His ex-wife had told him Winona was with her at the church where she was in a meeting. She was furious when I walked in the door and she saw me alone. "Who do you think you *are?* I'm not going to release my daughter to just *anyone.*"

I hurried down the church steps and put Bengie into the car. On the way home, I kept replaying the scene in my mind over and over. "How could she do that to me?" Ben was angry and hurt when I told him what happened. We felt helpless. Every time Winona visited us in Flint, she wore threadbare clothing—a direct hint from his ex-wife.

With some family matters settled and some in flux, cultural challenges loomed ahead.

CHAPTER 8

Liberia Enters the Picture

◇◇◇◇◇◇◇◇◇◇◇◇◇◇◇

If what we call love doesn't take us beyond ourselves, it is not really love.
—Oswald Chambers, *My Utmost for His Highest*

Wood Lane Drive, Flint, Michigan, March 1972

I called my parents to tell them, "Guess what? Ben wants to take me to Liberia this summer. I'm going to see his home and his people upcountry!"

They didn't say anything as they listened to my excitement, probably wondering what I had gotten myself into. I had no idea what to expect. Before I met Ben, my only impression of Africa came from an outdated 8th-grade geography book in which a boy in the Congo paddled a canoe and dug yams. Ben's snapshots of Monrovia showed a relatively sophisticated city of modern buildings and paved streets. I figured, "Okay. I can do this."

Monrovia seen from the balcony
of the Ducor Intercontinental Hotel at Mamba Point

#

My father was college educated, but it was my mother, who never had the opportunity, who loved learning and read constantly. Her interest and enthusiasm for the outside world rubbed off on me. In high school I dreamed of visiting Australia—the symbol of my escape and promise of exploration. In a high school essay titled, "What is Missing in my Education," I wrote, "I haven't traveled or experienced any other realm of life—from the Bowery in New York, to an Indian reservation. I want to travel the world while I'm young and live in a foreign country for at least a year, in order to fully grasp that one way of life isn't the only way."

The previous July of 1971, I was cooking supper when Ben walked in the kitchen door and said, "I just heard that President Tubman died."

William V. S. Tubman had ruled Liberia ruthlessly for 26 years. That's why Ben had no interest in going back home. All of a sudden, things were different. In an eager voice, he said, "The chancellor suggested I represent the University of Michigan at the state funeral, and I agreed. I'd like to see how things are. I'll only be gone a week or so."

I thought, *At least he'll be back soon.* Little did I know how that visit would alter the course of our marriage.

When Ben returned, he was enthusiastic and eager to share everything about his trip. The new president, William R. Tolbert Jr., had been a teenage acquaintance of his. During the state funeral, Tolbert warmly welcomed him as a representative of the University of Michigan.

During a dinner at Tolbert's home upriver in Bensonville, he admitted to his dinner guests, "Our country remains very divided. Our people are still being short-changed. I want all Liberians to feel like Liberians. I want to find a way for everyone to be paid for what he does and to have equal access to me as their president—their servant." It was everything Ben wanted to hear. His Mende and Gbandi villages in rural Lofa County were far removed from the political and economic clout of the Americo-Liberians concentrated in urban Monrovia on the coast and favored by former president Tubman.

He didn't have time to travel upcountry, so a nephew offered to put him on his Gbandi-language radio program. As they walked to the Ministry of Cultural Affairs together, a young man asked Ben in Gbandi, "What town are you from?"

When Ben answered in Gbandi, the young man laughed and said, "You see? He still knows Gbandi! He was gone before my older brother and sister were born, and he still speaks our language! Others who went to America pretend they don't understand after they've been gone two years. He's a real man who loves our people."

On the air, the nephew announced in Gbandi, "Here is our chief gone so long. We told you he was here, and he's really here. You will now hear him speak in our own language. We call him 'Dr. Dennis' now. You all listen. Chief, Dr. Dennis, say hello to all our people!"

As the microphone was thrust in his face, his mind went blank as he realized his people would hear his voice for the first time in twenty-two years. He gulped and said in English, "Hi, this is me."

The nephew insisted, "No, speak Gbandi!" and coached him, saying, "'A wa nai?" ("Are you all there?"). Ben repeated it and finally managed to say, "Malo ho" ("Good-bye. We will see each other.")

As he told me about it, he admitted, "I was never so embarrassed in my life."

I quietly listened to him speak, hearing underneath his voice his excitement and, especially, his desire to reconnect with his people.

That fall of 1971, as I began my junior year of college, I put it out of my mind. There it stayed until the following March, when he dropped the bombshell of wanting to take me to Liberia.

I had no real idea of what to expect. After all, what did I know of life around the globe? I was aware of Liberia's location within Africa and the tropical weather. At the same time, there was nothing that could adequately prepare me for what was in store—not being married to an African, not taking anthropology classes, not meeting African students, not even editing Ben's book. You might think I researched all I could on Liberia, a small country on the west coast of Africa about the size of Ohio. Located beneath "Africa's bulge" just north of the equator, the capital, Monrovia, lies on the Atlantic coast. As you travel into the interior, the land becomes mountainous. The rainy season is from May to October; the dry season, November to April.

The country was founded in 1822 by the American Colonization Society as a refuge for free Negroes and freed slaves. In essence, it was a "charitable" way to get rid of Negroes by sending them back to Africa. The capital was named for President James Monroe, a strong supporter of the society, who held office from 1817 to 1825. Although the settlers were rejected by America, they identified with the nation, calling themselves "Americo-Liberians." They survived by dominating and exploiting Liberia's 16 indigenous tribes.

The Americo-Liberians in Monrovia were the social, political, and economic elite. The 2nd tier of Americo-Liberians were those living upriver. At the bottom of the barrel were the Loma, Kissi, Gbandi, Mende, Gola, Kru, Krahn, Bassa, Kpelle, Gio, Grebo, Vai, Mano, and Bella tribes, as well as the Mandingo and Fanti people. Ben occupied a unique position, as he was simultaneously considered an Americo-Liberian and a tribal Liberian. As a Mende, he hailed from a small portion of that tribe located near Liberia's northern border with Sierra Leone. Through his mother, he was related to the adjacent Gbande tribe.

The government, technically a replica of the American system, was an illusion of democracy. With no effective checks and balances, the president ruled unhindered. Before World War II, the tribes were controlled by ruthless Frontier Force tribal soldiers commanded by Americo-Liberian officers. During the 1970s, the tribes had the vote, but it was often a sham. The Americo-Liberians, comprising 5 percent of the population, held 95 percent of the wealth.

Instead of learning all this beforehand, I was busy with a husband, a toddler, and college classes, content to see Liberia firsthand and trusting that Ben would take care of things. I told Joanna about the trip, and she said, "Anita, I can't imagine why anyone would want to go to Africa."

In contrast, Sandy said, "I'd like to go with you." Winona, 12, wanted to see Africa too. I wasn't excited about them coming along, since I wanted to share this trip privately with Ben, but I couldn't turn them down. In preparation, we were inoculated for smallpox, yellow fever, and tetanus. I bought a Bell & Howell movie camera with a synchronized cassette tape player, determined to record this journey in glowing color.

In June of 1972, our entourage departed from Detroit Metro Airport. Ben reluctantly paid $200 in overweight charges for our enormous amount of luggage with way too many clothes, including my portable hooded hair dryer, cosmetic case, and camera equipment. At JFK Airport in New York City, we boarded a trans-Atlantic flight on a Pan Am clipper with 150 passengers aboard and settled in for the 9-hour flight. Sandy and Winona watched the in-flight movie. As I held my sleeping 3-year-old, I became mesmerized by the moonlight on the airplane wing. The sunrise quickly approached. We arrived in Dakar, Senegal, that morning for a pit stop. With my tape recorder running, I asked Ben, "How do you feel?"

He said, "I'm happy. I'm going home!"

The time passed quickly on the 600 miles to Liberia. During our descent into Robertsfield International Airport, 5 miles from Monrovia, I marveled into the microphone, "The waves are pounding on the white sandy beach. I see marshes, clusters of palm trees. There are burned-out areas. They must have a lot of forest fires. (I had forgotten about slash-and-burn farming.) Oh, there are power lines and a Texaco gas station."

As we landed, the stewardess announced, "Those passengers going on to Abidjan, and Congo/Libreville, please remain on board. For those now deplaning in Monrovia, you are entering an area of malaria. Please take the necessary precautions."

Exiting the plane in my polyester pantsuit, I walked down the air stairs into a steam bath, struggling to catch my breath. By the time I reached the terminal, my curly red hair went limp and my suit was stuck to my skin. In Sandy's photo, with my smeared mascara and tousled hair, I looked like I'd been up all night.

A crowd of tribal people rushed around us, carting our luggage to customs. Ben's Americo-Liberian "cousin" Jimmy had his car and driver waiting. As I understood it from Ben's explanation, he was from the Dennis family, who had "adopted" Ben's father as a teenager in Monrovia. Ben's connection to the Dennises was murky, but there must have been some genetic link because he had the same fold of skin at the lower back of his scalp.

Jimmy worked for his father, Charles Cecil (C. C.) Dennis, a prominent Americo-Liberian who published the *Liberian Age*, considered the mouthpiece of the True Whig Party—Liberia's sole political entity. In addition to the newspaper, C. C. was responsible for government publications and magazines promoting Liberia and President Tubman. In fact, he was the uncle Ben had told me about at OU when we first met.

I noticed the Americo-Liberians began calling Ben "B. G.," which stood for Benjamin G. (After a clerk in the United States misspelled his middle name, "Ngombu," as "Gumbo" on his driver's license, Ben used G. as his middle initial.)

The paved road from the airport turned to red clay as we drove to Jimmy's house in the suburbs of Monrovia. I was exhilarated, despite my exhaustion, by the lush tropical landscape of various palm trees and brightly colored flowers. Here and there were modest concrete block houses with galvanized roofs. People in simple Western clothing stood around watching as we passed. Mansions scattered here and there provided a stark contrast.

We entered Jimmy's compound, his black Peugeot passing through a wrought-iron gate with a high white concrete wall on both sides, its top edge lined with glass shards. In the center of a massive lawn stood a modern 2-story white structure. Sandy and I stared in awe as the car pulled around to the back courtyard.

Ben opened the door and quickly got out. Jimmy called him over, and I heard him say, "B. G., let me talk to you a little bit. You shouldn't have done that."

Ben said, "Done what? Get out of the car?"

"That's what we have a chauffeur for. I pay him good money to open the car door. When we come back this afternoon, exercise a little patience. Let the chauffer get out and open the door and let you out. Please, for my sake, B. G."

"I'm not sick. It doesn't make sense."

"That's what he's paid for, and he's happy to do it. All the chauffeurs do it, not just him. B. G., you've been away too long."

I walked into a house unlike anything I had seen in America—a palatial mansion with 3 living rooms, wood floors throughout, and floor-to-ceiling windows with white drapes. The living room had oversized European upholstered furniture; the foyer was graced by a grand piano. A chandelier hung over the formal dining room, and the coffee table in the family room was the cross-section of an enormous tree trunk.

The 5 bedrooms on the 2nd story had private baths with marble-tiled walls. Our guest room featured a king-size bed with plenty of room for Bengie to lie between us. The dark brown floor-to-ceiling drapes and droning window air conditioner were conducive for sleeping.

On our way to dinner, Sandy spotted a tiny brown lizard on the hallway floor and let out a scream. The cook from the Bassa tribe walked over, took a look, and said with a grin, "That's a sign of good luck." We ate Liberian dishes in the formal dining room: Jollof rice, a cucumber-and-avocado salad, greens cooked in palm oil, fried plantain, and fresh pineapple rings for dessert. The table was graced with a bouquet of flowers, as were the bedrooms and bathrooms.

By then I was swaying from fatigue and had to excuse myself to lie down with Bengie, who was still airsick and retching on sips of water. As soon as he fell asleep, I tiptoed out to take a shower, only to discover there was no shower curtain. Even worse, my cosmetic case was missing. I went to bed in total exhaustion, wondering what was coming next. However, there was no turning back.

The next morning around 10 a.m., the Bassa cook knocked on the door and said, "What would you like for breakfast?" Ben had gone out with Jimmy, and I had no idea where they went.

I said, "Oh, just some toast and peanut butter."

"Boss Lady, there's no bread in the house. If you give me 30 cents, I'll get some."

I scrambled to find some change in my purse. After Bengie and I ate our toast and peanut butter, Sandy asked, "Why didn't you eat the scrambled eggs?"

I said, "He didn't tell me he fixed any."

Jimmy's staff included 2 houseboys, a nanny, a chauffeur, a cook, and a laundryman. Each of them worked from 6 a.m. to 6:30 p.m., six days a week, receiving $40 US a month in wages. His wife, Doris, a black American, kept the kitchen cupboards and pantry locked, so the cook had to ask permission for food supplies.

Doris spent much of the day lying in bed watching American sitcoms on TV. That evening, Sandy and I were surprised to find that the TV news focused on African and European issues rather than our "beloved" United States. Doris was civil to Sandy and me for her husband's sake, but our early faux pas made her lecture us on the rules regarding "servant etiquette": "Keep your things locked up. And for heaven's sake, don't put your bras and panties in the wash for that Bassa laundryman. That's too intimate. I always hand wash mine."

Ben and Jimmy returned close to lunch. In the meantime, several Mende and Gbandi people arrived to see Ben. We presented Ben's Mende "brother" Patrick with a watch.

After lunch, the chauffer drove Ben, Sandy, Bengie, and me downtown. On the way, the driver pointed out the Temple of Justice; the capitol building, where the Senate and House of Representatives met; and the real seat of power, the Executive Mansion, where the president lived—a white 7-story building surrounded by massive lawns. In the bustling traffic, the taxis paid little attention to the traffic signals, using their horns instead. The enormous chasm between rich and poor was evident in mansions that sat next to concrete-block hovels with a bare light bulb hanging from the ceiling and no indoor plumbing. Liberians couldn't get credit, so there were numerous structures in various stages of construction.

We stopped at the Cooper Clinic, where Bengie was given a sedative to settle his stomach. At the Pan Am office, I was hugely relieved that they had found my cosmetic bag left under my seat. Our next destination was the Office of Immigration, a two-story beige stucco building.

Sandy and I walked up the steps, passing a beggar on the way. The place looked impressive from the outside, but the inside needed a fresh coat of paint. We arrived during siesta—12 to 3 p.m. A few people were milling around, some sitting in the waiting room's wooden chairs.

I walked up to the clerk standing behind the counter, watching, and said, "We've come to report to immigration. We'll be staying in Liberia for 6 weeks."

He said flatly, "The minister's not in. Go, come."

I didn't know he meant, "Go, and come back tomorrow. You won't get anything done today unless you dash [bribe] me," so I asked, "When will he be back?"

"He might not be back today."

"Can we make an appointment?"

"No."

"Well then, we'll wait."

"The people sitting in those chairs'll be ahead of you."

Ben walked in with Jimmy at his side, and the clerk's demeanor changed instantly, "Oh, Boss Man, are these your people?"

Jimmy said, "Yes."

"I'll process the forms right away."

Sandy and I exchanged a "Can you believe this?" look.

Later that afternoon, Doris took Sandy and me to a modern supermarket owned by a Lebanese man. The women fruit sellers quickly spotted our white faces and began arguing for higher prices. I lifted my camera and they said, "No pictures! You'll take them home to laugh at us." An old man walked up and said, "You can take my picture for a nickel." Baffled, I didn't respond.

Those two weeks in Monrovia were a round of parties, receptions, and social affairs with government dignitaries, eminent Americo-Liberians, and important foreigners—polished Americans and Europeans employed in Liberia's iron ore and rubber industries. Suave and sophisticated, Jimmy hosted a reception to introduce us to Samuel Westerfield Jr., the US ambassador to Liberia. It was protocol before our meeting with him in the US Embassy at Mamba Point. In that mini-compound of America, Saturday-morning cartoons were shown on TV, and a cafeteria served hamburgers and fries. Its familiar scene touched a nerve of homesickness until I stepped back into the "other world" of the street.

Jimmy arranged numerous events to help Ben regain his connections to the Americo-Liberian elite. For example, one night Ben spoke at the Rotary Club. Another evening, Jimmy and Doris took us to a dance at the Monrovia City Hall, an impressive white-marble building. In a photo of the event, Jimmy was striking in a tux and Doris in a floor-length evening gown. Sandy and I wore Sunday dresses, and Ben looked dapper in his suit.

Early each morning, Mende and Gbandi people arrived at the house to see Ben, who was usually gone out on the town with Jimmy. The people waited on benches in the courtyard, sometimes until the afternoon. Our most prominent and persistent visitor was Hawah, a Gbandi chief's widow, who dressed in a head-tie and African Java print ankle-length dress. The first time she came, I asked her into the family room.

When Doris learned that I had invited Hawah inside, she demanded, "I don't want that woman in my house." I'm ashamed to say that after that, Hawah persistently sat in the courtyard in the sun for hours, no one offering her anything to drink.

One afternoon, I used my movie camera to pan Monrovia, from the 11th-floor balcony of the Ducor Intercontinental Hotel on the elevated Mamba Point. Beginning at the massive, gilded Masonic lodge on my near right, I zoomed out to the Executive Mansion on the Atlantic coast. Broad Street, in the center of town, was accented by its row of Poinciana trees sparkling with orange-red blooms. The new Trinity Episcopal Cathedral, with its modern concrete design, was hard to miss, next to the 3-story Treasury Building. Moving left, I closed in on the circular True Whig Party building in the distance, ending with the harbor of the Freeport, where large ships were docked.

English is the national language of Liberia, but it took me a while to get used to the local accent. Getting comfortable with "the lay of the land" was easier since Chase Manhattan Bank on Ashmun Street gave out handy tourist maps of the relatively compact downtown Monrovia. We soon discovered Diana's, an American-style restaurant on Broad Street that served milk shakes, hamburgers, and fries. Rosalie's, near the new post office, specialized in Liberian dishes. I was surprised at the number of Chinese, Lebanese, and French restaurants.

Stores in Monrovia were owned and operated by Lebanese merchants. At various times, you could find just about anything Western, from knickknacks to the most expensive goods. The bric-a-brac of affluent cultures that was brought in never ceased to amaze me.

The markets at waterside on the Mesurado River, close to downtown, held an equally large array of goods. Tribal women in brightly colored African dress commanded tables displaying everything imaginable. I was especially taken with the gorgeous tie-dye fabrics. Every street had a tailor shop where young men designed their own clothing patterns.

The taxis darting around the city displayed Liberian philosophy in slogans like "Aim High;" "The Lord is my Shepherd;" "Why Worry;" "Bear Patience;" "It leaves with you;" and my favorite, "Poor, No Friend." Shops showed off their personality with signs like "Play-Boy Saloon," "Soul Spot," and "Bedrango King of Shirts." In time, I managed a number of memorable photographs: a man with a tray of cigarettes, a boy selling coconuts out of a wheelbarrow, and my favorite, a woman walking down the sidewalk with her arms free, a large bundle balanced on her head and her baby on her back wrapped in a *lappa* cloth tied in front under her arms and around her waist.

One Sunday, Ben, Bengie, and I attended Providence Baptist Church, the first church in Liberia, founded in the 1800s. Ben had sung in the choir there as a teenager. During the service, women in hats and gloves and men in suits sang "Blessed Assurance" while sweating under the lazy circling fans.

We attended St. Peter Lutheran Church in the suburb of Sinkor. Before the service, we enjoyed the youth choir marching up the center aisle, singing, "We are soljahs in the a-r-my. We have to fight although we have to die. We have to *h-o-l-d* up the bles-sed bah-a-*nar*. We have to hold it up until we *die*," pausing in their steps to the beat.

One afternoon, we visited Ben's sister, Angie, who was spending the summer in Liberia. She said, "Brother, I'd like you to visit the Lott Carey Baptist Mission tonight. I sponsor it, you know."

We were sitting in the congregation of children when a deacon came over during a hymn and whispered to Ben, "Angie told us you are the speaker tonight. I'll usher you up front."

Ben said, "Really? She didn't tell me that." Rising to the occasion, he told the children how God had provided for him after he left Liberia, urging them to trust God too. I recorded the children singing the concluding refrain, "Heah our prayer, O Lord. Heah our prayer, O Lord. Heah our prayer, O Lord, and grant us Thy peace."

Liberia was winding down from its economic heyday, when the sale of exported iron ore and rubber brought profits to the elite. The limited public education was poor quality. Churches ran their own private elementary schools. Expatriates enrolled their children in the American International School in Monrovia. Liberia's welfare system consisted of beggars regularly making the rounds to businesses on Saturdays, asking for handouts.

I soon noticed gaps in Liberia's emulation of Western modernity. Electricity and running water went off and on sporadically. TV broadcasting was limited to late afternoon and evening hours. In the Temple of Justice, I was surprised that Angie, as Supreme Court Justice, had a spartan office with a counter, a desk, a chair, and a file cabinet—no pictures on the wall or drapes on the jalousie windows.

Men with machetes "brushed" the massive front lawn of the Executive Mansion. Toilets on its ground-floor reception area were stopped up and lacked toilet paper. On Front Street, old Southern clapboard houses with brick foundations were desperately in need of a coat of paint. Paved streets had large potholes, and many sidewalks were in disrepair.

For all the impressive space and accoutrements in their mansion, Jimmy and Doris had one of their servants hand wash their laundry in a galvanized tub in the yard. Their modern Italian kitchen cupboards sat empty because Doris made the cook shop day to day, ensuring supplies didn't "disappear."

Still, it was the lap of luxury compared to what I was about to experience.

CHAPTER 9

A Native Son Returns

<><><><><><><><><><><><>

If there is no struggle, there is no progress.
—Frederick Douglass

Upcountry Liberia, summer, 1972

As we approached Ben's father's village of Vahun, we heard celebratory gunfire. Everyone in our party picked up the pace. Suddenly a large crowd of men enveloped me, shouting with joy. I was rushed and swept along with them to a half-walled gravesite, covered by a corrugated roof, in the center of the village. The air inside was stifling from the afternoon sun, and the men crowded around me. Ben stood over the grave of his ancestor, Ngombu Tejjeh, weeping. I longed to wrap my arms around him, but I couldn't say or do anything.

Outside, around a 100 people stood reverently watching, yet filled with excitement. It was clear they were enthusiastic to see Ben. A week earlier, word had gone out that the son of Ngombu Tejjeh was coming home after 23 years away. The crowd was larger than usual since Mende relatives from Sierra Leone traveled there to see the return of their "native son."

In rapt silence, every eye was on Ben as he poured a large, expensive bottle of gin on the grave, gently coached in the ritual by his brother Patrick. More tears and ceremony followed. As the elders standing with

Ben began to leave, I realized how much his people meant to him—and he to them.

#

In Monrovia, our travel upcountry was arranged by Ben's friend Sumo, from the Loma tribe, who was the superintendent of Lofa County. I grew up on a farm but had never gone camping. I was trained in anthropology and yet naive about "the real thing" I was facing or how Ben's tribal people were going to be "my family."

We left the coast, heading into the mountainous interior—literally going upcountry. As usual, I took too much with us, including my hair dryer. Sumo rented an old migrant labor bus in order to carry everything; it was the epitome of a nag about to take its last gasp. Twenty miles out of Monrovia, the paved road turned into pot-holed red clay. The truck's shock absorbers were history. At our crawling pace of 25 miles an hour, we felt every jar of the ribbed road and every dip in the ruts.

Our air conditioning, consisting of open windows, ensured that we were soon coated with red dust from head to toe—including our hair, despite our head scarves. I quickly had that "I can't wait to take a shower and wash my hair" feeling. At the same time, I was charmed by the drier, pleasant weather and the lush countryside of trees and mountains, unaware that the farther we traveled, the more our accommodations would dwindle in sophistication and comfort.

We arrived late that night in Voinjama, the capital of Lofa, and were shown to the guest rooms on the 2nd floor of the county building. Sumo and his Lebanese girlfriend used the 3rd floor. I hurried to our bathroom and turned on the faucet—no water. Disgusted, I went to bed stinky and dirty.

The next evening, with the generator going, I washed my hair and used the dryer. I walked outside to the carport, reveling in the cool, still air now that I was fresh and clean. The Loma soldier guarding the place let me tape record him singing and marching in cadence. Afterward, in the formal dining room, we ate what became my favorite meal upcountry—peanut butter on fresh baked bread and tea with cream and sugar, the result of British influence before World War II.

Our bedroom windows opened to a majestic view of the town surrounded by hills. Mud-block houses plastered with concrete had zinc roofs. Dotting the red dirt roads, they were interspersed with palm trees. The Loma doctor, trained in Israel, offered to show us the local hospital, a prime example of medical improvisation. Premature babies slept next to hot water bottles. Amputations were performed with a saw sterilized by boiling water. The doctor took us by the bed of a woman on an IV drip for rehydration during early pregnancy. I looked into her haunted eyes, longing to say to her, "I've been there. It will be okay," frustrated that I couldn't speak Loma.

To reach Ben's mother's Gbandi village of Somalahun, we traveled the last 5 miles on foot. Leaving the motor road at Kolahun, we crossed the Kihala River on a monkey bridge high above the riverbed. Ben was in front of me, and Bengie behind on a young man's shoulders. Walking on thick vines tied together, we steadied ourselves by holding on to the large vine at the top of the side lattices of smaller vines, refreshed by the sound of rushing water below and birds singing above in the leafy canopy.

We walked the dirt trail single file, those with us carrying packages and buckets on their heads. I asked the young Gbandi man ahead of me, "What are those large mud cones over there?" When he said, "Termite hills," I shuddered.

It was late afternoon when we arrived. The village was quiet, except for gurgling water from a nearby stream. The only sign of our expected visit was a welcome arch of palm branches at the entrance. The 15 huts scattered here and there were round with thatched roofs.

At the sound of our voices, word spread quickly. Suddenly we were surrounded by a small group of old men, women, and children; the able-bodied men were hunting or at the rice farms. Faces with broad smiles beamed in anticipation. Children stared at the best entertainment around.

Ben's beloved Uncle Komah, a great hunter, walked up. I was eager to meet him since Ben had told me he taught him many things when he was a boy. Complaining in rapid Gbandi, Komah suddenly grabbed one of my breasts, letting go before I could react. I stood there speechless, looking at Ben for help. It was useless. He was completely oblivious, preoccupied with the crowd of women fawning over him. I suspected Komah was angry that I was white. When I told Ben, he couldn't explain since he hadn't seen what happened. I let it go, but I never forgot it.

A young man took Ben into a nearby hut while I watched from the porch of Ben's "brother" Morlu, the town chief. A few minutes later, Ben came out, wiping tears from his eyes. He had just seen his mother's grave for the first time in the dirt floor of the hut. In Gbandi society, loved ones remained nearby, becoming ancestor spirit mediators between God and their relatives.

Morlu quickly ordered a container of his fresh palm wine. When it arrived, he sniffed it and yelled "Booma Biangi!" in the face of the young man who brought it.

The young man blanched and stepped backward as if Morlu had punched him in the face. Ben, standing next to Morlu, turned abruptly to leave. I whispered to him, "What was that all about?" He quickly brushed me aside and stalked off.

We ate supper sitting on Morlu's porch and talking before the sun went down.

Me on Morlu's porch in Somalahun, 1972

The chief's youngest wife arrived with a large galvanized bucket of steaming water and led me to a bathing area enclosed with bamboo poles. By the light of a small kerosene lantern, I stood on large flat rocks, bathing Bengie first and then myself. I finished by pouring the bucket over us to rinse off. We walked back to Morlu's house wrapped in handwoven cotton country cloth. Morlu offered Ben and me his bed.

The bedroom was pleasantly warm from the light of the kerosene lantern; the wooden shutters were closed at sunset to keep out mosquitoes. Finally alone, I asked Ben, "Why were you so rude walking away from me?"

He explained, "Morlu was very angry. The young man, by carelessly bringing the wrong bottle of old palm wine, humiliated him in front of me. 'Booma Biangi' is the highest Gbandi insult. It means 'Your butt is as red as the setting sun.' It's been so many years since I heard it, I was struggling not to laugh when you asked me. I had to get out of there to keep my composure so I wouldn't insult Morlu more."

Slipping out of my flip-flops, I discovered a large animal hole in the packed dirt floor at the edge of the bed. I wondered what might come out of it in the middle of the night and snuggled close to Bengie and Ben, willing myself to sleep. The next morning, another hot bucket of water was sitting by our bedroom door. I never asked or found out what lived in that hole. I was simply relieved that I wasn't spending another night there.

That day, before we left, I took a family picture of Morlu on his front porch, his 4 wives and 20 children surrounding him. I filmed a Gbande band using a talking drum, which changes tone when the player presses the strings on its sides.

En route to Vahun, we stopped in Yandohun at the end of the motor road. The local Muslim imam offered us his house for the night. It was late, but I couldn't sleep. The sound of rain pouring on the zinc roof was deafening, and I was nauseated from my birth control pills. When the rain finally let up, Ben put a flashlight in my hand so I could go out the back door and use the forest bathroom.

The next morning, the town chief rounded up four hammocks to use on the 15-mile trail over the Kamboi mountain range.

Winona in a traveling hammock before going over Kamboi

We used 2 since Ben and Sandy insisted on walking. Our carriers loaded up. Bengie again rode on a young man's shoulders. My stomach was queasy as I lay in the hammock listening to scolding monkeys and strange bird calls in the towering trees. An hour later, one of the men suggested, "Ma, let the carriers rest a while." I got down and walked the well-worn path, carefully stepping over tree roots and rocks. We proceeded single-file through valleys and rainforest, up slopes and steep inclines, winding our way over the mountain. Suddenly we heard a roaring crack overhead. Sandy barely had time to lunge forward. I stood frozen in fear as an enormous tree branch thundered to the ground between us, raising a cloud of dust as it bounced, pounding the ground. Everyone stood still, staring in silence. I caught my breath, feeling God's protection. Both of us could easily have been killed.

Weak from diarrhea, I walked slower and slower until one of the men said, "Ma, I think you should get back in. You're slowing us down."

I gratefully obeyed. At each stream, I climbed out and walked the log bridge with water rushing below, encouraged by a steadying Mende hand. At the edge of a swamp rice farm, we came upon clusters of reeds, towers of bamboo, and the oldest cotton tree in the area, the air underneath its crown cool and fresh. I had to back up a ways to get it in my camera lens. The Mende man standing in front of its trunk looked like a speck.

I was walking the final 2 miles when we came across a column of driver ants—the African species of army ants—crossing the trail. I bent down and noticed that the ants at the outer edges linked themselves together, forming a border. Those in the center raced in one direction. I was captivated by the column, which was about 3 inches wide, until a young Mende man warned, "Don't get too close or step on them. They'll swarm over you. They've found a dead animal."

The gravesite ceremony honoring Chief Ngombu Tejjeh when we first arrived in Vahun ushered in 3 days of official welcome-home celebrations. Ben purchased a cow to feed the village since as the Mende people say, "You don't talk to a man on an empty stomach." I filmed it being slaughtered, with a young girl running up to catch the blood spurting from its neck in her small bucket. The men quickly stripped the hide and cut the meat into portions, laying it on fresh palm leaves. Distributing the meat equitably took twice as long.

At the feast, the men ate from large enamel bowls full of steaming rice covered with a beef-and-vegetable stew. Most of them used their hands to scoop the mixture into their mouths. A few used the tablespoon in their shirt pocket. Everyone carefully left some food in the bowl for the boys. The women and girls ate separately in similar fashion. After the meal, the drums came to life and the women began singing.

Sandy, Winona, and I were taken to rooms in the most modern building in town—the commissioner's house, a mud-block building with concrete-plastered walls, covered by a corrugated zinc roof. Their room was opposite Ben's and mine. Country cloth covered the Western mattress on our double bed. The packed-dirt floor was swept. I opened the drawer in the bedside table and was surprised to see a half-used packet of birth control pills. That evening, women in brightly colored lappa skirts delivered buckets of hot water for each of us. Winona went with Sandy. I took Bengie with me.

When Ben came into the room, I said, "I saw you weeping at the grave."

He said solemnly, "I remembered my father coming to the village and the horn blown for Ngombu Tejjeh along the way. I miss them all so much. I've come home, but they're no longer here to share it with me. My only comfort was the old women who remembered me as a boy, hugging me afterward and rejoicing."

"Who was in that grave? Your father?"

He said, quietly, "I don't know."

"And that grave here at the commissioner's house where they say 'Joe' is buried—is that your twin brother?"

"I don't know that either."

I sensed his anguish, suspecting there would never be answers for the unknowns. A friend once told us, "Anita, your identity is very strong even though it's limited. Ben, you have a rather broad but vague identity." It was true. I quickly learned that Ben's chief personality trait was his multiple identities. Not only was he related to 2 tribes through his mother and father, but he also had close ties with the elite Americo-Liberians through his father's government work.

However, he didn't know the exact Western name his father went by, suggesting "Ngombu Tejjeh Dennis." I found it strange that he knew few details of his father's life: how his father became a Dennis, how he attended Oxford University, and what work he did for the Liberian government after they returned from Germany.

In time, I discovered his network of contacts ranged far and wide, but unlike me, he had no real roots. There were gaps in his background. He told me that all Mendes living in Vahun and all Gbandis in Somalahun knew exactly how they were related to everyone else. He didn't. His "brothers" in both Vahun and Somalahun were his closest relatives, but they were not "same mother, same father"—a distinction made because of multiple wives. In the African extended family, male cousins on the father's side are brothers, while male cousins on the mother's side are nephews. Ben assumed that all of his brothers and nephews were somehow related to him. Since he was expected to know, I think he was embarrassed to ask.

This was hard for me to fathom since I knew every aunt, uncle, and cousin on both sides of my family. He explained it, saying, "The problem is, I never grew up there. I was always coming and going." It also made sense when he said he never knew the exact rituals of his tribal culture or the deep meaning of the Mende parables.

One thing he was sure of—he was a descendent of the great Mende chief Ngombu Tejjeh. He said that during the 1800s, that chief was responsible for Guma District in Lofa County remaining within Liberia's border when the British in Sierra Leone tried to extend their territory southward. In fact, "*Guma*" in Mende means "I have been able to keep it."

The next morning, I learned more about Chief Ngombu Tejjeh as the elders sat talking and Patrick translated. A brave warrior, he was so strong he used his sword with one blow to split in two anyone who defied him. In fact, his personal power made tribes in the area cohesive. His horn, made of a large elephant tusk covered with deer skin, was blown to announce his arrival in every village. He had 100 wives, and whenever he traveled and saw a comely girl, he gave the command and she was brought. I was shocked to hear men exulting about such ruthless power. Ben saw my face and offered to take me on a tour of the village.

I counted 40 round huts, randomly spaced in a circular area enclosed by high forest. In fact, the tree line wasn't far from our quarters. The brown dirt in the village was in such contrast to the lush tropical foliage that I asked him, "Why don't they have grass around the huts?"

He said, "They keep the ground clean so they can see snakes."

Scattered here and there at the tree line were orange trees and clusters of banana stalks. Each hut had a conical raffia roof, smoke filtering through it from the central cooking fire inside. I bent over and went into the small door of one of the huts, the acrid wood smoke stinging my nose and burning my eyes. In the dim light, I saw a pot of rice bubbling on the grate over the fire, tended by a woman perched on a small woven stool. Several smoke-covered rattan baskets hung above the fire for drying meat. Mud-block beds lined the wall, and the floor was scattered with cooking pans, woven bags, and farm tools—crude by Western standards. I used the gourd dipper to pour some water on my hand from the clay pot by the door. It was clear and cool, but I didn't dare drink it.

The small elderly woman watching the pot raised her wrist for me to shake since her hands had food on them. I greeted her and quickly snapped a picture. Outside I whispered to Ben, "Why do they make fires in the huts? What about all that smoke?"

He explained, "The smoke keeps the roof dry. It drives the insects away and the rats trying to get the rice stored up there."

Most of the young women were pregnant or carrying a baby on their back in a lappa. I watched, amazed, as one woman leaned over and positioned her month-old infant on her back, quickly wrapping her lappa around it. Women casually pulled down the necks of their *bubbas* (blouses), openly nursing their babies.

Me Relaxing in Vahun, 1972

Late that afternoon, the men gathered in front of the commissioner's house to tell Ben the news since he had left. Every death that had occurred in the past 23 years was solemnly announced, including the funeral payments made by neighboring villages.

At the end of each man's report, Ben had to have it confirmed by saying, "Is this true?"

71

Patrick and Ben's "older brother," Brima, took turns doing so by nodding and saying, "It is so."

Meetings where I was accepted into the tribe and renamed

Afterwards I was accepted into the Mende tribe. In a small speech, I was named "Baindu," which means "gracious one." In fact, the Mende town chief was gracious when he said, "We don't look at a person's skin; we look at their heart."

As an official wife in the tribe, I was presented with a handmade rattan stool the women used in the hut. Sandy was equally honored as my older sister. A Mende woman announced, "Now you must learn to spin thread to make a gown for your husband." Sandy eagerly attempted it and did pretty well. With the greatest pressure on me, I was so nervous I botched it; the women laughed in a good-natured way. I was not only discovering my husband's tribal identity, but I had acquired one as well—Mende woman and "chief's wife."

Patrick said, "Come with me. I've got something for Bengie. He's a chief, too, you know." This led to one of my favorite photos—Bengie in a tiny chief's gown standing in front of a hut, beaming at his mommy.

Each time Ben walked around the village, he had to greet everyone, asking how each person was. Patrick stayed by his side, helping with the language. He was fluent in English since he had served as a police captain in Freetown, Sierra Leone, a former British colony.

I became curious as elderly women walked up to Ben, calling him "My husband." I whispered in his ear, "It looks like every woman in this village is married to you."

He smiled with his usual charm, teasing, "A chief has many wives."

Ben hugging one of his "wives."

That evening, Patrick, Brima, and some of the elders were on the porch of the commissioner's house, sitting around talking. Suddenly, Brima, lying in the hammock, looked right at me and loudly announced, "Tonight you're spending the night with *me*."

Everyone laughed while Ben translated into my ear. Glancing at Brima's bald head and round stomach, I turned beet-red. Before I could say anything, Ben whispered, "Tell him you have to get your cover cloth. Then go into our room."

I eagerly complied.

As soon as Ben came to bed, I confronted him. "What was *that* all about?"

He said, "When a woman marries, she marries into a family. All of her husband's brothers are considered her 'husband' as well."

"What?"

"Don't worry. It's only a joking relationship."

The next morning, on our third day there, the men were back on the porch. Brima was grinning as he greeted me. "What happened to you last night? You went to get your cover cloth, and I never *saw* you!"

I was relieved when a round of hearty laughter followed.

An elder told Ben, "We thought you died. What kept you all these years?"

Ben said, "Jesus took care of me."

The elder asked, "Who is this Jesus? We'd like to meet him. Bring him with you the next time you come." Ben smiled and nodded. In time, he would share his faith with his people, who traditionally worshipped "Ngawoh," the Creator, and the ancestor spirits who interceded for them.

On the 4th day, after breakfast, I heard loud drumming coming from the forest. The village itself was dead silent; everyone was in the huts. Ben said, "Take Bengie into our room and stay there. Benii, the head masked being of the Mende tribe, is coming out of the forest to honor me today." No one knew which tribesman was in Benii's costume, except a very few elders of the entire tribe, including the majority of Mendes in Sierra Leone. Representing the highest moral standards, Benii had the authority to rebuke a paramount chief, if necessary.

I peeked out the window to see a muscular man in a raffia skirt and headdress leaping and dancing from hut to hut, announcing Benii's arrival.

Messenger for Benii, the Mende masked being

74

Eight young men came out of the forest dressed in loin cloths, with large scarves tied diagonally across their chests. As Benii's attendants, they enticed him forward by waving small scarves in their hands.

In a crescendo of drumming, Benii strode out in raffia dress with a leopard-skin peplum in front. His "face" was a round leopard-skin circle fringed with raffia. He swung his "arms" of leopard skin each time he turned quickly from side to side. Suddenly changing course, he veered, shaking his shoulders back and forth, the wooden pieces attached to his back clacking as he moved. Each time he darted, the men of the village jumped out of his way.

Benii dancing, egged on by his attendants

Adding to the frenzy was the row of men pounding drums. With his appearance complete, women and children were allowed to come out of the huts. I quickly grabbed my movie camera. As everyone followed Benii to Ngombu Tejjeh's gravesite, I was swept up in the crowd. Benii went inside, summoning Ben to join him.

During the festivities afterwards, the women danced single-file, dressed in matching, brightly-colored Java-print lappas, bubbas, and head-ties. The village was alive with excitement, the children gaping in wonder.

During the lull at noon, I asked a young man, "Where did Benii go?"

He said, "He's in that hut over there, resting."

I started walking over to take pictures. The young man quickly stopped me, saying, "Ma, no woman is allowed to approach him."

In late afternoon, things livened up again with more feasting, music, and dancing. That last evening in Vahun, a light-skinned Mende woman brought me a plate of fried sweet potatoes. I was familiar with the orange variety, but these were small and white. They tasted like candy, and Bengie and I quickly devoured them.

That night it poured. The next morning, it took forever to assign baggage carriers for the trip back over the Kamboi range. The light-skinned Mende woman walked up and said, "What farewell gift do you have for me?" I thought fast. Reaching into my purse, I gave her my small pocket mirror. I was relieved that she was pleased by it.

As we were about to leave, a group of elderly women scolded me in Mende, "You are taking our husband away too soon! We haven't had a chance to sleep with him!" When Ben translated in my ear, I stood there speechless while he laughed and hugged each one. He teased me about it, saying it was the only time he had ever seen me at a complete loss for words.

I had put up a good front considering my culture shock. The truth was, I was eager, more like desperate, to leave that "other planet" and get back to civilization. The anticipation of my return to Monrovia so energized me that I walked almost the entire way back over the Kamboi range, amazing even myself.

That time when we encountered the ants, they were scattered, running wildly in circles. A young man said, "They're looking for food. Even the boa constrictors search the area before they swallow their prey. If they don't, the ants eat them alive as they lie there, unable to move. Jump over them as fast as you can. Pat your pant legs so they won't travel up your clothing."

Sandy and I quickly obeyed. We thought we had made it until Sandy screamed, yanking frantically at her blouse. One had bitten her breast. When she pulled it off, the body snapped, leaving the pincers and head, twice as large as the body, in her flesh. She quickly pulled that out too.

The rain the night before had turned the mountain streams into raging torrents. At one point we encountered a log bridge that had washed out. The men helped Ben and Sandy, the rushing water rising to their chests. When my turn came, a man, smaller than I, squatted for me to sit on his shoulders. I reluctantly did so, holding my breath as he edged down the steep bank and into the water.

Those on the opposite bank watched tensely. As the water rose to his shoulders, he struggled to keep his footing with the strong current buffeting us. I sat still, knowing I would drown if he fell since I couldn't swim. At one point he stumbled, but he managed to regain his footing. We finally reached the other bank, where a multitude of hands grabbed us and pulled us up. The men sighed in relief, especially Ben. Once again, God kept me safe.

President Tolbert had invited us as his guests for Liberia's July 26 independence celebrations. On our way back to Monrovia, we took a taxi to Nimba County. Ben was assigned a room in the same suite as Frank Tolbert, the president's brother, who was an important senator. Sandy, Winona, Bengie, and I stayed in another part of the building with lesser accommodations.

When Ben and I met up in the morning, he said, "I was taking my turn in the bathroom when Frank said, 'Who boy are you?'—the expression used for a native servant. I'm going to say something tonight to Tolbert." That night, he said, "Tolbert apologized, 'Never mind, ya. That's the way he is.'"

We watched the parade from the balcony of the new government building. It was a perfect spot to film tribal women in tie-dye dresses swaying back and forth to the music, each with her characteristic version of the fancy footwork. Some of the masked beings in the procession walked on stilts with bells tinkling. The most menacing character was War; his body covered with chalk, and his front teeth filed to points. I was honored to photograph the presidents of 2 African countries with their wives: Tolbert of Liberia and Sekou Toure of Guinea, Tolbert's guest.

Back at Jimmy's house, Monrovia was familiar and manageable compared to upcountry. Ben proudly introduced me to other tribal Liberians, saying, "Her name is Bendu. She's been accepted by my people." Their broad smiles beamed with welcome.

Ben arranged for a meeting with President Tolbert to ask him to build a motor road to Vahun so his people would no longer be cut off from the rest of Liberia. When he returned, he told me they had spoken freely as friends, with Tolbert reminding him, "You're really needed here." Ben explained that he had a family in America and was teaching at the university. Determined to win him over, Tolbert offered, "I'd like to see the problem for myself. I'll visit Vahun if you'll join me. Then perhaps the road will be built. I'll let you know when the arrangements are made."

Ben told him, "Mr. President, I will do so by the help of God."

I listened while he talked, figuring it wouldn't happen.

During our last 2 weeks in Monrovia, it was obvious Sandy and I overstayed our welcome at Jimmy's house. Doris had little in common with "white tourists who went into the bush" and avoided us for the most part.

Even so, we heartily thanked them both, appreciating their generosity. The flight home was long, but I didn't mind. I was enormously grateful to return to my world in Michigan.

I suspected I was going back with a different husband than the one I married.

CHAPTER 10

What Had I Done? Who Was This Man I Married?

◇◇◇◇◇◇◇◇◇◇◇◇◇◇◇

Faith must be tested because it can only become
your intimate possession through conflict.
—Oswald Chambers, *My Utmost for His Highest*

Wood Lane Drive, Flint, Michigan, August 1972

As I stood for the first time back in our bedroom, with its white walls, light aqua carpet, yellow sheer curtains, and matching floral bedding, I thought, *How can the Mende people live so happily with so little—so few comforts and conveniences?*

The stark reality hit me that I hadn't visited Africa; I married it. My dilemma was that Ben was everything he told me—a bona fide chief and a favorite son of his people. I despaired knowing how much his people meant to him. I was helpless, trapped in a marriage with a man I no longer knew—someone radically different from anything I had experienced.

In light of all I would face, my love for him was slipping away. I longed to be in a regular, ordinary, everyday marriage in a white community. Thoughts tumbled through my mind: *What have I done? I can't deal with this. I'm young. I can start over.*

I knew divorce was wrong, but in my desperation, I contemplated it. My thoughts were suddenly interrupted when Bengie walked in and said, "Mommy, I'm hungry." I came back to my senses, realizing, *I can't do this to my child—take him from his loving father and bring him up without one.* I walked into the kitchen still in turmoil, forcing myself to do the next thing—prepare supper.

#

Africa made me come face-to-face with myself. What could I accept in another culture? In living conditions? I had entered another universe far removed from my own cultural experiences and values. For the first time in my life, I was a white woman in a country of black people. I was treated well but was still the odd man out—a foreigner unable to speak the language and ignorant of the customs. I was helpless upcountry, aware of how vulnerable I was, knowing I couldn't survive on my own. I was ignorant of what everyone else took for granted. The people of Vahun knew every animal and insect. I couldn't tell the difference between the dangerous and the harmless. Ben easily distinguished among tribes by facial structure. I couldn't. I was back in familiar surroundings, at the same time realizing there was a big world out there very different from mine. I was eager to ignore it, my sense of adventure having flown the coop.

I was equally torn as exciting memories from the trip flooded back at times. The truth is that once you've been to Africa, it lives in your veins. I had been treated royally in Monrovia, and I missed it. The Americo-Liberians knew how to party. No one did it better. I longed for those social events. I had become accustomed to everyone hugging me and kissing me on both cheeks, greeting me with the Liberian handshake with its distinctive finger pop, snapping the third finger during a handshake to show everything was okay between two people.

On top of this, I experienced reverse culture shock. I saw America with the eyes of an outsider and found it somewhat wanting. "Hi, how are ya?" seemed superficial and inadequate. Strange as it may sound, I almost felt as though I no longer belonged in the United States.

It wasn't the first time I had been thrust into a strange world. In New York City, the small Hispanic congregation I worked with was comprised primarily of Cuban and Puerto Rican immigrants. In the church basement,

Steve, the social worker, taught Spanish classes, which I joined. I had taken 4 years of high school Spanish, but I couldn't speak it.

In the beginning, most of my days were spent making visits to members' homes. One afternoon, I stepped off the bus at Prospect Avenue and found my way to an apartment building. The entry door was open, the hallway cold. I looked into the dark corridor and noticed that the bulbs in the light fixtures were smashed. The smell of urine assaulted my nose, and trash rustled at my feet as I walked. I barely made out the "203" on the door, which had been painted far too many times. I figured this must be the place, so I knocked.

A woman's voice answered, "Who is it?"

"It's Anita, from church."

Someone looked at me through the peephole. Then the door opened, and a woman quickly pulled me inside. She said, "You came here through that hallway? Are you *crazy?* Didn't you see the drug addicts have knocked out the lights? Never come here alone *again!*" In my naïveté, I had entered the building curious and unafraid. After that warning, I exited cautiously.

I reported the incident during an assessment meeting, and it was decided that Steve join me. Each Saturday, we made the rounds of our members, encouraging them to be in church the next morning. Steve's thin hair reflected that he was in his 50s, but he spoke Spanish fluently from his years in Mexico. In contrast, the language was a strain for me. I hated struggling for words and sounding stupid.

We got to know each other better as we shared some of our history. There was pain in his voice when he said, "I was jilted when the love of my life ran off with a Mexican military officer. I still think of her every day." I told him about Ben. Alcohol was his comfort, and he sometimes took me to his favorite bar, where we commiserated.

Sharing the tragedies of the poor had been heartbreaking. One Saturday, we walked up the cold stairway to the apartment of one of our faithful members, a tiny Puerto Rican woman in her late 40s. Her daughter answered the door and ushered us into the kitchen, where the woman was standing over a steaming pot on the stove, looking lost. She had just received word that her son was killed the night before in a street gang fight. The next morning, I was surprised to see her in church, but I knew that God and the church were her comfort and support.

I met warm and generous people. At Christmas, a Cuban family invited me to join them. I became homesick watching them celebrate as a loving family. My gift under their tree was a beautiful leather book cover. I felt ashamed that I hadn't brought anything for my gracious hosts, and I cried in loneliness on the bus ride home.

The strange world of Liberia had much greater ramifications. The study of anthropology no longer entailed interesting information about people far away. It was personal, affecting every area of my life. What had I done? Who *was* this man I married? In the coming months, I determined to unravel the mystery.

I began with his parents, but I never had the opportunity to meet them. In 1955, he received word in America that his father and brother had been killed in a plane crash over the Swiss Alps. He knew none of the details or where they were buried. His face was drained and his voice controlled as he said, "My mother had someone write to tell me not to come home since it would disrupt my education. I should never have listened to her. A year later, I received word that she died in Somalahun in Liberia. I walked around in a trance in those days." I put my arms around him as he wiped his eyes. After I got him to share these painful memories, he avoided the subject, saying, "Talking about it won't change anything."

I understood why his skin was chocolate brown when he told me, "My mother's light skin came from her Nubian [Arabian] ancestors, who migrated to the Gbandi area of Liberia generations ago. I loved her long black hair hanging below her waist. She was 4 feet 11 inches, and my father, 6 feet 4 inches. I used to tease them, 'Say, how did you two ever get together?' And my father would laugh and say, 'Shut up.'"

It was common for a man from the dominant Mende tribe to marry a woman from the adjacent Gbandi tribe. In fact, his mother was his father's second wife; the first died in childbirth. There were a number of children from the first marriage, but Ben didn't know where they lived or what happened to them. When I said how remarkable this was to me, he simply said, "I keep in touch with my sister, Angie."

His mother, Mali, was illiterate, but there was pride in his voice as he told me she graduated first in her class in the women's traditional school. He recited her Arabic mantra, which he knew by heart after hearing it so often.

What puzzled me most was that he had thought his grandmother was his mother until he was 5 years old since she primarily took care of him and his twin brother. Having had a stay-at-home mom myself, it sounded abnormal.

He went on. "I loved and respected my father, but I was a momma's boy. I adored my mother. When I was a toddler, I sucked on her breast to calm myself."

I was shocked. Who ever heard of a toddler nursing?

As I plied him with endless questions, he spoke fondly of his father. "He was bald except for a fringe of hair over his ears. I liked to tease him about it, and he laughed and said, 'Your time will come.'"

He remembered him always impeccably dressed in a business suit. In the evening, he played his favorite tune, "Drink to Me Only with Thine Eyes," on his violin in the study.

I was amazed. *An African playing a violin?* I thought. *How bizarre!*

His life was so exotic compared to mine. He had spent his childhood in Berlin, where his father served as the Liberian financial attaché during the 1920s and '30s. In 1929, when his mother was pregnant with him, she returned to Monrovia so he would be born on native soil. To everyone's surprise, she had twin boys—Joe and him. She returned to Berlin when they were 6 months old. From then on, Ben and his brother spent their winters in Europe and their summers in Liberia.

They were taught by German tutors who arrived at the consulate each morning. After classes that ran until noon, the boys spent the afternoons with their German friends. They wore matching suits, and Ben couldn't wait to wear long pants and "be a man." They loved their German governess, even though she made them make their beds in the morning and wash between their toes.

One day, Ben told me, "Joe was my built-in playmate. He was the musical one, and I envied his singing and guitar playing. No one could tell us apart, not even my grandmother, who invariably called us the wrong name. As teenagers in Monrovia, I fooled Joe's girlfriend and kissed her on the beach. When she found out, she refused to have anything to do with either of us."

Joe liked to talk big and pick fights. To keep him from getting beaten up, Ben bit the arms of German boys. He smiled as he said, "After those first few bites, whenever I clenched my teeth, the boys knew what I was up to and they ran. It was eventually reported to my father. I so wanted him to be proud of me that I stopped."

Ben's cross-cultural childhood had led to a confused identity. Until the age of 10, he thought he was a German. He recounted the story to me more than once of the time when his German friends brought him a khaki shirt, shorts, and a Swastika armband, saying, "Come on, Ben. We're going to join the Jungvolk to march for the Fatherland. Put this on."

Angie told his father what was happening. Just as Ben was about to run off with the boys, his father called out of his study window, "You're not going with them! You're not a German!"

Ben's friends said, "Of course you're a German! Your father must have just gotten up from his nap and he's not thinking well."

Ben yelled back, "But, Papa! All my friends say I'm a German!"

His father was adamant. "Take one step and you'll answer to me!"

Ben ran inside and told his mother, "Papa says I'm not a German."

She replied, "He's right. You're not."

"But then what am I?"

She said, "You're an African."

Ben was baffled and said, "You mean the place we go for *vacation?*"

In Germany, Ben had watched Adolf Hitler in parades. When America wanted to use Liberia as an air base for the North African campaign in December, 1940, his parents were given 24 hours safe passage out of Germany. He said with a catch in his voice, "As we packed what we could, our governess, Frau Decker, sat on the sofa with her face in her hands, crying."

The family fled to London. For 6 months they lived through the Blitz, during which thousands of people lost their lives. One day, he watched from a bomb shelter window and saw an elderly couple running to get there; they were crushed by a falling steeple before they made it. He almost cried as he told me. Perhaps this explained why he moaned softly at night when he had nightmares.

They arrived in Monrovia in 1942 and began living in a house on Gurley Street. Four years later, when Ben was 17, his father had sent him to Queens College at Oxford University to study pre-law and follow in his father's footsteps. Joe went to The Sorbonne in Paris to study medicine. Ben regretted leaving his family at such a young age.

As I plied him with questions over time, I listened to all of this, feeling sympathy for this lost man. I had no capacity to imagine such a life. In contrast, the only transition I ever made in life was as a 5-year-old in 1951, when we moved to the farm. During my childhood in the 1950s, no significant world event, injustice, or family disaster touched me.

Besides our faith, we shared that common German heritage. From his childhood, Ben had absorbed a great deal of the culture. He knew more about Germany than I did. In fact, German was one of his first languages. He recited lines from Shakespearean plays he had performed in German as a boy in Berlin.

He lived by German punctuality; he was never late anywhere. Students had to be in their seats when he walked into class. He was very methodical and didn't like being interrupted. He lectured me, saying, "Do one thing at a time. Then you won't make mistakes."

One Sunday, we visited a Lutheran church. Naturally Ben was the only black person in the crowded sanctuary. As the organ played from the Lutheran hymnal, everyone sang, "This is the feast of victory for our God …" Ben joined in from memory. A few minutes later, we overheard an elderly white woman standing behind us whisper loudly to her friend, "He knows the liturgy."

On the other hand, except for our Christian faith and German heritage, nothing else in our life meshed. My childhood years were well documented from earliest infancy in photos and home movies. He had no pictures of himself from before he arrived in America, because his father thought taking photographs of a person was testing fate.

I can't say I didn't have hints of cultural issues from the start. During our first year of marriage, the Liberian graduate student who was Ben's best man stayed with us for a semester while he was in town in between travels to different projects. One night, he cooked a Liberian dish in our kitchen, which included a large pot of rice. I sat at the table to keep him company while he ate and was astonished when he dished all of the rice onto his plate and poured the meat-and-vegetable stew over it. Staring, I blurted out, "Are you going to eat *all* that rice?"

Ben was on the couch reading in our adjacent living room. When he heard me, he glared with a scowl on his face. How was I to know tribal Liberians typically ate one large meal a day? The man smiled good-naturedly, taking it in stride.

One morning, we were in the bedroom when I asked, "Honey, what are those rows of scars on both sides of your backbone? They look like they go along the edge of your shoulders."

He said, "They show I'm a Poro man. I graduated from Poro school."

"What's that?"

He explained that it was the traditional Mende and Gbandi school, when boys are sequestered in the forest for 4 years, away from their families and village, to be trained in everything a man needs to know. A masked being called Landai symbolically swallows them at the beginning of training and excretes them when they graduate. Ashes are rubbed into the cuts on the boys' backs, the scars representing Landai's teeth marks.

When I asked what went on in Poro, he said, "I can only tell you that experts were called in from the various villages for the training. The rest of Poro is a sacred secret known only by the graduates. No woman or outsider is permitted to share in these things unique to our culture."

"You can tell *me*. I'm your *wife*."

"No, I can't. You're a woman. Don't even bother me to coax me about this, because I absolutely won't tell you."

"You mean you're going to keep secrets from me?"

He said yes so seriously that I didn't pursue it, but I thought, *This isn't fair. He's more loyal to his tribes than he is to me.*

In our 2nd year of marriage, in the fall of 1969, Ben received a call from Angie. She had been newly elected as president of the General Assembly of the United Nations for 1970 and wanted us to join her for United Nations Day on October 24 in New York City. A chauffeur met us at the airport in a limousine and took us straight to the UN. As we arrived, he said, "Angie's presiding over the Security Council, sitting in for the current president. Would you like to peek in?" What a question! It was exhilarating to witness such a seat of world power. I felt like pinching myself to make sure it was real.

Those 3 days were a whirlwind of UN functions, concerts, and parties. We sat in the balcony as she addressed the General Assembly. At one of the receptions, she introduced us to U Thant, the secretary general, and showed us the ivory-inlaid table donated by Liberia. We visited her spacious suite at the Plaza Hotel on the corner of Central Park. In the bedroom, I admired her wardrobe of gorgeous African gowns. Just before we left, she said, "When I go back to Liberia, I'll give you my mink coat. I won't need it anymore."

In the spring of 1970, she spoke at the Kennedy Lecture Series at Ohio University. In a photo taken with the African Association, she looked regal in her African gown surrounded by a group of smiling students and with me—the only white face in the crowd—sitting next to her. The university president hosted a reception at his home on campus, and his wife insisted at first that Angie stay with them, although we wanted her with us. She settled it by telling the president's wife, "I'll stay with Brother."

It was great having her with us, but I was nervous as I fixed breakfast the next morning. Rushing to pour the orange juice, I smelled the eggs burning. Angie put me right at ease. She walked into the kitchen, took the spatula, and turned them over, saying, "They'll be okay." From that moment on, I loved her.

After she left, Ben told me she had offered to take Bengie with her so I could go back to school. He explained that it was a common practice in Liberia for well-to-do Americo-Liberians to raise native children, and Angie had done the same for quite a number of them. Ben grinned in his teasing way as he said, "I told her, 'If you take that child, you'll have to take Anita too. She'll never part with him.'"

I was shocked. You might say I biblically "pondered this in my heart."

Ben's Mende and Gbandi child-rearing ways conflicted with modern Western life. During his childhood in the 1930s, mothers nursed a boy for 4 years and a girl for 3. Our babies weren't nursed, since giving them formula seemed easier at the time. Ben teased, "Cow's milk is for cow babies," but he didn't object.

In Mende culture, children slept with their mother until the age of 5. Ben didn't suggest we do the same—I suspect because it limited romance. I put my newborn son in a bassinet next to our bed at night, but I kept waking every hour to check if he was breathing. I was so sleep deprived after three nights that I put him in his crib in the next room.

Each night, I rocked him to sleep in Ben's famous rocking chair, which was covered with Naugahyde. The following year, when we rented a house, I wanted to simply lay him down at bedtime. Ben insisted I keep rocking him. It was our first big fight. He was adamant, and I was frustrated, thinking, *I'm a loving mother. How can he tell me how to treat my baby?* He was so determined that I grudgingly complied.

The summer we moved to Flint, I was busy painting and decorating the house and no longer had the time or energy to rock my toddler to sleep. Ben insisted I continue, and we argued about it. Finally, I said, "Let me try laying him down, and let's see what happens. If he cries 3 nights in a row, I'll rock him." He cried one night, and that was it.

Ben enjoyed holding Bengie on his shoulder and dancing around the living room in his distinct rhythm, singing Mende and Gbandi songs. Within minutes, Bengie's eyes drooped and he was fast asleep, secure in his father's arms and in his love. Ben enjoyed bathing Bengie in the bathtub until he was in the first grade before I convinced him to stop.

We were both raised in strong patriarchal homes. When Ben and Joe got into trouble, their father called them into his office. He told me, "I'd rather have a beating than endure his tongue lashing. He'd say, 'Do you mean to tell me you're *my* sons and you've done *this?*' We cowered and wished we could disappear under his desk."

As a result, Ben was gentle and passive, determined to be the opposite of his father. In contrast, I imitated my father's strict disciplinarian approach. As the parent who had to lay down the law, I was frustrated when Ben let Bengie talk back to me.

In addition to cultural challenges, there were racial realities. This may sound odd, but I first realized I was in an interracial marriage when I cleaned his kinky hair out of the bathtub. I had to buy him skin lotion for his dry "ashy" legs—something I'd never heard of before. When he told me black people could get sunburned, I was astonished. One day, I marveled that the palms of his hands and the soles of his feet weren't dark-skinned. While he knew otherwise, he told me a parable that had circulated in the Negro community during the 1950s, "When God created man, He told everyone to wash in the river. White people hurried in first. Then came the red- and yellow-skinned folks. Black people were so late that, by the time they arrived, they could only put the soles of their feet and the palms of their hands in the water that was left."

Ben had arrived in 1950, with America on the cusp of the civil rights movement. During the Montgomery Bus Boycott in 1955, he lived with Martin Luther King Jr. for several weeks, researching that "new social movement in the South" for his master's degree in sociology. In 1963, he debated Malcolm X at Michigan State University, countering the call for black separatism by arguing for integration, saying blacks had earned full-fledged citizenship. He had me read *The Autobiography of Malcom X*, and we were both saddened by his assassination in 1965.

Ben empathized with American blacks, but they didn't necessarily identify with him. In April of 1968, I was 4-months pregnant. We were on the couch, watching the national news, when we heard that Rev. Martin Luther King had been assassinated in Memphis, Tennessee. Ben was speechless, looking like someone had punched him in the stomach. After we listened to the details, he said quickly, "I've got to meet with the black students on campus."

Later that evening, he came back crestfallen, saying, "They told me I didn't understand. I was a foreigner. I told them I lived with Martin.

I marched with him. It didn't make any difference." He struggled not to break down.

I didn't detect racial bitterness in him. He was familiar with colonialism and experienced plenty of racism in the United States. He was hurt by it, but I think he was more objective because of his academic training and the fact that he hadn't grown up with it. I saw how charming and engaging he was in public, but I also sensed his underlying insecurity as a black man in America's white world.

On some level, I knew our son would experience life in ways I could only imagine. At the same time, racism didn't seem to apply to us. Its ramifications weren't personal, since I married a black foreigner rather than an American black. A white friend told me, "You married a black man with a steady income."

Our marriage—a blend of racial and cultural elements—had posed problems from the very start within the shadow of my parents' rejection. In my eyes, I had "married up." After all, Ben was a highly educated college professor. In the eyes of most whites, I had "married down." While I had access to the higher social world of the college community, at the same time, racism cut off ties to my familiar white community and culture. I was sheltered within the academic community, and yet I was gradually realizing there was a social price to pay for "breaking the rules." As the white partner in an interracial couple, I was something of an outcast in the dominant society. It gave me a perspective different from that of most of my white peers, opening my heart to black people and others who had been socially rejected.

People who met us never assumed we were married. As soon as they felt comfortable, the inevitable question was, "Say, how did you two meet?" I explained that we met in Ben's anthropology class, and Ben usually joked by saying, "She never left."

In our associations, we didn't have that free and easy crossover between races. Ben was accepted in the white community on a certain level, just as I was accepted in the black community. But he was never completely part of white society just as I was never completely part of black culture. There was always that racial and social chasm—mild at times, stronger at others. In essence, I was estranged from white society and on the fringe of black society. Ben was on the fringe of both white and black society.

And yet there were some strong connections and a few intimate friendships. My closest friends, when I had time for them, were white church women. Ben befriended students and had many acquaintances in the Flint community. His 2 closest friends were Edgar and Roy, the latter of whom was a German Lutheran who was a missionary in China for many years.

Ben was a member of different social groups in Liberia and America; he was never completely enveloped or limited by any of them. His training in anthropology and sociology enabled him to step back and understand people from an academic perspective. With his numerous connections, he bridged the gap in so many ways: between Americo-Liberians and tribal people in Liberia; among Africans, Liberians, and Americans; between blacks and whites in the United States; and between foreigners and Americans among the faculty and students. By marrying him, I became part of that world.

Our marriage wasn't perfect. The real difficulty for me was that he was focused on his career and professional obligations. He had his domain—academia and the larger community, along with his speaking engagements and travels. My world consisted of home and the handling of our affairs. I was the moth around the flame—his support personnel, as they say in the mission field. In the Biblical concept of marriage, I was his "help meet," performing the role I was taught as a child.

In some ways, he wasn't the encouraging support I needed. If I was depressed, rather than cheering me up, he became "down" too—perhaps because he relied on me for emotional nurturing.

I once complained, "Our relationship wasn't fair. You were so much older than me."

He said, simply, "I married you, didn't I?"

In time, I learned that, despite his German acculturation, he was primarily an African and a Liberian. It not only added a cultural richness to our marriage, but it also led to amusing exchanges.

The first time I wanted to make love in the morning, he said, "If I do, I'll be going against my Mende training."

I said, "What's that all about?"

He replied, "The Mende people have strict rules against sex in the daytime or in the bush. It gives the society a certain kind of order." It wasn't difficult for me to get him to break that rule.

One evening, I prepared lima beans for supper. He took one look and said, "The Mende people call them 'kola toa'—'sweetheart beans.' When a young woman wants to send a signal to a young man, she cooks these for him." He looked at me with a quixotic expression, and I burst out laughing.

My family always ate potatoes on the farm. Right after we married, Ben taught me how to cook rice, explaining, "A Mende man can snack on plantain, fruit, or other things throughout the day, but if he hasn't eaten rice, he hasn't eaten."

Other than rice at supper, he wasn't a fussy eater. I once told him, "I know I'm not the greatest cook, but you never get upset."

He said, "A Mende man never complains about what his wife cooks. She fixes whatever's available, and he never questions it. He's grateful there's something to eat."

Coming from an oral tradition, Ben was a consummate storyteller, complete with sound effects. He made me laugh, and I loved him for it. In one of his courses I attended, he told the class, "An anthropologist was giving instructions to his assistants and said, 'If a snake bites you, make a cross in the skin and suck the poison out.' One of the anthropologist's assistants asked, 'What if you get bitten on your behind?' The anthropologist said, 'Well, my dear, that's when you know who your best friends are.'"

The class burst out in an uproar.

The surprises of Ben's African behaviors and comments could be quirky. He refused to eat the heel of a loaf of bread, saying, "The Americo-Liberians call it 'the butt of the bread.'"

One day, when I opened my umbrella in anticipation of rain, he said, "In Liberia, when a white person uses an umbrella for shade, the Mendes call it a 'sun kitchen,' since the people build thatched-roof open kitchens on the farm to rest in the shade."

Another time, he was clipping his toenails and said, "If I were a true Mende, I would be collecting these clippings so no one could 'witch' me."

When I said, "Huh?" he explained, "If you have a part of someone's body, you can witch them."

As we listened to the birds in the trees outside our bedroom window in the morning, he said, "The Gbandi people say the birds are singing to praise God." We both knew they were staking out their territory, but I liked the notion that all of creation was constantly praising its Creator.

One day, he slapped a mosquito on his arm and said, "The Gbandi people say, 'When you smack a mosquito, you smash its insides. You can no longer examine it.' In other words, you've obliterated the problem without analyzing it. Whenever you deal with a situation in anger, you never learn the whole story."

I thought, *Wow. There's a lot of wisdom in that.*

If he was too tired to do something, he said, "Tired, not be lazy." I loved that Mende expression and often used it myself. I thought, *It shows their understanding of the human condition.*

Ben was aware I was desperately trying to figure him out. He sensed my dilemma and the change in me as I was conflicted by the negative and positive facets of our relationship. However, he never knew how close I came to ending our marriage. He didn't want to bring up a sore subject. I didn't either. We muddled through by focusing on what was at hand – him getting back to teaching and me beginning my senior year. I settled back into my role of student, faculty partner, mother, and wife, but my return to normalcy didn't last long.

I had no idea Liberia would encroach upon our lives so soon.

CHAPTER 11

From Doubt to Commitment

◇◇◇◇◇◇◇◇◇◇◇◇

I must learn that the purpose of my life belongs to God, not me.
God is using me from His great personal perspective,
and all He asks of me is that I trust Him.
—Oswald Chambers, My Utmost for His Highest

Wood Lane Drive, Flint, Michigan, December 1972

When semester finals were approaching, Ben phoned me from his office after a call from the Liberian Executive Mansion. With excitement in his voice, he said, "President Tolbert's going to visit Vahun. He wants me join him." I knew he had made up his mind when he added, "I told the officer who called, 'Tell the president I will come.' The secretary's booking my flight. I'll have to get my shots up to date. Hani and Bill will administer my exams."

#

I was happy for him, and at the same time, I felt swept up in the rush of events without any say. Still, I had sympathy for the Mende people, even though I didn't want to live in their village. Besides, what could I say? "Don't help your people?" or "Why go at Christmas?" I kept silent.

I admired Ben for wanting to help his people. I was equally amazed at Tolbert's response, despite his affinity with Ben. How many presidents of countries fulfill the wishes of a citizen returning home after an absence of many years? I could see how they served each other's purposes. Still, I thought it highly unusual.

Executive Mansion, Monrovia, Liberia

Our family with President and Mrs. William R. Tolbert Jr.

Mulling it over in my mind, I came to realize that somehow, this must be part of God's plan. Ben's purpose in life was greater than teaching college classes. What God was doing for the Mende people was bigger than Ben's or my role in it. I knew it was critical that I support my husband, so

I prayed, "Lord, this is so awesome. I'm willing to serve You through my marriage. But I'll *really* need Your help. I can't do it without You." And yet isn't that how God works?

That Christmas was subdued for me without Ben. I took Bengie to Mom and Dad's, keeping up a cheerful appearance for his sake. The day I was to return, Dad and I got into a discussion, and my glib approach must have irritated him because he retorted, "Do you think everything can suddenly be smoothed over? After all we've gone through?"

Stunned, I said, "I need to take a nap before I drive home." I fled to their bedroom to rest, my cheeks hot with indignation. Dad wasn't the only one who had been hurt. My father, who should have had my back through thick and thin, made every effort to force me to return home. Ben and I had apologized—for what, I'm not quite sure—but he never acknowledged doing anything wrong or hurting me. Tears ran down my cheeks as I prayed, "Lord, help me forgive."

I was exhausted, but I had to get out of there. I packed up and put Bengie in the backseat of our Plymouth Fury. After a quick good-bye, we pulled out onto Route 281, but the real relief didn't come until I walked into my kitchen.

Ben returned two days later, just before New Year's. He was exhausted but keyed up as he described what happened. He was sick from his shots on the way to Madrid, and the stewardess made a bed for him in the seats at the back of the plane. As soon as he landed in Monrovia, he was taken to the graduation ceremonies at the University of Liberia. He said, "I could barely keep my eyes open sitting next to Tolbert on the dais, when I was announced as the commencement speaker. I can't remember a word I said."

From there, the presidential entourage headed straight upcountry, stopping at Tolbert's farm in Bellefani for the night. Ben said, "I was finally lying down to sleep when Tolbert walked in, in his pajamas. We talked the whole night. He really shares my vision for Liberia."

Tolbert took a bush plane to Vahun, taking off at the small airport in Foya and landing on the new airstrip in Vahun. The plane carried only a few passengers, and Ben was to bring up the rear. When Ben suggested he go ahead to prepare the way, Tolbert said, "No, I want to see the people as they are."

The festivities were well under way, with music and dancing, as well as 2 cows being slaughtered for the feast, when Ben arrived. In the newly built *palava* (talking) hut, Tolbert stood and hugged him as soon as he walked in. Everyone applauded.

Tolbert had already toured the village and said, "You're quite right. The people of Vahun are so nice. They're loyal Liberians."

Ben said, "Yes, Mr. President, they faithfully pay their taxes, but it's a tragedy they're cut off from the rest of the country." He asked someone in the crowd to show him the money they used and was given a Sierra Leonean coin. He handed it to the president, saying, "They're not even using Liberian currency, because they do their marketing in Sierra Leone."

The next morning, as the national anthem was played while the flag was raised, Tolbert saw the children laughing and dancing. Soberly, he told Ben, "They've never heard our national anthem. I'll do my very best to include these people in Liberia. The road will be built. It's a worthwhile thing to do."

As I listened, I was happy for Ben since it confirmed his important role to play for his people. In my heart, I committed to be his partner and help him in whatever way I could. I believed God was in this, and I guessed it would require sacrifice. I already had a strong dose of that. Still, I struggled, afraid of how inadequate I was, how much I'd need God's help. I reminded myself how far God had brought us. I'd have to trust Him the rest of the way to give me the strength to do whatever His will required.

Tolbert kept his promise. In March of 1973, a Swedish company bulldozed a road over the Kamboi mountain range to Vahun. The project generated surprise and resentment in Monrovia circles; the Americo-Liberians questioned why national coffers were used on such an expensive project for a small, remote village and people who, in their eyes, could contribute little to the country. They wondered about Ben's relationship with their president. At one point, Ben overheard someone say disparagingly, "Who's this Dr. Dennis everyone's talking about? Vahun? What's *that?*"

It was early in Tolbert's administration, and he was taking a risk by reaching out to the tribal people. He needed the support of the Americo-Liberians to stay in power. For the time being, Tolbert prevailed and Vahun became his shining example of rural development, expressed by his slogans, "Total Involvement for Higher Heights" and "From Mat to Mattresses."

The following April, Ben's book *The Gbandes: A People of the Liberian Hinterland* was published. Nelson Hall, the publisher, used my photograph of a Gbandi woman displaying a woven basket on the cover. Not only that, I had spent umpteen hours typing and editing it. Ben inscribed my copy as follows: "The first woman I really loved and trusted completely was my mother. That's why I decided to write a book about her tribe. Nita, you are the second woman I love and trust as much, and even more."

In May I graduated with a BA in sociology with a minor in anthropology. The entire family was invited, but Dad was angry with Jim and told me he wouldn't come if he was there. Mom and Dad's absence dampened the occasion, but Jim and his wife and Sandy came. In the home movies Jim took, Ben is sitting up front with the faculty as I walk across the stage to receive my diploma.

Graduation from the University of Michigan–Flint in 1973

There was no resting on my laurels. We were heading back to Liberia for the summer.

CHAPTER 12

Chaperones—Summer Study Abroad

◇◇◇◇◇◇◇◇◇◇◇◇◇

Experience, travel—these are education in themselves.
—Euripides

Wood Lane Drive, Flint, Michigan, February 1973

To prepare for the Summer Study Abroad Program trip, we held several meetings in our home. Some of our advice was basic: "Don't drink any water that hasn't been boiled or treated with purification tablets, even if it comes from a faucet," and "Always carry your own toilet paper with you." Other recommendations included, for example, "Girls, don't wear short shorts or halter tops." Our final bit of advice was, "Be respectful because you represent the University of Michigan and America."

Of course, they didn't all listen. Donna said, "I'm going to wear shorts. It'll be too hot to wear anything else!" As I sat there looking at them, I wondered, *If something happens, what will we tell their parents?* It was one thing to risk our lives. It was quite another to put theirs in jeopardy. I believed it was God's plan that I get another look at Liberia. I would have to trust Him to take care of us.

#

In January of 1973, the University of Michigan–Flint approved Ben's proposal for a 10-week trip to Liberia for the Summer Study Abroad Program. Sabena Airlines gave us round-trip tickets to Liberia for $600 each. The students were to pay what they could, and the Pew Charitable Trust made up the balance. It also supplied the funds for food and housing, as well as a $500 stipend for me as co-chaperone. The 10 juniors and seniors who signed up were to receive 5 hours of college credit for researching some aspect of Liberian life related to their field of study and writing a term paper on it.

The 6 white students included a married couple who were sociology majors. Ken looked like Jesus with his chin-length brown hair and beard. Karen was a flower child with dark-brown hair over her shoulders. Phil, the political science major, became a lawyer. Julie, a quiet girl of Dutch heritage, had never traveled outside Michigan. Donna, an art student, took great photographs. Becky's goal was to shape up by walking the trails.

The 4 black students comprised Gary, with an Afro, who became a police officer; Eddie, who was "Mr. Cool" in his round sunglasses and entertained us during bus rides with his humorous imitations of people; Mary, who was sweet, quiet, and attractive; and Ophelia, who was shapely and vivacious.

Like most Americans, they had a limited knowledge of Africa, acquired via television and *National Geographic* magazine. Liberia was a great place for them to begin since it was called "Little America" and the official language was English. On my first trip, I had seen Ben's homeland. On that second venture, anthropology became a family matter—a way to understand my relatives.

We flew out of Detroit Metro Airport nonstop to Brussels, Belgium. From there we headed due south over the Sahara. For several hours, there wasn't a cloud in the sky—sand as far as the eye could see, the pale yellow waves of dunes lending a geometric beauty to the stark landscape. I saw a few tiny settlements and shuddered at the thought of living in such a barren, desolate place. At our stop in Conakry, Guinea, a few fighter jets flew overhead while we waited for our connecting flight. We were forbidden to take photographs, courtesy of President Sekou Toure.

At Robertsfield, the steamy air as I stepped out of the plane was all too familiar. Once again, my curls went limp, but I welcomed a tropical summer after our cold Michigan spring. A large crowd swarmed onto the tarmac. When Ben stepped out of the plane holding Bengie, the multitude erupted in shouts of glee. Gary exclaimed, "Hey! This guy must own this town!" When I reached the bottom step of the air stairs, I was kissed and hugged many times, and my bags were taken by eager "valets." Walking to the terminal, I looked back to see two of the black students kneel down and kiss the ground of Mother Africa.

A brand-new Toyota bus with air conditioning awaited us outside the terminal. A presidential staff woman had arranged our housing. The boys were dropped off at the Methodist youth hostel in Monrovia. The girls were taken to the new dorm at the University of Liberia, with the opportunity to get to know their Liberian peers.

The bus, available for the entire 10 weeks, facilitated our trip tremendously. We simply told our 30-year-old driver from the Vai tribe what time to arrive each morning. The kids usually made him turn up the radio so they could listen to "Lean on Me" by Bill Withers or African music. Several students from a Wayne State University summer program joined us at various times.

Five days after we arrived, there was an audience with President Tolbert in the Executive Mansion. We dressed in our very best: Ben in a suit and tie, and I in a tie-dye floor-length gown I made. Phil wore his powder-blue tux with matching bow tie.

As we sat in the presidential waiting room, we were duly impressed when 2 enormous ivory tusks were carried in as a gift for the president. Our young tour guide offered to explain the row of historic oil paintings hanging high on the wood-paneled wall. "This first one is Joseph Jenkins Roberts, the first president of Liberia."

I blurted out, "Why, he looks like a white man!"

He smiled and said, "We say he was 'light, bright, and almost white.'"

The students were quiet as they filed into the majestic presidential office. The tall windows were graced with gold brocade drapes, and the flag of Liberia was displayed behind Tolbert's desk. While he stood, greeting us warmly, a press photographer scrambled around snapping pictures. In one photo, Ben nodded in deference as he handed Tolbert a gift Bible and a world clock that displayed various time zones.

Shaking President Tolbert's hand,
Presidential Office, Executive Mansion

Just before we left, the photographer lined us up for a group shot surrounding the president. It was on the front page of several Liberian newspapers the next morning. From then on, our group was known as "Tolbert's kids."

Afterwards, during our private tour of the Executive Mansion, we began in the formal dining room, which featured a mirrored ceiling and wall of glass facing the Atlantic Ocean. The ornate desks in the 2 press-conference rooms stood in front of grand historic murals—one of the Frontier Force marching before the 1800s government building, and the other of Vai women in raffia skirts, dancing.

We stopped in at the president's wood-paneled personal chapel and later examined the exquisite wood and ivory carvings in his trophy room. As a special privilege, we were quietly hustled through his private bedroom on the 7th floor. I smiled at seeing a traditional southern US quilt on his bed.

Ben was Tolbert's darling, and doors opened everywhere for us. We dropped in on the American International School in Monrovia; its classrooms reminded me of my Midwestern upbringing. At the cultural center, we watched a dance troupe perform and met a tribal anthropologist who explained the significance of the movements. We walked around the landscaped national park on Providence Island, where the settlers first landed in Liberia in 1822. The next day, we inspected Liberia's National

Bureau of Investigation (NBI). I was appalled by the crime lab's lack of sophistication—one microscope and a few items of evidence on a wooden table.

We traveled upcountry by bus to Nimba County to learn about LAMCO, the Liberian-American-Swedish Minerals Company. From a peak in the Nimba mountain range, we looked down on the massive open-pit mining site and saw enormous trucks and equipment crawling around like ants. At the ore-processing center, the man in charge told us, "Liberia has the second-richest grade of iron ore in the world." I snapped a picture of the matching tie-dye drapes and bedspreads in the company motel. The large dining hall for staff and visitors was modern; there were tables graced with starched white table cloths, and Liberian waiters in white uniforms. The administrators' neighborhood looked like white suburbia with ranch houses and lawns, except for the tropical landscaping.

On a day trip to the Firestone rubber plantation in Harbel, we watched rubber being tapped. Workers visited each tree 3 times a day. We toured the refinery, learning how rubber was processed. I was intrigued by the different grades of rubber, the purest quality being used for crepe-soled shoes. The contrast was evident between the administrators' large homes and the small brick structures where the workers lived. Needless to say, the tennis courts weren't available to the workers. The next day, we stopped at a local rubber farm in Kakata, owned by an Americo-Liberian. The Morris family had tribal workers tap the trees and sold the rubber to Firestone.

The students were excited to explore Angie's diamond project. Phil asked, "Dr. D, if we find a *small* diamond, can we *keep* it?"

Angie's husband, Isaac, had had a dam built to gain access to the riverbed to harvest the diamonds, but the rain the night before had washed it out. Everyone was disappointed, but nothing could be done.

Acting as chaperones had its amusing moments. Ophelia was always running out of funds and often pleaded with Ben, "Dr. D., can I have some more money for souvenirs? I ran out."

Ben teased her, saying, "I'm sorry for whoever you marry!"

Donna made us nervous with her ultra-short shorts and halter tops.

At an Americo-Liberian party, a black student from Wayne State University was forced to leave for wearing cornrows since only women wore them in Liberia. When the hostess saw his plaited hair, she demanded, "Are you a woman or man? We don't like to confuse the two. Get out of here!"

One afternoon, the bus driver took the students and me to see Tolbert's private home in residential Monrovia. As I raised my camera for a shot, a soldier quickly strode over and grabbed it, saying, "What are ya doin'? I'm gonna rip the film outta this camera."

I said, "Oh no! My husband is a friend of President Tolbert. He'll be here in a minute."

As Ben walked up, the soldier said, "Oh, Boss Man. Is this your wife? I didn't know. It's okay, Boss Man. Don't be vex [angry]," and he handed the camera back.

On Tubman Boulevard, I attempted a picture of the women at the fish market. A woman behind the table spotted me and glared. "If you take that, I'll splash this bloody fish water in your face. You're just going to take that picture to America and laugh at us."

I said, "Oh no! My husband's a Liberian. I'll bring him here." Ben walked back with me, instantly charming the women. It was one of my best shots.

In between seeing the sights, the students worked on their research, reporting their progress and problems to Ben each week. Weekends were free time. Most Sundays, Ben and I attended the English service at St. Peter's Lutheran Church in Sinkor.

The students periodically eased their homesickness by watching American movies at the Relda Cinema or eating hamburgers and milkshakes at Diana's on Broad Street. They went to the beach on the Atlantic Ocean, where European women sunbathed topless.

I discovered more about the Americo-Liberian lifestyle. The summer before, Jimmy's house was Western with an Americo-Liberian flair. That summer, Ben, Bengie, and I lived in an authentic Americo-Liberian home. Our hostess, Etna, was the daughter of the Honorable Mac De Shield, the postmaster general in the Tubman administration, who was responsible for the massive new modern post office in Monrovia. A short woman in her 50s, she served as a clerk at the Temple of Justice; her gray-haired husband, Elliott, was an elementary school superintendent. They followed the typical Americo-Liberian work day, leaving late morning and arriving home early afternoon, the work rhythm of their household servants regulated by their coming and going. Elliott, originally from Ghana, was more Americo-Liberian than the Americo-Liberians; he rigidly followed the spoken and unspoken rules of domination, probably to keep his distinction from native Liberians.

A gallery of ancestral family portraits hung on their front parlor walls. Lining the room were chairs featuring crocheted doilies on the upper backs and armrests. Open wooden shelving separated the dining room from the parlor, and a swinging door led to the kitchen.

On the back porch, tribal servant girls squatted, washing and sorting greens in large enamel bowls. In the backyard, a young male servant in a T-shirt blazoned with a Confederate flag cut up a large fish on a small wooden table. Chickens cackled, a turtle roamed, and a goat stood tied to a tree nearby.

The one bathroom was at the end of a hallway, flanked by four bedrooms. Etna gave us her front bedroom and moved into Elliott's across the hall. Because of limited space, their son shared his room with the two male servants, one of whom was a student at the University of Liberia. The three servant girls slept in the room across from theirs.

Our room faced Clay Street, with people constantly walking by our window. Nonetheless, we had privacy because the street noise drowned out our voices. Each evening, Etna closed the jalousie windows and "flinted" our bedroom, using Flint bug spray, because of holes in the screens. I immediately opened the windows afterward, preferring to be bitten rather than asphyxiated—and bitten I was. One afternoon, I discovered a stream of ants proceeding across the top of the vanity. They had devoured the insides of a large rhinoceros beetle I was given as a souvenir.

Etna graciously included us in her social life. I attended a lavish Americo-Liberian wedding at Trinity Episcopal Cathedral on Broad Street, as well as the wake of Chief Justice Pierre of the Supreme Court. Ben and I accompanied Etna and Elliott to several Americo-Liberian gatherings. At one party, I was about to dish up some pungent soup to go over my rice when I saw a crayfish that appeared to be swimming in the ladle. I quickly lowered it back into the pot and took a generous helping of corn bread instead.

I did our laundry at the Laundromat at the Sinkor Shopping Center. On weekdays, we ate out in restaurants with the students. On weekends, we were usually around the house—in and out.

Every Saturday, in the household ritual, Philip polished all of Etna's and Elliott's shoes. Everyone gathered in the parlor for devotions on Sunday, the servants sitting on the floor. Etna invariably closed with, "May the words of my mouth and the meditation of my heart be pleasing in your sight, O Lord, my Rock and my Redeemer," from Psalm 19:14.

The servant girls then scrambled to make Sunday dinner while we accompanied Etna to her African Methodist Episcopal church. Afterward, we ate at the dining room table. The servants ate the leftovers afterward, standing in the kitchen or sitting on the back porch.

The news of Ben's arrival had spread like wildfire. The 2nd day we were there, 25 Mendes crowded into Etna's parlor, most of them sitting on the floor. Ben described his business plans and the importance of protecting the land for the heirs of Ngombu Tejjeh. He emphasized that it would take work on everyone's part. The visitors nodded in agreement.

One man stood and addressed Ben in Mende, saying, "You have indeed selected a good family woman. She's not like other whites, who always keep themselves aloof from Africans, never sitting down and talking with them." As Ben translated this for me, he explained that the silence afterward implied agreement. He was pleased. I felt accepted.

Some days, we returned in the afternoon to find 10 or so Mendes and Gbandis waiting on the front porch. Each claimed to be a relative, and they all wanted something: money, medical care, or the opportunity to live with us in order to become educated in America. Americo-Liberians dropped by as well.

One afternoon, we were walking home on Camp Johnson Road, nearing the intersection with Clay Street, when our Gbande companion told us, "You know Senator Frank Tolbert, the president's brother. He was speeding down this road and hit and killed a boy at this very spot, jumping out of the car, screaming, 'Have the parents clean this blood off my car *right now*. I just washed it. People don't keep their children off the street!'" Ben and I were speechless.

Midway through our stay, Ben walked into the parlor and told me with anger in his voice, "I just ran into Winona downtown. Her mother's staying at Jimmy's. She's going around town telling everyone she's my *wife*." I was shocked, but what could I say?

Etna took the busy traffic in stride, never showing exasperation that her home was being invaded without her permission. She and her husband were so gracious with us that I was surprised by how they treated their servants. Each afternoon, Elliott walked into the parlor barking orders: "Gwey! Take off my shoes! Nora! Get me a drink of water!"

The servant girls burst through the swinging door, hustling to comply.

He'd sit down to read the paper, saying, "Ophelia, where are my white gloves? Have you washed them?"

When she walked in with them, he scolded, "You're so *slow*. You know I need those gloves for the party meeting tonight." (He belonged to the True Whig Party, the only party in Liberia.)

One morning, we awoke to hear Etna screaming at 10-year-old Nora because she wet the bed again, "I'm sending you back to your village! Now wash these sheets before you go to school!" Tears ran down Nora's cheeks as she knelt, scrubbing the sheets in a tub on the dining-room floor since it was pouring rain outside. The other girls had sympathetic looks on their faces and wanted to help, but they couldn't because they had to get to school.

Ironically, the original black migrants from America brought with them the mentality of white Southern plantation owners. When slaves feigned gratitude, it implied the master treated them well. The modern descendants of the Americo-Liberians expected the same.

A few years later, Ben and I accidentally met up with Etna as she sat in the presidential waiting room. When we asked about the children, she lamented, "I had to send Nora back to her village. I'm especially disappointed with Ophelia. Instead of finishing high school, she took up with a high government official and has two children by him. I never see or hear from her. I don't even know exactly where she's living.

"Gwey's gone too, now that she's grown. That's what these kids do to you after all you've done for them. I've given up on all of them, although Daniel did well. He put himself through college and graduated from the University of Liberia."

Ben and I looked at each other. I was grateful to Etna, but this gave me some understanding of the conflict between the Americo-Liberians and the tribal people.   That summer, we stayed with Etna. I put Bengie down for his nap one afternoon and discovered he was burning up with a very high fever.

Ben said, "It's malaria."

I sponged Bengie with cold cloths, and we took him to the clinic run by Dr. Cooper, whom Ben knew and trusted. I was consumed with worry until Cooper assured me it was treatable with chloroquine. Bengie quickly recovered, but I was shaken by this new threat to our health.

As we left the clinic, Dr. Cooper privately complained to Ben, "Your wife asks too many questions."

Ben said, "She does that to everyone."

I was concerned since we were about to make a 10-day trip upcountry with the students. Any tourist could visit Monrovia. We wanted to give them the rare opportunity to visit a remote tribal village, hosted by its native son.

CHAPTER 13

Welcomed Once Again

◇◇◇◇◇◇◇◇◇◇◇◇◇

Fools rush in where angels fear to tread.
—Alexander Pope

Yandohun, Lofa County, summer, 1973

That night, one of the Peace Corps girls traveling with us had a high fever. We convinced her to rest on our bed. Then Julie told Ben, "My kidney disease is worse. My pills are gone, and I'm not urinating much."

Donna, her pal on the trip, chimed in. "I'm not feeling well either."

Ben arranged for the 3 of them to be taken to the hospital at the Holy Cross Episcopal Mission in Bolahun.

#

After 2 weeks in Monrovia, it was early June when we began our journey upcountry that morning. How different it was traveling in an air-conditioned bus with cushioned seats and new shock absorbers! The rainy season was getting under way, with downpours almost every night; but it was clear during the day, and the dirt roads were still passable. Along the way, the students munched on peanut-butter-covered bread, baked in brick kilns and sold in Lebanese stores.

We entered Lofa County and passed through a number of tribal villages before reaching Kamatahun, where we had to change vehicles. The people there heard that Ben was coming, and for his sake, they delayed a ceremony to honor a local police chief. As soon as our bus stopped, we were mobbed by Gbandis rejoicing with gratitude for the new road over the Kamboi mountain range. Ben and I were ushered to honorary seats in the town hall and presented with rolls of striped country cloth in various colors. Ben gave watches as gifts to the chief and the Alahaji, the Muslim imam, who solemnly prayed for us.

I tugged on Ben's sleeve. "I'd like to say thank you." He conveyed my wishes to the assembled crowd, which listened with rapt attention as I addressed them. However, when I finished, I was met with a multitude of blank stares.

A young Gbandi man said apologetically, "Ma, they can't understand your accent. I'll translate." When he did so, heads nodded in agreement; smiles broke out all around. I was flummoxed. I so wanted to be able to communicate directly with them!

After the ceremony, Ben, Bengie, and I climbed into the Land Rover of Ben's nephew, Thomas, the under minister of rural affairs. The students piled into a local police jeep and a Peace Corps jeep driven by a tanned and handsome blond-haired volunteer.

Our intention was to reach Vahun by nightfall, but it was 8 p.m. by the time we reached Massabolahun on the far side of the mountain range. There was still some light as the jeeps carrying the students zoomed around us, but Ben and I couldn't simply pass through.

After that welcome ceremony in Massabolahun, and the harrowing trip over Kamboi, which I described at the very beginning of my story, I awakened to the sound of drums pounding and the Land Rover coming to a halt. We had made it over Kamboi. I breathed, "Thank You, Lord." It was 2 a.m. A huge bonfire blazed before me, flames and sparks dancing upward in the heat haze and smoke. Men milled around, energized by our arrival. The crowd quickly enveloped Ben the minute he got out. I was led to the commissioner's house carrying Bengie, relieved to see the students sitting on their backpacks on the porch. They looked confused, exhausted, bedraggled, and frankly scared, but alive and safe. As soon as Ben and I arrived, they were assigned to different huts to spend the night.

By the light of the bonfire, I noticed a fresh coat of white paint on the commissioner's house, probably the result of Tolbert's Christmas visit. I walked into the same bedroom as before, only this time there was a new linoleum floor and screens on the windows in front of the closed wooden shutters.

I lay next to Bengie until he settled down to go back to sleep. When I heard him breathing deeply, I got up and went into the small room across the hall, which had been converted into a bathroom. It was sheer paradise; the sink was lit by small florescent lights, powered by the roaring generator outside. A large bucket of steaming water sat on the linoleum floor next to the tub and toilet, which both drained to the outside. I stood in the tub, quickly washing up and pouring the water over me to rinse. The commotion outside was deafening, but feeling clean and fresh, I went dead asleep. I never heard Ben stagger in at 4 a.m. and drop into the bed next to Bengie.

The next morning, I watched from the porch as the groggy students gradually made their way back to the commissioner's house. The festivities, which had lasted the whole night, included masked beings and dancers gamboling throughout the village. Phil, who shared a hut with Gary, said, "With that bonfire going and those devils coming around our hut each time we dozed off, I sure hoped Dr. D. was everything he said he was. I even saw Gary wake up once and go right into a karate stance."

Ben purchased a cow, and Patrick arranged for a table and the school benches to be brought over for our meals. In the daylight, as the students looked around the village, they eagerly snapped pictures, the boys gaping at bare-breasted young girls and old women. (Married women of childbearing age kept their breasts covered unless they were nursing.)

At noon, Patrick leaned over with his tall frame, setting the table with enamel plates and cheap silverware, even paper napkins. Several Mende girls marched up the porch steps, balancing on their heads large enamel bowls of steaming rice with a beef-and-vegetable stew in the center. The meal was topped off with plates of fresh, candy-sweet pineapple rings and bananas. Enamel mugs of hot tea with cream and sugar were passed around—safe to drink since the water had been boiled.

After lunch, several students joined Ben and me as we walked to the new airstrip on the hill at the end of town. On our way, a young man called out, "Baindu!" several times to see if I responded to my new name. Each time I looked over, he laughed. In our lovely view of the wooded mountains around us, I saw that land had been cleared. Trees no longer formed a close circle around the village

I stubbed my toe walking down the path in my flip-flops, taking off quite a bit of skin. Ben took me to the new clinic, and the medical "dresser" dipped a cloth into his gallon of mercurochrome and tied it around my toe.

At the yard in front of the commissioner's house, the additional school benches that were brought over were full of men waiting for the welcome ceremony to acknowledge the students. The girls, including the2 Peace Corp teachers who joined us, received Mende names, which pleased them. Ben gave a speech, and I spoke briefly, with a young Mende teacher at the new school translating.

Ben's gift of numerous rolls of country cloth, woven by hand in 4-inch-wide strips, colorfully displayed varied stripes of red, yellow, white, blue, black, and brown. He was bedecked in a royal country cloth chief's gown with machine embroidery at the neck and on the front pouch, and then crowned with a peaked hat with a tassel. That afternoon, I took one of my favorite pictures of him.

Ben gowned by his people in Vahun

Hawah, the Gbandi chief's widow, clothed Bengie and me. I received a black-and-white-striped country cloth lappa wrap-around skirt and a V-neck top with white machine embroidery. Bengie grinned when she put a striped shirt and country cloth skullcap on him.

My gown and Bengie's shirt and cap

Afterward, Ben and I, with a few of the students, inspected the new school. I took note of the painted blackboard and especially the large switch lying on the small table in front. I assumed the teacher was strict.

That night, it was back to kerosene lanterns at the commissioner's house since the generator ran out of gasoline—a common occurrence. The glow of the lantern in our bedroom made it cozy and romantic. With the light shining gently on Bengie's sleeping face, I felt safe and at peace.

The next morning, the real festivities began. The students quietly watched from the porch as the messenger made his rounds of the village three times and the "scarf boys" teased Benii out of the forest. They followed the crowd as Benii strode to the gravesite, again summoning Ben inside to join him. At "Joe's" grave near the commissioner's house, Benii leaned over, laying his head on it in respect. The entire day was taken up with great rejoicing and display. The eager student spectators snapped pictures, probably pinching themselves to see if it was real.

Ben dancing in celebration

Late that afternoon, we said our good-byes and packed into the Land Rover and 2 jeeps for our return over Kamboi before the evening rains made it treacherous. In the daylight, I saw how perilous our journey had been 2 nights before. The road was dry. Even so, traveling over its valleys and peaks was the scariest roller-coaster ride ever. If the incline wasn't steep, the driver accelerated going into the valley, gunning the engine to make it over the next hill—with us hanging on for dear life. When the incline was steep, he paused at the bottom, shifted into four-wheel drive, and edged up carefully.

At one point, the driver of our Land Rover misjudged the steep incline, stalling a few feet from the top. I held my breath while he braked, grinding into 4-wheel drive; I was sure that we would plunge backward. When he quickly and masterfully let out the clutch and it caught, carrying us over the top, the relief in the vehicle was palpable. One of the jeeps did the same thing. That time the students jumped out while the driver managed to get it over the top, and they then climbed back in.

My mind was greatly eased when we reached Yandohun on the other side of Kamboi. From there it was a short, easy stretch back to Kamatahun in Gbandi territory and our waiting driver and bus. Bengie and I arrived first in the Land Rover. A little while later, I was ecstatic to see Ben get out of one of the jeeps. The group spent the night there, while Ben took Julie and Donna to the hospital in Bolahun, which I mentioned at the beginning of this chapter. I sat with the students, listening to ELWA (Eternal Love Winning Africa), a Christian radio station with a transmitter near

Monrovia, singing along softly to "How Great Thou Art." My eyes welled with tears of gratitude for God's protection as I heard, "This is the Billy Graham Hour," before the station began to fade in and out. I was moved that God could speak to me this way in such a remote place.

The next morning, everyone quickly pulled out his or her camera when a whimsical Gbandi masked being arrived to honor us before we left. He jiggled about, shaking a series of raffia rings on his arms and legs, nodding so the tiny mirrors on his "head" glistened.

Masked being in Kamatahun

As I was about to board the bus, 2 women walked up to me speaking Gbandi. A young man nearby said, "They're talking to you," and he translated.

One of the women gave me a small chicken with the legs tied, saying, "It's too small to give to the Old Man [meaning Ben], so I'm bringing it to you."

As I turned to step into the bus, she quickly said, "What remembrance will you leave with us?"

Thankfully, I had purchased several pocket mirrors for gifts, and I gave them each one. Smiling, they held my hands in gratitude.

We stopped at the hospital in Bolahun to find out what had happened to the 2 girls. A Gbandi nurse told Ben, "They're staying at my house."

In the nurse's living room, Julie told Ben, "They did *nothing* for me at the clinic. I'm *worse.*"

He decided to take them to the Lutheran Hospital at Zor Zor, with the rest of us staying overnight in Kolahun. The commissioner had been unaware we were coming, but Ben spoke to him before he left. The commissioner's house on top of the hill overlooking the town was impressive with its 3 stories. Ben, Bengie, and I were given the room on the third floor where President Tolbert stayed during official visits. Our lavish lodging had a king-size bed with embroidered pillowcases, a huge mirrored dresser, a chifforobe, and drapes. However, it lacked the comforts of home: electricity, indoor plumbing, and hot running water.

It was dark by the time Bengie and I bathed. On the concrete stairs outside the building, he insisted on carrying the lantern while navigating the steep steps with his little legs. We entered a circular corrugated zinc enclosure in the yard, stepping onto a pile of large stones. The night was peaceful, the air still and cool. I sat the lantern on one of the rocks, bathing Bengie first. As I washed myself, I looked up at the white stars and the rising moon in the open sky. Its glow softened the forest in the distance, making it appear gentle and welcoming. I cherish those wonderful moments that made me fall in love with Africa.

Bengie fell asleep just before Ben returned exhausted and angry. Julie didn't have kidney disease. She was dehydrated from refusing to drink water upcountry. She and Donna had confessed they feigned illness because they didn't like the lodgings. Ben's driver had sped for miles to get them to the hospital in Zor Zor, where the medical staff had run all kinds of unnecessary tests. Ben was so upset that he left the girls at the hospital to be picked up on our way back to Monrovia. The other students were disgusted as well when they found out.

The next morning, at a local Lebanese store in Kolahun, Ben bought a lantern and lappa cloths to present to Morlu's wives. Just as we walked out, Morlu arrived to escort us to Somalahun on the trail. The students talked excitedly among themselves as they crossed the monkey bridge, hanging onto the sides.

Monkey bridge en route to Somalahun

We soon reached the big rice farm; the swamp and cocoa trees along the trail looked familiar. At one point, a cloud of yellow butterflies danced around my head, glints of sunlight on their wings.

The village sprang to life when we arrived. The rest of the morning, we sat on Morlu's porch talking and eating pineapple rings and strips of fried ripe plantain, the men drinking palm wine. As a sign of respect, Ben purchased a large plastic jug of cane juice for a funeral taking place later that day in nearby Danbu. He demonstrated for the students a Gbandi woven sling like the one he had used as a boy. When I heard the stone snapping through the tree leaves, I thought of David, in the Bible, knocking Goliath unconscious.

In late afternoon, we were about to leave when Morlu strode toward us, carrying a piece of old, dirty country cloth. He unwrapped what appeared to be a huge fuzzy "deer antler," which looked unimpressive until he told Ben, "I want to give you this elephant tusk as a farewell gift." Later, in Monrovia, at a shop on Front Street, we had it polished and carved with animals and palm trees.

As we headed to the trail, I felt a sudden urge to use the bathroom and yelled to Ben, "You all go on ahead. I'll catch up." Afterward, I followed the trail alone trying to catch up. When I reached the fork in the trail, I was in a hurry and confused and turned right. I quickly realized my mistake when I approached a washed-out bridge. The thought of facing a deadly bush cow or driver ants on my own made me panic. I screamed for Ben several times. No answer. *How could the forest be so still and Ben not hear me? He and the students couldn't be that far along the trail.*

Mustering my courage, I told myself, "You've walked this trail several times, Anita. You can find your way back." I quickly backtracked and took the other fork. To my relief, I saw Ben up ahead waiting for me and gave him a hug. We walked on together, catching up with the students before we reached Kolahun, where a Gbandi "uncle" presented me with a black goat. Everyone piled into the bus for the ride to Monrovia.

Ben and I gave the goat to Etna, along with the chickens and turtle. However, on the plane ride home, we couldn't possibly carry the other gifts and purchases we had accumulated: 20 rolls of country cloth, 5 chief's gowns, wood carvings, a large tribal xylophone, and a fragile weaver bird nest.

I had gotten carried away with Monrovia's shopping intrigue; when the seller stated a high price, I countered with a lower one, finally meeting in the middle to save face. With my pale skin, I expected a jacked-up price and sometimes asked a Liberian to buy something for me. At first the market women, suspecting my ignorance, said to Ben, "Oh Boss Man, let your wife shop by *herself.*"

We hired someone to build a plywood box and packed everything in it. The next challenge was shipping it to Michigan. At one office, we needed a stamp. At another, it was a letter. Then it was a filled-out form. Nothing could be done on the spot. It was always, "Go, come."

Later that day, a Gbande man reminded Ben, "Doc, you gotta dash [bribe]. Have you forgotten?"

We went back to each office. The minute Ben slipped some money into the clerk's hand, it was, "Yes, Boss Man!" It took less than an hour.

The grand finale for the students was the July 26 independence celebrations in Robertsport, on the Atlantic coast—a perfect site because of its spectacular view of the ocean.

In my movies, 10-year-old girls in raffia skirts and wide gingham straps crisscrossing their chests twirl and dance to the relentless beat of drums.

At one of the local balls that evening, the students joined the grand march, dancing single-file, their hands on the shoulders of the person ahead of them. As the band played, women with straightened hair in floor-length gowns and men in tuxedos snaked their way around the room, which was draped with red, white, and blue bunting. The students were duly impressed with the Americo-Liberians in their grandest display.

At the airport waiting room, everyone was delighted and honored to visit with Miriam Makeba, the famous South African singer, who was on a layover for her flight home. We boarded the plane exhausted, but giddy with a lifetime of memorable experiences.

Our box of carvings and gifts arrived in Flint several weeks later. Ben's tuxedo shirt and dress shoes that we had tucked in were missing, but everything else was intact. From then on, I displayed African art in our home. A friend called my style "African-Modern."

We hosted a program at the university that fall, showcasing our journey. The room was packed and the students proud as our African memorabilia was displayed on tables and we showed our slides. The students did well on their research papers, for the most part, which made Ben happy. Overall, the trip's success added to his mystique on campus.

My broader view of Liberia mitigated my culture shock. It had been an amazing time touring with the students. I captured many aspects of Liberian life in movies and photographs and felt more connected to Ben and his heritage.

During the trip, a generous impulse expanded our household beyond our nuclear family. A young Gbandi man working as a stenographer at the Executive Mansion had regularly stopped by Etna's house, pleading for an opportunity to better himself. In my naïveté, I encouraged Ben to agree that Solomah could live with us while attending the University of Michigan–Flint.

We assumed he was single. Instead we learned he had 3 children and a wife who was pregnant with twins. We felt terrible—even worse when he told us the twins died in childbirth. That December, near the end of his first semester, the university contacted Ben saying Solomah had flunked all of his classes. As a favor to Ben, the administration waived the tuition.

Ben insisted that Solomah get a job—anything he could find—and move out. Solomah worked for GM in Flint for a while and had a good income. He visited Liberia several times. However, he never returned to his home country, because he was an academic failure with no opportunity in Liberia. Instead he married a young black woman in our neighborhood, and they had a baby girl. A year later, he brought over his 3 children.

In the long term, nothing ever worked out for him, possibly because of his alcoholism. He called Ben at all hours of the night, drunk and rambling incoherently. Everything was Ben's fault because we never helped him enough.

There was more trouble ahead, but that time it wasn't due to my ignorance.

CHAPTER 14

A New Direction

◇◇◇◇◇◇◇◇◇◇◇◇◇◇

The greatest enemy of the life of faith in God is not sin,
but good choices which are not quite good enough.
—Oswald Chambers, *My Utmost for His Highest*

Wood County Hospital, Bowling Green, Ohio, July 1974

I was 2 months pregnant and desperately thirsty as I lay in a hospital
bed with matted hair and no makeup. I didn't dare take a sip of water,
because I knew it would make me start retching again. The med tech
had made several attempts to insert the IV, but my vein collapsed from
dehydration. Finally the head of the department succeeded in putting in
a mesh shunt, and life-giving fluids were flowing into me. Mom walked
in later that afternoon and handed me a blue air letter from Ben. I eagerly
tore it open and read it under the fluorescent lights.

The words jumped off the page: "My dear Nita, I hope you are managing.
The guys are staying with Angie. She told me they're out every night until
late, running wild with Liberian women. I'm so ashamed of them. I'm not
even going to take them up to Vahun. When I think of the moral damage
they could have done, I thank the Lord that this was revealed in Monrovia.
My biggest mistake and regret is that I knew nothing of their beliefs or
character. I can't wait to get home."

I realized his life was as bleak as mine. A week later, another air letter announced that as soon as the men got the truck out of customs, they sold it for airfare home. I sighed. Ben's rice-farming venture had been a complete disaster. I was extremely weak. Life was dismal, and I felt all alone in the world. We needed each other's comfort, only he was halfway around the world and wouldn't be back until August.

#

During the Summer Study Abroad Program trip in 1973, the tribal elders of Vahun deeded Ben 5,000 acres of local land—privately owned— in gratitude for the new road over the Kamboi mountain range. This was unusual since land was communally owned. Once a man harvested his rice crop, the site went back to the tribe.

That land deed, coupled with Tolbert's friendship, ignited Ben's plans for the Mende people. He wanted to better their lives before introducing mission work. His idea was a nonprofit communal rice farm, which would benefit the entire village during the annual "hungry time" until the next harvest. Mende farmers produced enough rice for local consumption, but they had to sell their grain to pay taxes. Subsequently, they were forced to buy seed grain. Ben's communal farm would supplement the local harvest and generate income. I never wanted a farmer for a husband, but I had one then.

That fall, Ben, in his exuberance, mentioned the project to one of his anthropology classes. A student followed him to his office, expressing interest in supervising it. Ben needed someone who would be financially accountable solely to him. He strongly suspected that if he turned over the project funds to his "brothers," the money would disappear because no one had to answer for it. In the tribal mentality, it was "one for all." Men worked to provide for their families, but ultimately their efforts were for the benefit of the tribe.

The student's only qualification was his willingness to go. He soon recruited an old army buddy. With Ben's $6,000, they purchased supplies and a used truck. I had misgivings about the guys and the whole project, but I trusted Ben to handle it. The truth is that I ignored the whole thing. My focus was on having another baby.

That fall, after we came back from the Summer Study Abroad Program trip, Bengie began kindergarten. Ben encouraged me to attend the University of Michigan in Ann Arbor, an hour away, for my master's degree. I dismissed it. There was no way I could handle the commute and the studies while fulfilling wife and mom responsibilities. It was time for another baby, but the months dragged on and I didn't get pregnant. At the Eastland Mall, tears came to my eyes when I saw the knitted baby booties and blankets on the craft-show tables. I rushed to the car, crying.

In May of 1974, my gynecologist told me, "The birth control pills have suppressed your ovulation too successfully. I'd like to try a fertility drug." Ben and I agreed, and I soon became pregnant. Our second baby was definitely planned. From what I know now, I'm thankful I didn't have twins or triplets!

Since I was pregnant, we decided that Bengie and I would spend the summer with my folks while Ben took the men to Liberia to get the rice-farm project going. How I managed to drive to the farm with Bengie, his bike, and a vomiting cat in the backseat, I'll never know. I was relieved when I arrived, but the situation quickly deteriorated. Mom and Dad were tense because the crops desperately needed rain. Bengie missed Ben and kept hanging onto Dad's leg wherever he went. Finally Dad lost all patience and said, "Will you keep him off of me? He's always underfoot." Thinking, *Typical Dad*, I walked over, put my arms around, Bengie and kept him near me.

Our tomcat, Henry, became weaker. The vet said, "He'll need a hernia operation, and it costs $400." I steeled myself and had him put to sleep. I couldn't deal with it, so Mom comforted Bengie and helped him bury our butterscotch Henry near the shed.

It was a lonely time for Bengie with no other kids around. His summer highlight was learning to ride his bike on the sidewalk after Dad took off the training wheels. I watched from the back door as he weaved precariously. Just as it looked as if he would topple over, he suddenly righted himself. After that, he confidently rode his bike around the farmstead on the gravel driveways. I thought, *That's my boy,* and I wished Ben were there to see it.

Mom had her hands full fixing meals, keeping house, and entertaining her grandson. It was hard for her to see me struggle to keep food down since she had gone through the same thing the entire 9 months. Under their own pressures, Mom and Dad couldn't cheer me up; my loneliness and anxiety were taking their toll.

Two weeks into our visit, as with my first pregnancy, I could no longer keep liquids down. During my first hospital stay, our home pastor visited, quoting Isaiah 55:8: "'For My thoughts are not your thoughts; neither are your ways, my ways,' declares the Lord." It didn't help. Things looked bleaker as the thought crossed my mind, *Is God against us?* I regained enough strength to go home, but 2 weeks later had a relapse and ended up in the hospital again.

Ben's failed venture certainly added to my stress. The truth is that the men he took to Liberia knew nothing about rice farming or Africa. I figured they were losers looking for a colonial-type money-making adventure. They probably saw themselves ordering around native people who meekly followed their bidding. In the final outcome, with "outsiders in charge," the money disappeared with no explanation.

I gradually recovered my strength during my 3rd stint in the hospital. The doctor had ordered complete bed rest. Frustrated with hospital protocol, I hated sponge baths and longed to take a shower. Finally I was given permission. As the shower water poured over me, I was filled with momentary gratitude.

Back at the farm, my heart beat so rapidly one afternoon that I called the gynecologist the hospital assigned to me. The best he could offer were these comforting words: "The reason for your morning sickness is that you are too psychologically dependent upon your parents. You told me your husband will soon be home. Just hold till then."

I thought, *Boy, he's no help.*

I managed to get through one day at a time, struggling to survive until Ben arrived in August. Mom and Dad took Bengie with them when they picked him up at the Toledo airport. I was overjoyed when I heard them coming in the kitchen door. Just seeing his face was balm to my soul. The next day, he drove us back to Flint. I was still weak as I lay in our hammock on our back porch. The nausea continued for a while, but it was heaven to have Ben back and be in my own home.

He was disheartened about the rice farming fiasco, and quite frankly, neither of us wanted to talk about it. We had assumed that whatever he proposed would be successful since God was leading him in saving his people. We were wrong. I realized I would share in my husband's mistakes as well as his triumphs—with ramifications for both of us.

It wasn't easy to see my husband in that lesser light. He had been my mentor and unflagging support in the "education of Anita Dennis" in so many ways, encouraging me to get my master's degree and beyond. In Liberia, I was helpless without him. I put my disappointment in him behind me, figuring we were both foolish. He had only observed rice farming. I was a housewife. What did we know?

At the same time, I was comforted by the joy and satisfaction of having another child. That fall and winter, things fell into their normal routine. Ben was back teaching, and I was preparing for our new arrival.

At Christmas, I empathized with Mary being about to deliver—while riding on a donkey! In mid-February, I had a tremendous burst of energy, cleaning house while it snowed all day; our neighborhood was a quiet winter wonderland by the time I went to bed. As I relaxed, I felt that familiar twinge of pain and said, "Honey, I think I'm going into labor."

There was panic in his voice as he looked out the window and exclaimed, "Why does a baby have to come at a time like this?"

I called my cousin, who managed to make it through the snow. As soon as she arrived, we headed to McClaren Hospital across town. Flint looked abandoned. Streets were empty as we crawled along in our Plymouth Fury, pushing through the snow. At one point, we skidded down a street and right through a red stoplight at the bottom.

Our 2nd child was born at 1 a.m.—another baby boy with dark hair and big brown eyes. In fact, he looked so much like Bengie that I had trouble, years later, sorting the baby pictures.

At our house that morning, Ben took Bengie into our bed and told him, "You have a little brother."

Bengie's face brightened, and he said, "I know. Let's name him Friendly Dennis!"

I called Dad when I came home from the hospital. "One of the baby's names will be Harold, after you."

He said, "Great!"

His first name was Joe, after Ben's twin brother, and then Harold. Tribal names followed. And so Joseph Harold Boaki Kovah entered our lives.

In late spring of 1975, Ben and I attended a series of Christian lectures called "The Institute of Basic Youth Conflicts" at Cobo Arena in Detroit. The director described wisdom as "seeing life from God's perspective." He explained, "Sometimes, God lets us fail in our vision so we can focus on *His* vision." We suddenly saw our rice-farming failure in a new light. From then on, we resolved to focus solely on sharing the gospel. We'd "seek first the Kingdom of God" and trust Him to "let all these things be added unto us"—in His will and in the fullness of His time.

Painful reminders of Ben's first marriage continued. That spring, his ex-wife announced by phone, "I've moved to Nashville since I've taken a position at Meharry [Medical School]." Ben knew he had "lost" Winona once again.

Two months later, he received a late-night phone call. Winona, 16, had attempted suicide. He walked back into our bedroom, the soul drained out of him. He told me briefly what happened and then flopped into bed, his grief radiating in the narrow space between us. I put my hand in his as we lay there, but there was no way to comfort him. There was nothing we could do about it except pray—and he did plenty of that on his knees.

In the meantime, our faith was growing. We held daily devotions at the supper table. Each night, I read a chapter from the Bible. When we reached the book of Revelation, we began again in Genesis. We took turns praying out loud.

We were in church each Sunday. After kindergarten, Bengie went to the first grade at Our Savior parochial school. For Christmas festivities, he participated in two church programs: one at our church the week before, and one at Mom and Dad's church on Christmas Eve. As the people at Our Savior came to love and trust Ben, they chose him to be an elder. From there he was elected to the church's board of directors.

During the 1970s, conservatives and liberals in the Lutheran church debated the infallibility of the Scriptures. Ben was chosen to participate in a Michigan district task force convened to work things out. From there he was selected as a delegate to the national convention in the summer of 1975.

He was excited when he phoned me from California. "I've just been elected to the mission board. Evidently, people were impressed when I expressed my belief in the truth of the Scriptures."

From then on, he traveled to the church headquarters in St. Louis every 6 weeks, flying out of Flint on Thursday after his last class and returning late Saturday night. He came back excited, but exhausted, with little time for me and the boys. I gave him time for a nap on Sunday afternoons since he'd be back in class on Monday morning. To keep the house quiet, I took Bengie and Joe to the mall.

Key leaders of the church came to know and trust Ben at those mission board meetings. They listened as he repeatedly insisted, "My Mende people need to know Jesus." The board decided to check things out when Ben offered his five thousand acres of land. Two missionaries accompanied him on a two-month survey trip during the summer of 1976, exploring mission opportunities in Liberia and five other African countries.

It sounded like a marvelous adventure, and I wanted to go along. I asked my folks to keep the kids for the summer, but Dad said it would be too much for Mom. I was deeply disappointed but had to accept it.

Ben encouraged me to do something special with the kids while he was gone, so I signed up for a week at Camp Arcadia on the shore of Lake Michigan. It was a disaster. We slept on cots in a large building, which made me a nervous wreck. Joe was a fussy 18-month-old that entire week, demanding my constant attention. I couldn't get him to sleep at night and worried about him keeping the other campers awake.

Thankfully Bengie, then 6, ran off to the camp activities each morning and had a good time. The other campers were kind, and the teenage counselors were so sympathetic that they offered to babysit Joe one day while I went on a canoe ride—my one peaceful activity. I was extremely relieved to be back home in Flint without an audience witnessing such an inadequate mother.

Joe's diarrhea wouldn't stop, and he was admitted to the hospital. I tried to keep him quiet as he lay there with an IV in his arm. I was scared, worried, and tired—tired of having a sick child and tired of having my husband halfway around the world when I needed him. Ben was so much on the go that his blue air letters were few and far between.

That evening, when I came home from the hospital, I was distraught, and I prayed like Gideon in the Bible: "Lord, please give me a sign that You'll heal my son. When I tip over this button jar, let there be 2 buttons on top that are just the right size to replace the ones missing on his jacket."

I pushed over the large container. Hundreds of buttons tumbled out on the bedspread. On top were 2 perfect white buttons.

The next morning, before heading back to the hospital, like Gideon, I asked for a 2nd sign to confirm the first. "Lord, if that garbage truck comes back to pick up the missed trash across the street, I'll know my son will be okay." I walked back into the kitchen 15 minutes later and saw that the trash was gone.

That day, the doctor told me Joe was lactose intolerant. It made all the difference. From then on he was fine, as I adjusted his diet.

In August, I finally got my husband back. That first night in bed, he told me, "On our flight home, the plane suddenly dropped 200 feet. Things were flying all over. Everyone was yelling or dead silent in fear. After we regained altitude, the pilot came on and said something about an air pocket. When we landed at JFK, everyone applauded."

I was shocked, but the incident confirmed for me that "the Lord is with us."

I ached to have Ben all to myself, but I wasn't the only one happy to see him. Before his fall classes started, he held court with people stopping by. I was so frustrated that one afternoon, I put Joe in the car seat and took a long drive out to Fenton. I wanted Ben to miss me, but he was clueless when I returned and started making supper.

The survey trip was wildly successful in Liberia, much less so in the other countries. Based on the findings, the board recommended a team of missionaries to go to Vahun—an evangelist, an agricultural missionary, a medical missionary, and a teacher. The evangelist would be first, followed each year by an additional missionary. There seemed to be no limit to Ben's aspirations and the church's cooperation. With our newfound sense of purpose and trust in God's care, we were happy in our life together, anticipating the path it was taking.

As plans for the new mission in Vahun firmed up, we headed to Liberia in the summer of 1977 to announce its arrival; Bengie was 9; Joe, 2 and a half.

CHAPTER 15

Great Expectations

◇◇◇◇◇◇◇◇◇◇◇◇◇◇◇

Love is not just looking at another;
it's looking in the same direction.
—Antoine de St. Exupery

Vahun, Liberia, summer 1977

That afternoon, the children celebrated our arrival wearing their new
T-shirts and badges. Following each other in a circle, they chanted,
"Baika, Baika," which means "Thank you, thank you." Patrick occupied the
center of the circle, prompting the teenage song leader. In typical African
call-and-response, the young man began: "Eyah! Ey-a-ah!" The children
replied in a lower key, "Eyah! Ey-a-ah!" They concluded with a prophetic
song in Mende that meant "The Old Man is coming. He's bringing good
news."

Children celebrating in anticipation of the coming of the mission

#

That June, for our trip to Liberia, my new family passport photo with the kids showed a young, skinny woman with eyebrows so plucked they were hardly visible. Joe, sitting on my lap, had his finger in his mouth. Bengie, his glasses too big for him, leaned on me, his smile displaying his new adult-size front teeth.

We spent 2 enjoyable days sightseeing on our layover in Frankfurt, Germany, but our taxi driver was so slow we missed our connecting flight to Liberia. J. Rud, Ben's Gbandi nephew, met us at Robertsfield at 1 a.m. The others had all gone home. He quickly showed us our quarters at his new house in the suburb of Monrovia called Paynesville, and then headed off to get some sleep. Our room was spacious and clean; the guest bathroom, modern. I turned on the faucet in the sink to wash up—cold water. I turned on the spigot in the tub—more cold water. Once again, cleaning up would have to wait.

As a businessman, J. Rud wore a suit and tie. His Vai wife, Gladys, was a lawyer who preferred fashionable Western dresses with a satin Liberian head tie. Tribal women wore head ties, and many Americo-Liberian women used them as a fashion statement. Matching the fabric of an African gown, they could be quite elaborate. The Johnsons had met and married while in college in America. In their impressive home, which reflected Americo-Liberian grandiosity, it took me 5 minutes to walk from our guest wing into their spacious living room.

In their situation, the child servants were tribal relatives. Within the tribal reciprocity system, those who became urbanized and successful were obligated to provide opportunities for family and other tribesmen to do as well in Monrovia. In return, the hosts were provided free household labor. The bedrooms for their 4 children and the servants were on the 2nd floor. Each morning, a Gbandi chauffer drove the children to school and dropped Gladys off at her office.

J. Rud and Gladys were busy with their careers. Except for special occasions, we spent more time with their children and the household staff. Each day, our kids disappeared to play with theirs.

I came better prepared for the heat this time with 6 simple cotton dresses I had made from Java-print fabric purchased on earlier trips. That summer, I added the current fashion to my wardrobe—batik and tie-dye T-shirts with matching wraparound skirts.

Even then, when we visited Gladys's church, the hot, stifling air in the packed sanctuary sucked the breath out of me. As I sat perfectly still, rivulets of sweat ran down my cheeks. The open door and cracked windows didn't provide any ventilation to speak of, and Joe's hot body on my lap certainly didn't help. I wanted to run out of the building to breathe, but I couldn't embarrass Ben or Gladys. It was a long service, and I found it hard to concentrate on the pastor's message. As I glanced around, I saw that the Liberian audience looked calm and comfortable.

A week later, our family attended a mission Sunday school held in a small, corrugated metal shack with a flat matching roof, the only light and air coming from the small open door. The stifling heat did nothing to dampen the enthusiasm of the young teacher or the children singing enthusiastically while crowded together on benches. Stooping slightly to go through the door as we left, I was grateful for a breath of fresh, but humid, air.

One day, Ben's sister, Angie, and her husband, Isaac, took us to their new home nearby. As we pulled up in their large black Cadillac, I stared at an immense skeleton of concrete block—comparable in size to the Executive Mansion—with openings for doors and windows. We climbed the concrete stairs to a 3rd-floor balcony overlooking the massive living room. Isaac's eyes lit up as he said, "The floor will slide away to reveal a swimming pool. I've ordered the chandeliers from Europe. Those crates over there hold some of the furniture that's been delivered."

I was surprised that Angie lived in one of the bare-bones upper-story bedrooms. She complained, "I'm tired of paying rent waiting for this house to be finished"; her husband's dream had remained empty since the money ran out.

The next day, on our way to Vahun, the driver of the Land Rover stopped at a juncture in the road for gas at the small station there. A 10-year-old tribal boy ran up to my front passenger window as we pulled up. Lifting an egg carton tray, he said, "Ma, boiled eggs, ten cent, ten cent. I give you salt in a paper." Glancing at my tie-dye outfit, he continued eagerly. "What's your name?"

Assuming my Mende identity, I said my new name: "Baindu."

He looked puzzled and then smiled.

I walked into the forest bathroom behind the gas station and overheard him tell his friend, "You see that white woman over there? Her name is Baindu."

The friend said, "Aww … ain't no white woman named *Baindu!*"

We were about to leave when the 2 boys ran up to my window. The egg seller said, "Ma, what's your name?"

"Baindu."

With a broad smile, he elbowed the other boy in the ribs and said, "You *see?*"

In Zor Zor, we toured the Lutheran hospital. I saw women patients sitting along the walls of a large room. In the center were open holes in the floor. I was baffled about their use until one of the women walked up and squatted, defecating into one of them. I turned my head, embarrassed for her, but she was unfazed. I shouldn't have been surprised, because at times, people urinated by the roadside or on the beach.

At Kolahun, we stopped at the familiar commissioner's house. Joe needed a nap, and I laid down with him in one of the bedrooms on the 2nd floor. As he dropped off to sleep, I noticed a large insect with iridescent wings sitting on the inside of the screen. It didn't move or look menacing, so I ignored it. We both slept until late afternoon, when the doves outside our window woke us with their haunting cooing.

We rode to Somalahun in an old covered pickup on the new motor road. A concrete bridge had replaced the monkey bridge, which was no longer maintained and in disrepair. I was sad to see it go.

When we arrived, Morlu surprised me with a special gift—a concrete latrine. He had been embarrassed during our earlier trips to have a white woman bathe outdoors in a bamboo enclosure. No one had been allowed to use it until I christened it. I teased Ben, saying, "*You* never built me a concrete latrine!"

We met John Corey, a Sudan Interior Mission missionary, holding a conference that day. Morlu told us, "I'm happy to learn how God created the world. It makes sense." The small, thatched-roof town hall was full as Ben opened the 1 o'clock session by saying, "What he's teaching is good for all of us. I'm one of you. I'm a follower of Jesus Christ, and I affirm that what he's saying is the truth."

In the question-and-answer session afterwards, Corey struggled to speak Gbandi, nervously pushing up his lower denture with his tongue. A murmur arose in the group, and an old man spoke up. "Did your teeth just go up and down in your mouth?"

Corey said, "Yes, I can take my denture out and put it back."

That statement signaled the end of religious theme of the meeting. From then on, it was chaos.

The old man said, "Do it! Do it!"

Corey obliged, and a woman exclaimed, "Oh, the man can take his teeth out!"

Everyone rushed up to get a good look.

A teenager pulled on his teeth and concluded, "Mine can't come out."

An old woman asked Ben, "Can *all* white people take their teeth out and put them back easy like that?"

Ben was at a loss for words because there's no Gbandi word for "false teeth." Finally he offered, "Those aren't his own teeth."

The old woman said, "What do you mean? We saw them in his mouth. They look like his teeth. Whose teeth could they be?"

The 3 o'clock session was shot too, as those who gathered sat chattering about the amazing phenomenon. Ben scolded, "Don't look at his teeth, *please!* Listen to what he's saying." It was useless.

Corey later told Ben, "People are welcoming me into all the other villages."

Ben replied, "I hope it's not because of your teeth."

He said, "Well, they *do* ask, 'Is he the one with the removable teeth?'"

On our way back to Kolahun, the boys and I sat in the back of the pickup, jostled by our gifts: a turtle, 3 chickens, and a goat. Ben had to hang his head out the window of the front passenger seat, as he was carsick from the animal scent.

Heading to Vahun, the Land Rover stopped at the highest peak going over Kamboi. I jumped out with my camera and captured miles and miles of vast green forested hills stretching out before me under an open sky, a mist hanging in the valleys from the recent downpour.

As I opened the car door to get back in, I felt a twinge of diarrhea and asked the driver to wait. I banged the door closed in my haste and felt the vehicle slide slightly sideways in the wet clay mush. Slipping my way across the road, I stomped up the steep muddy embankment and into the bush. On my way there, I yelled, "Honey! I forgot the toilet paper! Can you toss me some?"

He called back, "I can't find it! You'll have to use Mende toilet paper [meaning big, soft plant leaves]!" I thought, *Men can never find anything.*

Ben and the boys were standing by the roadside waiting as I came out of the bush, using my feet to ski across the road. After taking a quick picture, I swung open the car door, and the Land Rover suddenly shifted and started moving downhill. I quickly backed away, slamming the door. Time stopped as we stood watching the vehicle slide down the mountain sideways. We stared, holding our breath, until it wedged itself into an embankment at the bottom. We slithered down the side of the road, Ben carrying Joe and I grabbing onto Bengie's arm.

Land Rover sliding

Land Rover at the bottom

The driver sat there shell-shocked as I exclaimed, "I'm so glad you're okay!" He smiled slightly but said nothing. The worst of our drive over Kamboi was over, and I knew God had protected us. After all, weren't we doing His work?

I was surprised to see how much Vahun had expanded. Land around the village was cleared, and a few new houses were under construction. The accessibility of the area meant Mendes were returning from Sierra Leone. Additional rice farms were planted, and the new health clinic was close to completion.

The next day, the town hall was full, not only with Mendes from town, but also with those from nearby villages interested in the mission. In fact, the meeting had been postponed from the previous day so everyone interested could attend.

In Flint, we had used church money to buy 100 badges and yellow T-shirts bearing a drawing of Jesus on the cross. They read in Mende, "Jesus mia ae mu balo moe," which meant "Jesus is the one who saves us completely." In Monrovia, we had purchased gifts for the women: laundry soap, head ties, combs, and mirrors. We brought a $200 cash gift for the village from the Lutheran church.

After the children marched in their T-shirts, singing, "The Old Man is coming; he's bringing good news," we presented our gifts to key people in the village, the large crowd on the benches watching. As Patrick handed them out, I stood in front with Joe hanging on my leg, hoping he wouldn't say "I have to go potty" before the ceremony was over. My friend Hawah came forward, and I rushed over and gave her a big hug. Ben told me later, "The people were impressed by that."

Everyone listened attentively as Ben said, "When I came home, you asked me, 'Why did you come back after you were successful and prosperous in that other country?' I told you, 'The best thing I found when I was away from you is Jesus.' It's because I love Jesus that I've returned to share His love with you. I want you to know Him, too, because He loves me and He loves you. I'm here to tell you that the Good News about this Jesus will soon be told. The church is coming."

That evening, as Ben sat talking with the elders, a young girl came and served him the palm wine first. When she left, one of the elders said, "You see that young lady? She's pretty, isn't she? How many wives do you have in those people's country?"

Ben said, "Just Bendu."

The men looked at each other and laughed. One of them said, "You're in a bad place. We're looking to you as chief, and you're sitting over there with one wife? Is Bendu satisfied?"

"Yeah."

"She *can't* be. She's got to do all the work. She's your eyes, your feet, your mouth. She thinks for you. How can she do all this when she's by herself?"

Patrick came to Ben's aid, saying, "I know that's the way it is in the white people's country."

The elder disagreed. "But he's a *Mende!* He can get all the wives he wants. That girl could become his wife—and her younger sisters too, since she's the oldest."

Brima chimed in, "You know only poor people have one wife."

Another elder said, "It would be better for you to come home. We're a big family, and we want to increase. With just Bendu, you can't do much."

That night, as Ben told me about it, he had a mischievous look on his face when he said, "I told them, 'I'll have to talk to her.'"

I playfully tapped him on the shoulder and said, "I *bet* you will!"

The next day, Hawah presented us with a bedspread woven in a traditional African design. She smiled as she watched Joe running around and said, "My husband's back. He was just like that—determined, with a temper."

Ben whispered in my ear, "Young children are considered reborn ancestors."

Patrick accompanied us when we traveled to nearby Sierra Leone to meet Ben's Mende relatives, gathering the elders as we stopped in each village. The money bus, a van carrying 30 people, pulled up in Vahun, and I thought, *It's already full*. Ben paid the driver, and we boarded, so I assumed he was making an exception for us. I scrunched between 2 women with Joe on my lap. When he picked up 15 more passengers, I realized how wrong I had been!

Money Bus on the way to Sierra Leone

We bounced our way into Sierra Leone, stopping first at the small village of Geihun. Children crowded around us, pointing and calling to me, "Pu moi!"

I looked at Ben, and he said, "It means 'Western person.' Call them 'Mende moi'—Mende person.'"

I called it out enthusiastically, and the kids laughed and jumped. From then on, it became my mantra in each village.

While Ben and Patrick met with the elders everywhere we stopped, I sat on a wooden bench, watching, with Joe sleeping on my lap and Bengie leaning on me. I couldn't understand what was said, but I sensed the people were enthusiastic about having missionaries come and teach their children.

At one village, the entire group posed for a photo so we wouldn't forget them. I was beginning to understand Ben's and my role in representing these people to our national church.

Meetings in Sierra Leone

At another stop, there was so much rejoicing that the people urged me to "jump in the circle and dance." I knew the pony from my college days, but to be honest, I felt ridiculous dancing that way to the beat of the drums. In the town of Bo, we hired another truck driven by a young, handsome Mende man with beautiful white teeth. I sat next to him, straddling the gear shift with Ben by the window. He looked at me with his dazzling smile and exclaimed in jest, "So you're a Mende woman!" I smiled back.

At Kenema, we entered the chief's compound unannounced. In the courtyard, I noticed 3 gorgeous leopard skins drying on an elevated grave and snapped a picture. As we left, I saw that they were gone, prompting me to wonder if hunting leopards was banned.

Everywhere we traveled in Liberia and Sierra Leone, young people invariably quizzed Ben about education in America. He liberally handed out his professional cards, saying, "Write me." This resulted in a 100 letters or so asking us if they could be our houseboy while we put them through college.

It was late at night when, covered in sweat and grime, we reached Freetown, the capital of Sierra Leone. I longed for a decent place to stay. The Paramount Hotel with its British colonial ambiance was heaven-sent. The lounge was spacious, and the dining hall lovely. I relished the hot shower and clean white sheets.

The next morning, in the gift shop, I bought 2 small pink-and-blue coiled baskets—favorite souvenirs. I was admiring the enormous cotton tree towering over the town square when the Mende man with us said, "They rounded up slaves under that tree to carry in ships to America." I shuddered in horror, imagining their suffering.

In the nearby marketplace, an intellectually disabled man in his 20s walked up to me, a group of teenagers in his wake. After a silly, ridiculous dance, he stuck his tongue out of the corner of his mouth, put his finger on top of his head, and balanced on one leg, with his right foot on his left knee. He stared, waiting for a reward. I was embarrassed to see him humiliating himself and angry with those who had put him up to it. I looked down, refusing to acknowledge or reward any of them.

That afternoon, Joe had severe diarrhea. I was thankful there was a local clinic nearby. The doctor took a culture of his stool and said, "I think it's dysentery, but it'll take several days for the results. Since you're traveling, I'll give you the medicine for it anyway."

At the hotel, Ben booked tickets for Joe and me to fly directly to Monrovia. He said, "I'll take Bengie with me back to Vahun. When you land at Robertsfield, take a taxi to the Lutheran Guest House. Stay there until I come to get you." As the plane descended, I watched the waves crashing on the sandy beach and prayed, "Please be with me, Lord, and heal our son."

I arranged for a room at the Guest House and moved in. That afternoon, I took a city bus into town for groceries. Joe was on my lap, and I felt my skirt get wet, a familiar smell assaulting my nose.

Upon exiting the bus, I saw a Lebanese woman standing in a doorway next to a store. I figured she lived upstairs and asked if I could use her bathroom. She nodded, and I'll never forget her kindness. I rinsed Joe's underpants in the bathtub and put his wet shorts back on.

At the Guest House, Joe grew increasingly cranky. He couldn't stop scratching the red bumps on his arms, which I assumed were mosquito bites. A day later, he was unable to sleep more than 15 minutes at a time. I moved in a trance of sleeplessness, trying to calm him each time he awoke.

After 2 nights of that, I took him to the bishop's wife, who lived in a house at the compound. She was a nurse and quickly explained, "Oh, I know what that is. You can't tell until the bumps become elongated. A large fly has laid its eggs under Joe's skin. Worms are growing there. Let me get a match." I realized it must have been that large insect on the screen at the commissioner's house in Kolahun.

She killed the worms by putting a flame to their heads in the small openings. After squeezing out 6 of them, she put alcohol on each opening. It was an ordeal holding Joe down, but he was finally able to sleep.

At the Guest House on the Atlantic Ocean, the window shutters facing the beach were kept open. The waves crashing and retreating in time for another to arrive were a soothing backdrop that I sorely needed. Those 4 days seemed to last forever. Watching Ben and Bengie walk through the front entrance brought me a rush of joy. Ben quickly took us back to J. Rud's house.

A week later, we boarded a flight to Accra, the capital of Ghana, to visit 2 missionary teams—both kind and gracious hosts. As we drove to a remote mission station, the grassy flatlands and cornfields were in stark contrast to Liberia's rain forest. Joe was skinny. When I carried him in a lappa on my back, the missionary's wife said, "We've got to fatten him up." She did her best in the short time we were there.

Rainy season was in full force in Monrovia that August; sheets of rain pounded the earth relentlessly as far as the eye could see. Laundry hanging on J. Rud's back porch stayed damp for days. We were eager to get home. Ben's shoulders and neck ached. I was weak from a bout of malaria. Joe was still recovering. I was thankful that Bengie was unscathed.

The travel agent in Flint had warned us that our return flight would leave at 1 a.m. We needed to get to the airport the night before the date of our flight to catch our plane. If we missed it, we would overstay our 6-week travel rate. Of course, with all that had transpired, we forgot and had to pay an extra $1,500 airfare. Ben charged it on our credit card after receiving approval from the company in New York City.

We spent the night with a Mende man in nearby Harbel instead of going back to Monrovia. While I was walking around the area, milky water in a trench splashed into a bleeding mosquito bite on my ankle. By the time we reached JFK Airport in New York, I could hardly walk. Sores were breaking out on different parts of my leg. I kept saying to myself, "You'll soon be home; you'll soon be home."

I hobbled into my kitchen door, overwhelmed with relief. Ben ordered, "I'll watch the kids. Soak your leg in the hottest saltwater possible." I stuck my leg into a tall plastic wastebasket and felt the salt burning into the sores. After 3 days of soaking off and on, the sores were almost completely healed.

A week later, my malaria returned. We hadn't brought any chloroquine with us; nor could I get some at the local drugstore, as we had done in Monrovia. Our doctor finally located a supply at a local hospital. As usual, it did the trick. Getting malaria in Africa is like getting a cold in America. You know the symptoms and you know the cure. Our trip had been trying but successful. With God's help, we came home in one piece.

I didn't look forward to returning to Liberia; nor did I consider *moving* there. However, God had a different plan.

CHAPTER 16

Moving to Liberia

◇◇◇◇◇◇◇◇◇◇◇◇◇◇

God is always more than He seems.
—Eunice Graham

Wood Lane Drive, Flint, Michigan, January 1980

We were lying in bed one night, and Ben said, "I want to serve God in Liberia. What do you think?"

In faith, I said, "This must be God's plan for us. We'll go with you."

In Ben's eagerness to permanently return to Liberia, his utopian dreams for his 5,000 acres of land resurfaced. "My nonprofit corporation, called Jesus, My Friend, will include a cooperative rice farm, fields of fruits and vegetables, a sawmill for lumber, poultry coops, coffee and cocoa for cash crops, and a rock-crushing business."

I lay there pondering how that would come about, and whether I would survive it.

#

During the fall of 1977, after we returned from Liberia, I was happy and content to be home. I had a new sense of freedom with Bengie in 4ᵗʰ grade and Joe in nursery school 2 mornings a week. We bought bunk beds for the boys, and I turned our 3rd bedroom into an office for Ben. I shopped for new fall clothes and was busy refurbishing the house.

At the next mission board meeting, Ben was elected to serve on the Black Ministry Commission. A while later, familiar waves of nausea swept over me. We were both hoping for a girl when the gynecologist confirmed my pregnancy.

Ben said, "Let's name her Mali Anita for my mother and you."

Once again, I couldn't keep anything down. My condition spiraled downward until I ended up on IVs at the hospital. Ben visited as much as he could. I looked strange as my plucked eyebrows grew back, and I stopped plucking them after that.

In my absence, Ben did as well as he could with the kids, despite his full teaching load. When I returned home, a neighborhood friend was a godsend. I wanted Joe's picture taken at nursery school, and she saw to it. It's one of my favorites, with his curly black hair, red turtleneck, and shy, sweet smile. One day, she brought over her sister-in-law and they moved the boys' bunk beds to the other wall and changed the sheets.

I was depressed, lying in bed—helpless with more "family" dependent on me. When Ben came home, I longed for him to sit by my bedside and hold my hand. Instead he was busy feeding the boys and getting them to bed.

In 1976, during the mission survey trip, Ben had become acquainted with a young Vai woman while traveling in Lofa County. He gave her his card after they helped push a taxi out of the mud together. That November, Meita, as she was known, called us from Philadelphia asking for help. Immigration officials were on her tail because she had overstayed her visitor visa. I was touched by her plight and agreed when Ben invited her to come and stay with us. A month later, she returned to Liberia for a new visa and came back with malaria. While she lay sick in her bedroom in the basement, I lay upstairs in my bed, equally weak. She became part of our family as we went through tough times together. In between her classes at the University of Michigan–Flint, she occasionally babysat Joe and helped around the house.

She was not only charming and lovable but also Lutheran! She attended Our Savior with us, and the people there became attached to her as well; they held a fundraiser for her college tuition. She eventually became a registered nurse in Columbus, Ohio, after she married a Mende man from Sierra Leone.

I had to pace myself when I was able to eat again. The house was quiet with the boys gone, but there was a lot of cleaning and sprucing up to do. I needed to get ready for the baby. I worked until I became short of breath and then rested on the couch. A few minutes later, I was at it again. Ben's new office became a nursery, and our3rd baby had a new white crib and matching dressing table. In April of 1978, I was 9 months pregnant before Ben chose a boy's name just in case—"Peter," after his favorite disciple; "Morlu," after his maternal grandfather; and "Brima Sao," two Mende family names.

Baby #3 came into our lives in the middle of May 1978, but it took forever to arrive. I went into labor several times, with Ben rushing me to the hospital, only to bring me back when my pains stopped. One afternoon, while taking a nap, I was awakened by a warm liquid washing over my legs. On the phone, the doctor said, "Come to my office." Ben drove me there with a towel between my legs. She took one look at me and said, "Your water broke. Go straight to the hospital."

My labor pains stopped again, and Ben lay on the couch in the hall, waiting. He told me he overheard a nurse tell the other, "Look at that man—sleeping while his wife's in such pain."

A few minutes later, my doctor walked in and said, "I'm going to induce labor." My other 2 deliveries had been routine, but this was the shortest. As I was wheeled out of the delivery room, I told Ben, "Honey, it's another boy. I hope you're not too disappointed."

He said, "Of course not! I'm happy! I have another son!"

The next day, as I laid in the hospital bed holding Peter, Ben exulted, "Well, now that we've had all our babies, we can write books together!"

I said nothing, but I thought, *Are you crazy? I'm holding a newborn, and we have a three-year-old toddler and a ten-year-old in fourth grade. What are you thinking?*

I celebrated that Mother's Day in the hospital with a carnation in a vase on my lunch tray. Ben's tulips were blooming bright red and yellow under the pine tree when we pulled into our driveway. I thought, *Spring is a wonderful time to have a baby.*

That June, we had a visit from Allen and Mary Lou, the 1st missionaries to serve in Vahun. We gave them an introduction to the Mende people via our slides and movies. It was exciting that things were finally getting under way.

There was more good news. During that summer, Ben would accompany the chairman of the mission board and the executive secretary in awarding President Tolbert, a Baptist minister, an honorary doctor of laws degree from Concordia Seminary in recognition of his support for Ben's mission interest. The bad news? I was facing 3 weeks that summer without him.

How could I object? I completely supported his mission efforts. I believed God was orchestrating the events. With the help of friends, I somehow managed to prevail with 3 small children.

That summer, Allen and Mary Lou arrived in Liberia as well. However, the construction of their house in Vahun was delayed when a bridge on the road to Kamboi washed out. Ben's nephew, Thomas, then superintendent of Lofa County, told Ben government funds were tight because of the upcoming summit of the Organization of African Unity in Monrovia.

That fall, I recruited my ladies' Bible study group and our church's prayer chain to begin praying for a new bridge. One night, I told the women in faith, "When the Lord gives us the new bridge, I'm going to have a party to celebrate!"

On New Year's Day of 1979, Ben and I boldly prayed, "The bridge, this year, please, Lord." That January, Ben wrote President Tolbert, describing his discouragement about the poor condition of the road. He never mentioned the bridge. In March, he received a letter from him saying a new Bailey bridge—a prefabricated steel bridge—would soon be installed.

I hosted my promised party with 21 women attending. That prayer effort made me realize I could be a bridge between the people in my church and those in Vahun. I saw my role as one who encourages and prays while sharing news between groups.

Ben and I were eager to promote the mission effort in any way we could. During the summer of 1979, I was to meet him in St. Louis for a mission fest since he had gone ahead to attend the mission board meeting. I arranged for my neighborhood friend to take care of the kids. Late for my flight, I drove our Plymouth Duster over the speed limit on I-75 as I headed to Detroit Metro Airport. A mile from my destination, smoke rose from the hood. I pulled over at the side of the freeway and locked the car. Convinced that God didn't want me to miss my flight, I was bold—the more accurate term would be "reckless." Faith makes us that way sometimes.

I jumped out, frantically waving my arms to hitch a ride. Within minutes, a rather rough-looking young man in a pickup stopped, and I said, "Would you please drop me at the airport? My car broke down."

He was obviously heading somewhere else, but he smiled and said okay, and he dropped me at the front entrance. I ran to the United Airlines ticket counter. There was no one in line since the flight was about to leave. The agent said, "I'll alert them and send your bag on. If you hurry, you'll just make it."

I rushed down the corridor to the empty gate, where a stewardess ushered me into the plane. The flight was full. I found the only empty seat and buckled up, whispering, "Lord, thank You." Our dear Christian neighbors towed our car home.

For me, this experience, along with the Bailey bridge, symbolized God's ability to carry out His will. Ben and I began to think, *If missionaries can move to Vahun and serve God, why can't we? What had the Lord not done for us?"*

At the same time, there were rumblings of discontent in Liberia. Ben ignored them just as he had done years prior at Ohio University when a visiting Kru student told him, "My father worked at the mansion, so that's how I got a scholarship. Dr. Dennis, my eyes are opened. You, me, all of us—we have to serve Liberia."

Ben said, "How?"

"Not only through education. We have to change the government. Our leaders are like blind men. Their behavior is molded in such a way that they can't go up or down, right or left. If we don't change the government, *nothing* will change in Liberia.

"Our (tribal) people are getting masters [degrees] and doctorates in all *kinds* of fields. We're the most educated. Why should we let these archaic men rule? We've shown them and the world that we've got brains by virtue of our degrees. There are others who feel like I do. There's a community of Liberians in Maryland and some in the Washington, DC, area who are working on a project to take things over."

During our various trips to Liberia, we had observed that government corruption was rampant. Ben heard someone say about a government official, "Come on, man. You mean he's been in office 4 years and hasn't built a house?"

Our hostess, Etna, had complained, "All these foreigners—the Lebanese, the Indians, even the Nigerians and Ghanaians, and all the white people as well—are paying bribes to stay in business. The government's getting money for nothing. The only ones who aren't paying are the country people—the market women and those who sell tie-dye. You can't stay in business here without bribing."

We were also aware of the undercurrent of simmering resentment between the Americo-Liberians and the tribal people. When Ben met up with that Kru student in Liberia in the summer of 1978, he was going by his tribal name, Togba Nah Tipoteh. As they sat together in Rosalie's Restaurant in Monrovia, he said, "Dr. Dennis, I know you're very qualified. If you could run a department of white professors in a conservative university like OU, you can certainly help run a government of old men with no brains."

Ben said, "If they have no brains, that makes it much more difficult."

"Don't you see my point? This is your country too. Look at this place. Tomorrow I'll take you to visit some government offices so you can see for yourself."

After their visit, Tipoteh told Ben, "Did you see that the heads of those offices were Americo-Liberians and their assistants were our people? Mark my words; we're going to take over. They call us country people. Yeah, we're country people—the country belongs to *us*."

Ben cautioned him, saying, "Be sure to analyze everything. Have a blueprint for how this is going to work. You must build Liberia rather than simply instigating destruction based on hate. If that happens, we'll have nothing."

Several weeks later, President Tolbert told Ben, "I'm interested in you for vice president, but the majority of people in Liberia know too little about you. You need to return home for a year or two so people can see who you are. Think about it."

When Ben returned home, he mentioned Tolbert's comment to me, and I said, "Honey, I'm a white woman. How could I be the wife of the vice president of Liberia?"

Still, the possibility fueled Ben's ambition. Several weeks before Christmas of 1978, Tolbert visited the Liberian community in Detroit, and Ben and I attended his speech at Wayne State University. As Tolbert walked up to the stage, he saw Ben sitting in the audience and broke the line to shake hands with him. Ben was elated. The Detroit Liberians were pumped up by Tolbert's visit.

Family Photo taken in 1979

By April of 1979, Liberia was in turmoil. Crowds in Monrovia rioted over the rising price of rice, and the police called in to quell the rioting joined the protestors. Tolbert used troops from Guinea to restore order, but not before $40 million worth of damage was done.

Tolbert had served as 2nd in command under President Tubman for 20 years. In the same Americo-Liberian mindset, he took advantage of his position, as had every leader before him. After the riots, he followed typical tactics to retain power. He had the leaders of the protest arrested, the university closed, and due process suspended. At the Organization of African Unity summit that summer, the leaders of the riots were released, and the university reopened, but the die had been cast.

In contrast to this, everything was going well in Vahun. In January of 1980, Allen and Mary Lou, along with their 3 children, moved into the new mission house in Vahun near the airstrip on the hill. They flew to and from Monrovia on the bush plane nicknamed TILLY, which was owned by the Institute for Liberian Languages. In time, Allen conducted services with 39 – 40 in attendance. There were Bible study classes on Friday evenings, and the local children were "learning Bible" in school. Nearby villages expressed interest in Christianity and were eager to build their own church.

The success in Vahun, along with Tolbert's promise to make Ben vice-president, rang louder in Ben's ears than the gathering storm clouds. We preferred to believe the best. In the Bible, God used wicked rulers to accomplish His purposes. Couldn't He use President Tolbert, a leader who professed to be a Christian for his own advantage?

We made preparations to move to Liberia. In March of 1980, Ben intended to resign at the University of Michigan–Flint, until the chancellor convinced him to take a 2-year leave of absence to see how things went. We put our house up for sale and sent Bengie to Florida for a week's vacation with Mom and Dad since we didn't know when he'd see them again.

We had faith in the success of our venture, but I still had misgivings. It was daunting to think of raising an 11-year-old, a 5-year-old, and a 2-year-old in a foreign country. Of course, there was the lure of Africa—a carefree, indulgent life in Monrovia with house servants. At the same time, there was considerable uncertainty about how Ben's dreams were going to play out.

His standards of excellence as a professor were clear to me. What I couldn't fully understand was his ambition for himself in Liberia and all it entailed. Everything so far had been cloaked in missionary zeal. I was frightened that Ben was no longer the husband who listened to me and weighed everything. His mind was set; his focus was on his plans rather than how he would support me and the kids. I knew there had been times in America when we were essentially on our own.

I wondered, *How is this new venture going to affect our marriage and the raising of our children? Will Ben and I truly be partners in this? Or will he be wrapped up in his work there with no time for us? Is our marriage really ready for this?*

Ben was a compassionate man who believed in the importance of his role and destiny. I admired him for his self-respect, which stemmed from his heritage as a chief. He controlled his temper, never speaking rashly. In fact, it was hard to get him to talk if he was angry or didn't want to discuss something. Because of my German heritage, I was used to arguing things out. However, whenever I wanted to do that, he withdrew, which was terribly frustrating. Sometimes I calmed down and he responded. Other times, we left things unresolved, as in the current situation.

I no longer had blind faith in my husband. When we put our house on the market for $41,000, I asked for a sign from God to confirm our move. "Lord, if it's Your plan that we go there, let us get the full price for our house." A young black couple insisted on $40,000. Owing to the pressure of time and the lack of other offers, we signed a purchase agreement for that amount.

Things moved ahead out of my control. I dismissed the sign. However, God was still in charge.

CHAPTER 17

The Coup

◇◇◇◇◇◇◇◇◇◇◇◇◇◇◇

God will make a way when there seems to be no way.
—Don Moen

Wood Lane Drive, Flint, Michigan, April 13, 1980

The wall phone in the kitchen rang at 2 a.m. Ben went to answer it. I heard him say, "Hello," and then there was silence. He plodded back into the bedroom and just stood there, his eyes staring and vacant as if in shock. In a voice of defeat, he announced, "President Tolbert's been assassinated."

I was stunned by the news—and simultaneously relieved, as I instantly realized we weren't moving to Liberia after all. I stared at the man I loved, who appeared to be devastated, looking like a forlorn, lost child. He came to bed, and we lay there together in the silence for a few moments, trying to absorb the shock.

I reached over to hold his hand and said, "Who called you?"

"I'm not sure. I think the call was from London. Samuel Doe, one of Tolbert's security guards from the Krahn tribe, shot him and appears to be in charge."

#

149

Overnight, Liberia descended into chaos. We were desperate to learn what was happening to our friends and relatives, but getting fast and accurate news on American TV was almost impossible. Much of it was horrible; wild rumors abounded. President Tolbert had been shot in the head. Tribal soldiers shaved Victoria Tolbert's head and put her in a jail cell, naked. Tolbert's son, A. B., was beheaded. In the stockade, soldiers stripped government officials, making them jump, like puppets, at gunpoint.

Ten days later, another call in the middle of the night told us that Cecil Dennis, Ben's cousin who was minister of state, had been shot by a firing squad on the beach along with other government officials. Angie's former husband, Richard Henries, the speaker of the house, collapsed from a heart attack before they shot him. Uncle C. C. was chained to the back of a pickup and dragged to his death.

News about the coup trickled in. An Associated Press report titled "Thirteen Liberian Ex-Officials Killed by Firing Squad," said, "The executions may have been the opening round of a bloody purge of the old regime by the military men, led by Master Sergeant Samuel Doe, who toppled the government April 12th and killed President Tolbert ... Doe, twenty-eight, is the son of an impoverished farmer from the small Krahn tribe ... A red and white banner draped on a building in Monrovia reads, 'Our eyes are open: the time of the people has come.'"

Ben's nephew, Harry, working at the foreign ministry in Monrovia, wrote us: "Thomas is still in detention at the Barclay Training Center. Today he faced the military tribunal for corruption, misuse of public office, and abuse of the people's human rights ... We now await the verdict." Thomas was eventually released. The other good news was that the missionaries in Vahun were okay.

From that first phone call, Ben became a robot going through the motions; his personal dreams and those for Liberia had been smashed to smithereens. He was also mourning the death of his friend. Day after day, he sat in the living room with his short-wave radio on his lap, trying to tune in *World News* on the BBC. He said nothing about Liberia. It was too painful.

The local interest story in the *Flint Journal* read, "Dennis, who has taught at the U of M-Flint since 1970, said he could not discuss the situation in Liberia now because of his fear for the safety of family members still in the country ... In happier times, Dennis was Tolbert's special envoy during visits to public officials in Michigan."

A former student sent a note: "During your class lectures, you spoke so often of your family and your country and with such obvious pride in both …" A letter arrived, stating, "Resolved, that the Board for Missions regretfully release Dr. Benjamin Dennis from his one-year special assignment to Liberia."

With him incapacitated, I had to take over. I was glad the kids were young. Ben ate and slept. He dressed each morning. But he was a shell of a man.

He called the university, revoking his leave, and his fall classes were quickly posted and filled up. Had the coup occurred a month later, we would have been in Liberia. Who knows what would have happened to us? I realized God was there, protecting us—even when my husband had made a disastrous mistake.

We no longer needed to sell the house and contacted the couple through their black realtor. He told us, "A purchase agreement is a legal contract. They'll sue you in excess of $10,000 if you don't sell them your house. They really want it."

We were appalled. How could they be so hardhearted? We weren't moving to Liberia, but we would be moving after all.

Ben found a realtor through the university, but he made no comments or suggestions concerning the homes she showed us. I realized I'd have to make the decision and chose a tri-level house in the East Court Street area, closer to campus—with well-maintained homes, manicured lawns, and other faculty as neighbors.

Our new home had great potential, and I emphasize "potential." Essentially, it screamed "work." Constructed in 1950, it had been a builder's showcase model, decorated in art deco style. At a Flint home show, a young couple won it for $1 raffle ticket. We found the sign in the attic reading, "Win this house for a dollar."

Befitting a college professor, the spacious L-shaped living room had a white marble fireplace and 2 walls of floor-to-ceiling windows, the dining room accented by a brick wall. The spacious foyer, separating the public and private areas of the house, had a built-in mirrored vanity. Completing the house were 2 bedrooms and a full bath on the upper level and another bedroom and utility room on the lower level.

That was the good news. The downside was that it needed a complete overhaul. The former owners were an older, childless couple who preferred gold brocade drapes covering the living and dining room windows, and a brown-and-cream sculptured plush carpet. The walls of the main-level bathroom were covered with black foil wallpaper featuring dancing pink poodles. The accent wall of the kitchen eating area displayed enormous banana stalks on a maroon wallpaper background.

In June, when we moved in, one of Ben's students laid cream-and-gold simulated-marble floor tile diagonally in the foyer and kitchen. I ended up painting almost every inch of the place, including baseboards, kitchen and bathroom cupboards, and the bedroom closets—ivory this time, instead of white. The thin-slat venetian blinds throughout the house weren't installed for a month. Our neighbors, and indeed all of Flint, zipped by on Court Street, watching our renovation progress.

Ben and I lived in 2 different worlds during that time. He was mentally in Liberia. I was preoccupied with my new decorating project. That summer, he helped as much as he could with cleanup and the kids, but he had to prepare for fall classes. In my desire to have things done and in order, I pushed myself to exhaustion a number of times. In August, I lay in bed 3 days with incapacitating back spasms.

Things returned to normal on the surface when Ben resumed teaching and most of the house was in order. However, news from Liberia reopened agonizing wounds. The boys were at school one morning—Bengie in 6th grade, Joe in kindergarten, and Peter in a nursery program—when I heard a thump at the front door. I picked up a large brown envelope sent airmail from Liberia.

In the bundle of Liberian newspapers, I was stunned to see the front-page photos: bodies of government officials in their underwear, tied to poles on the beach—slumped over and riddled with bullets. Ben's cousin Cecil was among them. I felt sick to my stomach. Facing the stark reality of the coup, my hands shook. It was as if those soldiers had marched into our house, firing their rifles. I pondered showing them to Ben, yet I knew I couldn't keep them from him.

The renovations were complete in October, and we held an open house to dedicate our home to the Lord. Our theme was "… as for me and my household, we will serve the Lord" (Joshua 24:15). Ben was his usual, charming self, circulating among our relatives and friends—ignoring my struggle to serve the food. Adding insult to injury, he told a student to park on the lawn, and he chewed up the grass as he backed out to leave. When the guests were gone, I was overwhelmed with fatigue and stress. I lost it, bawling Ben out royally for leaving everything to me. It wasn't a shining moment in our marriage.

A week later, Ben invited a tall, young African student to dinner. Well-spoken and personable, he was charming with an inviting smile. Ben offered to do the dishes, suggesting I drop the student off at his host family's house. After months of drudgery, I was vulnerable to some excitement. During the ride, his passionate account of his homeland was infectious; and after dropping him off, the scent of his cologne filled the car.

I thought I'd never see him again, but a week later, he casually stopped by. Ben and I were moving boxes of books into the attic. When he smiled at me, I became literally speechless. I was shocked by my reaction.

He called a few days later and asked if he could stop over. Ben was at the office. I knew I shouldn't, but I agreed. Thankfully, Peter was home running around and nothing happened between us. I thought of him often after that but said nothing to Ben. A week later, when he called suggesting a rendezvous, my conscience thankfully said, "Stop!" I told Ben everything that night. He was understandably angry, considering what his first wife had done to him, but he was also relieved to have the upper hand.

The next day on campus, Ben confronted him. "I know what you're doing. My wife told me." That was the end of that. From then on, he avoided me like the plague. I found out later he was quite an operator, living off of women he seduced.

As life returned to normal, Ben and I grew close again. I focused on serving church members—befriending a mentally ill woman and one who was disabled. Ben prayed at the kitchen table, "Lord, please bless Anita in her work with the 'unlovables.'"

We spent Christmas as a happy family, exchanging gifts by the large tree in front of the wall of windows, the fireplace hung with stockings.

In January of 1981, a Liberian friend loaned us her videotape of the execution of government officials on the beach in Monrovia. Ben wept as we watched. I sat there frozen like a statue, unable to tear my eyes from the gruesome, horrific scene.

Vahun's remote location protected it from the immediate effects of the coup. Despite the tragedy, God's work had progressed there. When Allen and Mary Lou returned to the states the summer of 1981, 300 souls had been baptized. A church was built in Vahun, and preaching stations were set up in the nearby villages of Gbongoma and Seema.

That fall, Carol and George, the 2nd team of missionaries, visited us in Flint for their preview of the Mende people. They were gracious, and we felt confident God's work would continue through them.

We were settled in our new home and neighborhood. Life was moving along. The boys were growing and involved in school and church activities. As a taxi Mom, I took Ben Jr. to confirmation class, and Joe to after-school religion classes at Our Savior, as well as chauffeuring the two boys wherever they needed or wanted to go. I was active in our church prayer chain and women's Bible studies. Ben was busy teaching and serving on the mission board and the Black Ministry Commission.

I was sure the door to Liberia was forever closed, and I dismissed any thought of returning.

CHAPTER 18

Assurance from God

◇◇◇◇◇◇◇◇◇◇◇◇◇◇◇

The will of God will not take you where the
grace of God cannot keep you.
—Rebecca Nolt

814 S. Vernon Avenue, Flint, Michigan, fall 1982

One afternoon, Ben came home from the office and announced, "I've got a sabbatical coming up next year. I can take either 6 months off with full pay, or 9 months with half pay. I'd like to spend a year in Liberia investigating what's happened to the Gbandi people since I published my book.

"I know the young people have been abandoning traditional tribal life in favor of urban centers like Monrovia, the mining sites, and the rubber plantation. It's made them marginal people, unable to contribute in either society. Of course, while we're living in Vahun, we'll do lay missionary work."

#

That fall, Ben was 53 when he turned my world upside down. I was 37, and the boys 16, 8, and 5. I stood there listening to him, and the thought of Liberia once again entering my safe, secure world felt like a volcano erupting without warning. *Boom!* I wondered, *Can things have settled down that much?*

I wasn't initially enthusiastic about going, but whenever Ben came up with one of his ideas, I pondered whether God must have a plan in it. My life was captive to my husband's, and ultimately to God's, will. Did I struggle in being submissive? Yes! I made my peace with it by believing that God would help me through whatever was His will.

A year there seemed manageable compared to a permanent move, even if we lived in Vahun rather than Monrovia. It was a golden opportunity for the boys to learn about their father's side of the family. More importantly, it would give us time to personally witness to the Mende people about their Savior. Recovering my spunk, I guess I saw it as another anthropological adventure.

As Ben and I grew closer to the Lord in our devotions, we bonded in this venture. The preparations went smoothly, confirming God's plan. An African couple, who were good friends, agreed to rent our house. The mission board approved the funding for Ben to do a year of lay missionary work while reporting on other mission opportunities. Twenty-nine members of Our Savior signed up as prayer partners. The pastor of my home church gave us a missionary send-off.

I reminded Ben that I had always wanted to go to Europe, and he said, "Okay, I'll take you there on the way." My high school dream came true as we arranged a week's visit at the Liberian embassies in Paris, Bonn, and London. I finally saw in person the landmarks I had drooled over in picture books.

In September of 1983, we walked the narrow streets of Paris, with its florist shops, windows covered with lace curtains, and wrought-iron balconies full of flowerpots. We ate at outdoor cafés, struggling to decipher the menus. At the Eiffel Tower, we shaded our eyes while scanning the romantic city. I took a picture of the boys with the *Venus de Milo* at the Louvre. A magical photo of us, smiling, in front of the Palace of Versailles, sat on my dresser for years.

Highlights in Bonn, Germany, included a tour of the castle at Drachenfels (Dragon's Tooth Mountain,) a visit to the Bundestag, and a leisurely boat ride on the Rhine River, with castles dotting the wooded hills. In Belgium we boarded a ferry for England. On the train ride to Victoria Station, the white cliffs of Dover in the evening fog made me hum the World War II song: "There'll be bluebirds over the white cliffs of

Dover …" Beefeaters stood guard as we filed past the crown jewels in the room-size vault at the Tower of London. At Windsor Castle, we walked through the lavish staterooms, where armor, swords, and pistols were mounted on the walls. Sheep grazed in the fields on our bus ride through the Cotswolds, and I read all the plaques at Shakespeare's home in Avon.

Three weeks later, at the Charles De Gaulle airport in Paris, we checked in for our flight to Liberia. The UTA agent told us there was a 12-hour delay and they'd put us up in a hotel. When he began lugging our huge array of 13 bags onto the scales, I blurted out, "They told us at Detroit Metro Airport that UTA was an affiliate of TWA for this route. Our luggage has been checked all the way through to Liberia."

He countered, "That applies only if you're on a connecting flight. Because of your layover in Europe, we'll have to recheck your bags." He finished weighing them and gave Ben the bad news, "I'm sorry, sir. That will be $1,200 in overweight charges."

We stood there, stunned. Frantically, I offered, "Our bags are heavy because we're going to Liberia for a year to do lay missionary work. I packed extra supplies. We had no idea this would happen."

He said, "Missionary work? Let me talk to my manager. Maybe she can help. She's not on duty right now, but she'll be here before you board."

At our hotel room, we all knelt by the beds, praying for the Lord to rescue us. We didn't have extra money; nor did we want to leave any goods behind. The boys kept praying when we returned to speak with the manager. That night, she expedited our check-in, waiving the fee. We thanked her profusely and saw it as an answer to prayer, as well as a sign that the Lord would be with us in the coming year.

Ben struck up a conversation with an Episcopal missionary heading to the Congo, while we waited to board the plane. He told him we were going to Liberia, and the missionary said, "I've been there. What area are you going to?"

I butted in. "Oh, I'm sure you haven't been where we're going. You've probably never even heard of it. It's a very remote village."

He said, "Try me."

I said, "Vahun in Lofa County."

He said, "I've been there. We walked there and back from the Holy Cross Mission in Bolahun."

Ben and I and the boys looked at each other, trying to absorb such an amazing coincidence. We took it as another assurance of encouragement.

At 5:30 a.m., I was awakened by the pilot announcing our arrival at Robertsfield. It was dark, with the windows quickly steaming up. We were greeted by Ben's nephew, Thomas, along with the welcoming party of 30 tribal people who had stuck it out from the night before, the other 70 having gone home.

The Lutheran church's business manager was there with his VW bus. Our first stop was Harbel, near the Firestone rubber plantation. I knew I was home as I took in the scent of moist, fecund air, people's sweat as they hugged me, and burning rubber from the plantation. I remembered the African chants, accompanied by a small band. I watched the masked dancers cavorting to pounding drums.

In Monrovia, as we rode through the wrought-iron gate of the mission compound, I spotted the crate of books we had shipped ahead, stacked by the surrounding concrete-block walls. The manager took care of financial affairs and kept track of the missionaries upcountry by short-wave radio. He and his wife had their own Sunday school ministry in town.

The changes in Monrovia were obvious. Mold crept up the outer walls of government buildings. The Masonic lodge at Mamba Point was a squatter's paradise, with velvet drapes flapping out of windows. Vacant storefronts here and there flanked Broad Street, and the Poinciana trees in the center were missing. Other stark reminders of the coup were lavish homes that had been gutted and abandoned, garbage everywhere, and limited medical services.

When we reported to Immigration, the clerk said, "Resident visas and work permits are now $50 each. You need both of them. It's the same price for your kids' resident visas." We filled out the forms and the clerk told us, "Go, come," until a Mende man walked in, introducing himself as Ben's brother. He convinced the clerk that we had come to contribute to Liberia. We paid nothing.

From conversations with Liberians, we sensed there was a great deal of fear and uncertainty in political circles, as well as anxiety for the country as a whole. Liberia was deeply in debt. Instead of the usual repartee, people on the street looked tense, passing each other without looks or greetings.

The only thing flourishing was the military headquarters at the Barclay Training Camp. New facilities there included offices, 20 houses for military personnel, a church, a PX, and a nightclub.

We suspected that Liberians were tolerating the military until the supposed return to civilian rule in two years with presidential elections.

In the meantime, the new government, with its troops, wielded power indiscriminately. Streets in Monrovia were cleared whenever Doe—the new strongman who had killed Tolbert—drove through, speeding at 80 miles an hour.

I was surprised that most consumer items were still available. When I went to market, women with piles of imported Irish potatoes called out, "Potatoes, Missy? Potatoes here, Missy." In the Lebanese supermarket, I found frozen Amour-beef hot dogs; Wyandot popcorn from Marion, Ohio; and cellophane-covered Easter baskets that had arrived the previous May. Stores sold Donna Summers and Kenny Rogers cassette tapes. Lebanese clerks hadn't changed either; they were friendly to me, a Western white woman, while ignoring tribal women.

Our 2-bedroom apartment on the ground floor of the mission house was compact. The more descriptive term would be "claustrophobic." Monrovia's usual challenges included worms in the Bisquick, black weevils in the flour, and mold growing in the underarms of Ben's suit coat and the "footprints" in our sandals. I wondered if the electricity would go off each time I put a load in the washer or frozen meat in the small fridge.

The steady stream of Mende and Gbandi visitors made our cramped quarters a beehive of activity. As a good hostess, I was expected to offer juice or at least cold water to everyone right away and feed those who happened to be there at mealtime.

Six men squeezed together on our small couch, often staying late. Our tiny bathroom opened onto the living room, and I usually waited until visitors left before taking my shower. One night, I was extremely tired and decided to chance it. I stepped out of the shower, reaching for my robe hanging on the door, only to realize I had left it in the bedroom—much to my chagrin. With the steam choking me, in desperation, I wrapped a huge bath towel around me. I'm sure the eyes of 6 men were glued to me as I sprinted out of the door and into the bedroom. After that incident, Ben ensured that visitors waited and visited on wooden benches in the carport.

Because of Ben's ties to Tolbert, he wanted to allay any suspicion on the part of the new administration concerning our year in Vahun, before we headed upcountry. It took 3 weeks to arrange a meeting with Doe, who was then chairman of the People's Redemption Council. Ben asked me to go along for moral support.

I noticed the ragged front lawn as our taxi pulled up to the Executive Mansion. Grim-faced soldiers milled around the reception area on the ground floor as we passed through metal detectors. Gone was the easy exchange of former days, when security guards joked and called Ben "Boss Man."

The lavish European furnishings were no longer there as we walked to the presidential waiting room—the brocade drapes fluttering at the open windows. A spray of bullet holes covered the exit door of the presidential office. On the mahogany paneling in the waiting room, the historic oil portraits of Americo-Liberian presidents were missing, replaced by another spray of bullet holes.

We were kept waiting several hours. As we walked into the familiar presidential office, Doe, then in a business suit instead of his camouflage uniform, rose from his desk and extended his hand in greeting, waiting. I looked over at Ben, whose arms were clenched by his side; he was unable to shake the hand of the man who had killed his friend. In the uncomfortable silence, I reached out my hand, and Doe shook it. That brief interlude allowed Ben to regain his composure and do the same. During our brief visit, Doe listened and nodded as Ben described his goals in Vahun.

Ben explained things when we were back in the privacy of our apartment. "Shaking his hand was one of the hardest things I've done. What you saw today at the Executive Mansion is the suspicion and subdued spirit of the Liberian government, all because legitimacy is missing. And yet everything seems the same since one-man rule has simply changed hands." Before we left for upcountry, we registered with the US Embassy in case there was another coup.

Thomas arranged for a government truck to carry our luggage—particularly the 1,000 pounds of books we had shipped—after we reimbursed the business manager the additional $350 in customs charges. At Kamatahun, the truck became mired in mud. Men from the village had to unload it before they could push it to solid ground—and then reload it! We followed a day later in a taxi, our clothes for the trip in 6 woven plastic rice bags.

At Kolahun, Ben paid for a small pickup to take us to Somalahun; 15 other passengers tagged along for the ride. Morlu was at his rice farm, and there was great celebration as soon as he returned. The women found out Peter's middle name was "Morlu" and gave him hugs. Troops of kids followed him as if he were the Pied Piper.

Morlu told us, "The missionary comes regularly. I have trouble understanding how God could give His one and only Son for us. I have 20 children, and I can't imagine giving up any of them."

Late that afternoon, before we left, a hunter from the nearby village of Danbu presented us with 2 deer legs and thighs—hooves, fur, and all! We turned them over to Morlu as a farewell gift.

The roads were gutted and treacherous. In Kolahun, our only possible ride to Vahun was with J. D. in his Toyota Land Cruiser. The gears began crunching as we bumped and sloshed our way to Popalahun, his hometown. There he walked 5 miles to a nearby village where a man had a Land Cruiser, no longer drivable, and returned that evening with its gearbox.

By flashlight, and with a minimum of tools, he drained the oil from his vehicle's gearbox into a bucket, took the box apart, and reassembled it with the new gears, straining the oil with a thin cloth before replacing it. I was astonished.

We waited on the porch of the town chief's house, every child staring at us and any movement or gesture bringing instant giggles. The chief's son offered us his bedroom for the night, and the next morning, J. D. said, "Let's get going."

The first steep incline of Kamboi looked so threatening that I insisted on walking to the top with the boys. I soon gave up and stayed inside, despite worse areas that followed. We made it without a hitch, and I breathed a sigh of relief as we rode into the outskirts of Vahun—our home for the next year.

CHAPTER 19

Destination Vahun

◇◇◇◇◇◇◇◇◇◇◇◇◇◇

Stress is the gap between what you expect in life
and what you're actually getting.
—Gary Smalley

Downtown Vahun, November 1983

It was pitch black that night as I lay in bed in the house Ben's nephew had given us for the year, the buzz of swarming mosquitoes droning in my ears. I tucked my face deeper under the covers, knowing my soundly-sleeping husband and children were "fresh meat." Trying to control my panic, I told myself, "This place is filthy. There's no bathroom, no kitchen—not even water to drink. What are we going to do?"

The next morning, exhausted and desperate, I told Ben, "Honey, we can't possibly stay here."

#

That afternoon when we arrived in Vahun, it was easy to see the place had flourished since my last visit. More land had been cleared, opening up the area. Before the coup, the foundation of President Tolbert's summer home had been constructed on a hill near town. Vahun's budding suburbia on the road to Sierra Leone included several homes under construction.

162

Soldiers guarding the border lived in the new row of barracks by the marketplace. The paramount chief made a statement with his bright-pink house near the town hall.

The mud-block church was packed with everyone gathered to greet us—Muslims and all. My eyes welled with tears as the people sang hymns in Mende. We were exhausted, filthy, and starved, so Patrick told everyone to come back at 4 p.m. for the welcoming ceremony.

Carol, the missionary's wife, walked over and handed me 2 letters that had arrived on the bush plane. It was nice to know we were still in contact with the outside world. She smiled and said, "How about lunch?"

We walked up to the mission house near the airstrip on the hill. Her hospitality, coupled with Western familiarity, was not only welcome but also a huge relief. The boys wolfed down her spaghetti and rushed off to play with their children—a boy, 8, and a girl, 11. We bathed in the tub in their modern bathroom as quickly as she heated water on the stove. The house, built by an American contractor, was an oasis of civilization, with electricity via a generator, running water from an elevated water tank, safe drinking water in the rainwater cistern, and cold food in 2 kerosene-powered refrigerators. Other features included a gas stove with an oven, a wringer washing machine, and a separate building for George's study.

The welcome ceremony had fewer participants than the greeting party since the Muslims didn't return. "Mama" Carol had baked 550 cookies and made 30 gallons of Kool-Aid, served in Heineken beer bottles; all of the latter was consumed, nonetheless. Afterward, Patrick walked us to our new house in town. His wife, Nancy, brought over our supper. We ate sitting on the tan vinyl couch since there was no table or chairs. With a small kerosene lantern, we quickly looked the place over since night was fast approaching.

It was obvious Ben's nephew rarely used the place. The red and green checkerboard linoleum floor tiles were filthy. Red dust coated the jalousie window slats and torn screens. It was an insect heaven, with spider webs festooning the corners of the fiberboard ceilings, termite mud tunnels running along the cement plaster walls, and 100s of flourishing cockroaches scrambling from the lantern light when I opened a cupboard door in the mahogany buffet.

The bare kitchen had a dirt floor, as did the bathroom, with its mud-block walls and rose-pink bathtub (with no drain) sitting on the floor. The matching pink toilet sat in the hall next to a porta-potty. In three of the bedrooms, Carol had put sheets on the cheap, but usable, Western mattresses on the beds—the only cleanliness around.

It wasn't my only experience with a less-than-ideal house. In 1951, at the age of 6, my life changed drastically when Dad decided to work one of the farms Grandpa Meyer had acquired during the Great Depression. We went from a new brick home in suburban St. Louis to a 440-acre farm in northwestern Ohio. That March day was overcast, damp, and cold as we pulled into our 100-year-old farmstead dotted with bare elm trees. Soupy mud sucked at our feet until we reached the narrow sidewalk leading to a dilapidated house—a perfect movie set for *Ma and Pa Kettle on the Farm*.

Sounding too cheerful, Mom said, "This old house is a piece of *history*. The moving van's coming next week. We'll move in as soon as Dad puts in running water. We can use the outhouse out back until he finishes the bathroom. Go on upstairs, kids, and pick out your rooms."

Sandy and I climbed the steep stairs. Out of 6 bedrooms, we chose the one with the heat vent coming from the new oil stove in the large kitchen. Mom said, "We'll put up fresh wallpaper to perk things up. Look how spacious the living room is."

We got used to the sulfurous water in the well out back, but we were scared every time we used the rickety, wasp-infested outhouse—or the chamber pot at the foot of the stairs at night. Our one and only dial phone sat on Dad's desk in the living room; the party line was shared by ten neighbors.

In the winter, Sandy and I waited in our toasty bed until Mom called up the vent for us to get up. We raced over the ice-cold wood floors and down the stairs, warming our bare feet and dressing in the heat of the oil stove. After breakfast, Jim yelled, "The bus is here!" and we scrambled down the front-porch steps, our coats unbuttoned over cotton school dresses, running in the snow in tie shoes and ankle socks.

However, in Vahun, I wasn't 6 years old. I had a husband and children to care for. After our nightmare that first night, we lugged our suitcases, stacked in the extra bedroom, back up to the mission house. I blurted out, "That house isn't *livable*," when Carol met us at the door.

She said, "I feel the same way. I tried my best, sewing the curtains for the windows and loaning you the sheets and porta-potty, but I know just what you mean."

"May we stay with you for a while until we get the place in shape?"

"Sure! Come on in!" From that moment, I considered her a friend for life!

I happily settled in, sorting the stuff in our suitcases and doing laundry. That evening, we washed the red dust from our hair, and I used the clippers to give Ben and Ben Jr. sorely needed haircuts while the generator was running. Carol was gracious when Peter wet the bed that night, and I greatly appreciated her every kindness.

The next morning, Ben headed to Sierra Leone to buy cement and nails. For the next 4 days, I had the privilege of supervising 9 men in bright-orange jumpsuits as they cleaned and painted the house. The first time I saw them, I asked Patrick, "Why are they dressed like that?"

He said, "They're local convicts doing community service to work off their sentences." I shuddered, wondering at their crimes, but was afraid to ask any more.

In the nick of time, the business manager sent up 15 gallons of white paint and 5 gallons of Acqua on the bush plane from Monrovia. As the men painted, I mixed in more white paint, with each room turning out a lighter shade of Acqua. The house really looked spruced up with its fresh white exterior and red trim.

In the kitchen, we put the new counter-high table under the large window, and a smaller table on the opposite wall for the 2-burner kerosene stove. Each morning, the scrubbed-out oil drum by the back door was filled with buckets of water from the swamp well. George and Carol loaned us one of their kerosene fridges, and it sat in the opposite corner on the new concrete floor.

The local carpenter also made us a dining-room set, bathroom table, and desk and chair for the extra bedroom, as well as three benches for the carport. It took him a month since he walked to another village each day to cut his cocoa, using the cash crop to provide for his family.

The bathroom had the biggest transformation, with its concrete floor, cement plastered walls, and woven rattan ceiling. The pink tub and toilet drained into a ravine behind the house; the toilet was "hand flushed" with a bucket of water. The pièce de résistance was a small mirror, "made in China," hanging over the plastic washbasin on the bathroom table. A large galvanized bucket of water on the 2-burner kerosene stove in the hall took 20 minutes to simmer. We bathed by mixing hot and cold water, standing in the tub, and pouring the bucket over us to rinse. With careful planning, I washed my hair, shaved my legs, and bathed with 2 buckets of water.

In my haste to get settled, I overdid it and spent 2 days in bed with malaria—one of several bouts that year. I lay in the extra bed in George's study, burning up with fever and trying to get some sleep, until the chloroquine tablets kicked in. When I finally moved around again, I was demoralized, my strength sapped.

There was no choice but to bounce back. Thankfully, screens were repaired, windows washed, and floors scrubbed without me. Final touches included an Acqua tie-dye tablecloth on the dining room table, rattan chairs on the front porch, an oil drum to catch rainwater, and a landscaped front courtyard with a low hedge that read "Jesus Saves."

The curtains were removed, except for those in the bedrooms. The back of the house looked out at a breathtaking, majestic tree-covered mountain in the distance. The side windows faced our neighbors. One of them, Momo, drove the Lofa County Co-op produce truck. From my window, I watched his wife, Kpanah, spread cocoa to dry on her concrete slab and shoo chickens when she fanned rice.

Men from the village built a thatched-roof palava hut in the backyard, complete with hammocks and stools. I figured it would be an excellent tool for child evangelism. The boys used it for a playhouse.

We stayed with George and Carol a week and a half, moving into our house just before Thanksgiving. The next morning, they left on the bush plane for 2 weeks in Monrovia. We knew nothing about operating a kerosene fridge, so it sat empty until they returned. In the meantime, we drank lukewarm water. I mixed only enough powdered milk for one serving at a time. We ate canned meat, supplemented by an occasional scrawny chicken. The fresh deer meat we were given had maggots on it, but it didn't smell, so we boiled it thoroughly and ate it. Porcupine meat cooked in a tomato-onion sauce didn't go over well with the kids; nor did the turtle.

The house was wired for overhead lights and had a few wall sockets. However, we used our small kerosene lanterns until George and Carol returned and showed us how to operate the backup generator they had loaned us. When it was up and running, it seemed as if we lit up half of Vahun from our windows.

Life in Vahun was an anthropologist's dream. I quickly discovered that everything was made by hand—mud blocks for housing, rattan fish and animal traps, and country cloth woven from carded cotton spun into thread. Coffee and cocoa cash crops were harvested, fermented, and dried before sale. The local tailor made dresses from lappa-size pieces of store-bought cotton fabric, with tie-dye and Java print designs.

Kids amused themselves by creating toys out of odds and ends. Boys played by guiding an old tire with a stick. They shaped soft bamboo into a money bus, complete with tires made from old flip-flops and a curtain flap in back. Their bamboo "tape player" had old batteries inserted and a wire antenna. My favorite bamboo toy was the airplane with a leaf propeller and a tiny Liberian flag on the antenna.

Western local fashion was equally creative. I saw Nylon winter parkas worn during rainy season, T-shirts with slogans like "Camp Acorn" and "Charlie's Angels," and an elder sporting a knit cap that read, "Pittsburgh Steelers." The first prize for fashion follies went to the man wearing a maternity top labeled "Mom" with an arrow pointing downward, and the second prize to the man wearing pink satin bedroom slippers.

I dealt with the challenges of living in Vahun by doing what I had to do, learned from growing up on a farm. During my childhood, my most loathsome task was hoeing—the most boring activity on planet Earth. I would sooner have cleaned house every day than spend time in the fields, but Dad gave us no choice.

In high school, my other dreaded chore was gathering eggs. At our new farmstead, Dad had a modern chicken coop built, which housed 5,000 chickens—2 per wire cage, each cage suspended over a manure pit. Feeding and watering them were somewhat automatic. Collecting the eggs was another story. Dad built a cart to roll down the concrete aisles to hold the 100s of eggs we gathered twice a day. The manure ammonia stung our eyes, and despite our coveralls and red bandanas, our hair and clothes picked up a lovely scent.

During those first 6 weeks in Vahun, I periodically got down on the kitchen floor to check the kerosene flame under the fridge, hoping it hadn't gone from blue to yellow again which meant it would soon go out. I pleaded, "Please, Lord, don't let it go out! I've got meat in the freezer!" I classified the fridge as holy since I prayed so much over it. Carol taught me how to trim the wick and relight it when it went out, but the flame lasted only several days at a time.

A week after Christmas, our family flew to Monrovia in the TILLY bush plane owned by the Lutheran Bible Translators.

Bush plane at the landing strip in Vahun

Our pilot was very faithful about weighing us and our supplies. It looked like the plane wouldn't hold much more than us, but it was amazing what he could tuck in. I enjoyed our flight to Monrovia, looking out over villages dotted here and there in the midst of mountains covered with trees that looked like broccoli from the air.

After the quiet of Vahun, bustling Monrovia seemed like New York City. I wrote home, "We spent the first week at the mission apartment, the next at the Lutheran Guest House where I stayed when Joe had worms under his skin. We're close to the beach, and the boys bounced in the waves a number of afternoons. They're happy with room to roam around and kids to play with."

One afternoon, I decided to have a professional haircut. I entered a modern salon downtown that had young male hairdressers. As a walk-in customer, I was assigned to the new guy who spoke French and understood only a little English. I sat in the chair, carefully instructing him, "Don't cut my hair too short." He heard only the word "short." There was no going back after he cut off the hair by my ears. From then on, I let him do what he wanted since he couldn't understand me anyway.

I told Ben, "Honey, I hope you can stand this hairdo."

In his usual charming way, he smiled and said, "Don't worry. It'll grow out." That haircut lasted until we returned to Michigan.

I wrote home, "I'm sorry we can't connect on the short-wave radio or even by phone. Nine times out of ten, the phones here are out of order. If they work, it's a pleasant surprise. The only sure thing is the telecommunications center downtown. We took a taxi there to call you, and our 3 minutes cost $15. It was nice to hear your voice, however briefly."

I returned to Vahun with 15 pounds of frozen meat, hoping to make it last until we made our next trip to Monrovia in 3 months. Of course, the flame went out after we got back. Ben brought over a man in Vahun who had a kerosene fridge. He not only offered to let us temporarily use his freezer, but he also noticed that our fridge wasn't level. Even after we solved that, the flame continued to turn yellow. The meat was thawed and refrozen so many times, I finally cooked what remained—3 packages of beef and 6 pounds of hamburger. When our supply of kerosene ran out, we discovered the real problem—it had been tainted from storing it in a gas can. A fresh supply kept the flame blue and the food cold.

The fridge wasn't our only challenge. After a week or so, the generator began burning oil and rattling so loud that we went back to kerosene lanterns. My curly wash-and-wear hair meant I awakened to a new style each morning. After it grew out and got too out of control, I whacked on it with a scissors.

I wrote home, "Things move at a different speed here, and I usually don't know what time it is. We have one watch among 5 people that's still working, so we usually say, 'Okay, who's got the watch? I need it.' Time flies doing ordinary things. And yet I don't feel like I'm doing much."

Life in Vahun was full of either surprises and challenges or peaceful boredom. There was no in between. Every time life seemed to be progressing at a steady pace, the next crisis caught me off guard. I was fully aware that I was in a very different place—trapped in an unfamiliar environment. Desperately vulnerable, I was barely able to maintain a facade of day-to-day calm and normalcy. Numerous times, stretched to the limit, I was unable to survive without God's help.

In the States, Mom had confidently gushed, "Oh Ben, we're not worried. We know you'll take good care of your family." I knew better. I knew how challenged he was with household problems. I felt doubly helpless in Vahun because there he was clueless. To his credit, he never hesitated to ask people for help. I learned that year how much of life was out of my control, though I may have imagined it was. My faith and naïveté— as well as telling myself I'd be home in a year—sustained me, although at times, my return to civilization seemed a long way off.

CHAPTER 20

Communal Living

◇◇◇◇◇◇◇◇◇◇◇◇◇◇◇

Who could deny that privacy is a jewel?
—Phyllis McGinley

Our house in Vahun, November 1983

O ur generator—assaulting the African night with its roar—was both
a blessing and a curse. Open windows with bright lights made us a
reality TV show for the kids in town. When I lay on the couch trying to
read, 25 pairs of little eyes stared over my shoulders. Feeling invaded, I
went out and said, "Shoo!" The bevy of children scattered into the darkness,
only to regroup 5 minutes later. I chased them again. When they ran away
laughing, I knew it had become a game—and I lost.

Carol told me, "They did the same thing to us. The first thing I did
was sew curtains for all the windows."

#

In some ways, Vahun's rural setting reminded me of our old farmstead,
which had something to discover each day. In the summer, as Sandy and I
amused ourselves, our vast "playground equipment" included an enormous
red barn with a haymow and horse stables, a derelict concrete silo with
a ladder of iron rods up the side, two notoriously stinky hog barns, a

170

chicken coop with a box for each hen, a granary converted from a one-room schoolhouse, a corn crib with slatted sides, a repair shop full of old tools, and a damp, gloomy cellar.

One day, we scooted backward up the low slanted roof of the hog barn, looking out over the place from the gable. Realizing how high we were, we slowly came down on our fannies, using our tennis shoe soles to grip the shingles. We explored the hog barn by poking our heads into the doors until the stale manure made our eyes water. Some afternoons, we swung on the pulley ropes in the haymow or played school in the granary rooms. In our adventures, we imagined what the farm once was: cows drinking out of the concrete water trough, horses being hitched to a plow, hogs grunting in the barn, and the farmer's wife chasing the chickens out of the boxes to gather the eggs.

Except for our family, days on the farm were spent in social isolation. Sandy and I were by ourselves in the house while Jim and Dad were in the fields, and Mom took Joanna with her when she brought them lunch. We weren't only sisters; we were each other's only playmate for miles around. Many times, I played by myself.

In Vahun, I was once again in a rural setting, but in a very different community with its set of social rules. The Mendes did their utmost to make us feel welcome as we adjusted to a new climate, germs, insects, food, and customs. The main path to the farms passed right in front of our house. People heading out in the morning stopped by to say "Boowa" ("Are you up?"). People going out of town came to say "Malo Ho" ("Good-bye"). They never stayed long, but it was important to meet and greet each one, which certainly broke up our day. One morning, I excused myself to dress and closed the bedroom door, but I forgot to pull the curtains. The woman in the living room who had stopped by—determined to continue her visit— walked around to our front bedroom window and stared in as I dressed.

At the same time, that path was a photographer's paradise. Every once in a while, I ran out the front door snapping pictures, for example, of a hunter with two blue-faced monkeys slung over his shoulder, teenage girls with piles of greens on their heads that looked like bouffant hairdos, little girls parading single-file just like Mommy with small buckets on their heads, and boys bringing in firewood by also balancing small logs on their heads.

Photographer's paradise

Visiting Vahun was one thing. It was quite another living there in the thick of things, enveloped by a group-oriented people with no concept of Western privacy. In contrast to the mission house on the hill, living "downtown" was a circus with us in the center ring and the Mendes our audience. We might be awakened from a nap on Sunday afternoon by kids screaming outside our window or by someone walking into our bedroom to say hello. On the other hand, we were never disturbed by a ringing telephone or a doorbell. I sometimes longed for the sound of water running, a toilet flushing, or the Saturday afternoon football game on TV.

Kids were everywhere, congregating at the drop of a hat. They peered in the windows each day, calling "Morlu!" or "Ma Bendu," and saying "Bessia" ("Hello"). The hammock in the palava hut was a great place to lounge in late afternoon, but we had to check it before getting in since it was usually occupied by a youngster. Peter pushed me in it to make it sway, asking, "Mommy, have you got your seat belt on?"

Family relationships were everything in that closed community. Because of this, everyone was super polite. Kinship reciprocity was either direct or circular and subtle, depending on the situation. Obligations pursued to the extreme made family ties burdensome at times. An abundance of palava might include begging or assuming an obligation from other people.

The town's primary form of entertainment was conversation—passing on rumors, which made their way around the village at lightning speed. I was often the topic since nothing escaped their attention and I was unfamiliar with local customs. The people were amazed when they saw me cutting Ben's hair since the usual practice was that men cut men's hair and women cut women's hair. One day, I heard about a complaint circulating that I cut Peter's hair too short. Old men would rub the fuzz on his head and say, "Your mother should let it grow." I just laughed. The men sitting in our living room were shocked by my public display of affection when I put my arms around Ben as he stood there weeping after George came down with the news that Ben's friend Edgar had died suddenly in Flint. Mende men didn't openly hug their wives or hold hands.

As we settled in, I began teaching Joe, who was in 4th grade, and Peter, who was in kindergarten, long before homeschooling was the vogue. We purchased the materials from the Calvert School in Baltimore, Maryland, which served missionaries and others overseas. My supplies included a teaching guide for each grade as well as books, paper, pencils, crayons, and construction paper. Joe completed periodic tests, which we mailed to Baltimore to be graded, so he could enter the fifth grade when we returned. While the guides were specific and detailed, I adapted lesson plans because Peter finished his simple work so quickly.

School with Joe and Peter

Ben Jr. completed his high school junior-year classes through a correspondence school in Chicago. Basically on his own, he was quite disciplined, doing his lessons each morning and running with a gang of boys in the afternoon. He regularly sent in his tests; Algebra II was his only difficulty.

Ben Jr. with his pals in front of our palava hut

That fall, he wrote his grandparents: "I sure do miss home. I miss the fall leaves, the cool, crisp air, the brisk winds, and the frost covering the lawn. I miss all my friends, cross-country running, and the school routine."

There was so much commotion at our house each morning with people dropping by that I shifted our "classroom" from the dining room table. I moved Ben's desk table into Joe and Peter's room under the window and closed the door each day until noon. School gave our days consistency and a sense of normalcy in Vahun's chaotic life. I found teaching my children very satisfying as I learned along with them.

The books we had brought to Vahun became a treasure—my own personal library. Early on, I unpacked eight of the boxes and kept them at our house while the library was being set up in a room at the back of the church. My intent was to list and shelve the books, but the time flew by as I did ordinary everyday things. I read whenever I could and was especially moved as I reread *Through Gates of Splendor*, that classic tale of eight missionary martyrs killed by South American tribesmen.

From the minute we arrived in Vahun, it was blatantly obvious that I couldn't manage the household on my own. Patrick arranged the hiring of three 14-year-old boys—Moses, Timbeh, and Salia. For a US dollar a week, they worked Monday through Friday. Their first chore was to fill the two oil drums in the house by carrying buckets of water on their heads, making numerous trips to and from the swamp well in the valley, a 100 yards away. After that, they wiped the living room, kitchen, and hallway floors and swept the bedrooms. They danced while doing their chores when we played "Electric Boogie" or "African Typic Collection" on our battery-operated tape player—turning up the volume to share with our neighbors, which resulted in an instant audience of kids.

Their Mende Liberian English banter endeared the three helpers to me, giving me a glimpse of their culture as I listened while they worked. They teased each other about their girlfriends, with Moses telling Timbeh, "Your girlfriend is looking like dry stick." Timbeh quickly retorted, "Your girlfriend's head looking like Landai's own." (Landai is a masked being with a ferocious face.) Saliah usually chimed in, saying, "Your girlfriend got big stomach," and everyone laughed.

I made notes of their colloquialisms. One day, they told Ben Jr., "What you say, Boss Man? This place is looking cold [There's no action here]. Leggo [let's go] walk-about."

When I fed them, they told each other, "Eat your rice and gris [greens]," and, "Drink your Dutch Baby [bottled milk from Holland]."

During arguments, they jested, "You're giving me hard time," or "I'm going to frog [flog] you." When upset, it was, "Don't humbug me, man. Move behind me [Get out of my way. I'm angry]." Sometimes they asked, "Why are you vex with me?" or they said, "Don't abuse me [hurt my feelings]."

I was happy when they told me, "I enjoy [like] you," or comforted me with, "Let me sorry for you."

For our Liberian chop [food], I hired Patrick's 30-year-old daughter, Miriam, because I didn't know how to prepare it and it was time-consuming.

Miriam in our kitchen

175

I paid Patrick's wife, Nancy, to wash our laundry in the Mawa River, laying it on the grass to dry. I sorted it, folded it, and put it away each Friday when she delivered it. I paid both women 10 US dollars a week.

I wrote to Mom and Dad, "You'll never get your money's worth out of soap or deodorant as we do here. The smell of our laundry pile would knock you down. Hand washing's hard on elastic, so the boys have 'pin and wear' underwear and shorts. Please send some Sears Best men's and boy's briefs."

I was helpless without Nancy, Miriam, and the boys, so I appreciated what they did. In like manner, they relished the income. Weekends were quiet without them.

In a favorite photo, Nancy and I stood by the town hall with our arms around each other, smiling—quite a contrast in sister-in-laws.

Nancy and me in "downtown" Vahun

That year, I didn't iron, wax floors, vacuum, dust baseboards, or wash mirrors. Instead, I sprayed mattresses for bedbugs, fried popcorn in palm oil, brushed down spider webs every week, spread clothes on the grass to dry, kept a tight lid on sweet things, and sifted weevils out of rice, spaghetti, and flour before I used them. Many of the people thought I didn't do anything because I stayed in the house so much, but by the time I walked to someone's farm, I was exhausted from the heat.

Fresh produce was nothing new to me after life on the farm. Mom and Dad had pored over seed catalogs before we moved there. That first year, Dad planted every garden plant known to mankind, including pumpkins and raspberries. He was more selective in the ensuing years, but every summer, for lunch and supper, we feasted on freshly picked corn that was so sweet it tasted like candy. There were strawberries, peas, green beans, tomatoes, and cucumbers. In the winter, we ate them from Mom's supply in the chest freezer in the garage. We girls ate more strawberries than we picked. We shelled peas while sitting in the glider on the front porch. Dad had beehives installed for optimum pollination, but he later removed them when we kept getting stung.

Vahun was another fresh-food paradise. In the early months especially, people stopped by with gifts of yams, plantain, beans, and country rice. Occasionally they sold us fresh meat: porcupine, deer, and sometimes catfish. Our first week there, we must have accumulated a bushel each of fresh oranges, lovely large tangerines, and grapefruit, as well as a huge stalk of bananas. The cucumbers looked like small footballs.

The first time I tasted fresh, ripe pineapple, it was if I had never eaten pineapple before. It was sweet and soft and melted in my mouth, as opposed to the familiar tart and chewy canned stuff. Some Liberians salted it to cut the sweetness. I savored the fresh papayas, called *"pau pau,"* that the boys brought around for purchase.

Early on, Patrick, who had the same fringe of hair over his ears as Ben's father, told everyone that I liked plantain and pau pau, so I received both almost daily. Maintaining our digestive balance with new and unfamiliar foods was a struggle between too loose and too tight bowels, and this sapped our energy. We countered looseness with green plantain slices fried in palm oil. We also enjoyed the small white sweet potatoes Bengie and I had eaten years earlier. Nancy's roasted peanuts were so fresh—straight from the garden and roasted in an iron pot over the fire—that it was like eating peanuts for the first time.

Every 3 months, we took the bush plane to Monrovia, where I purchased Western food supplies, such as crackers, sugar, seasonings, Ovaltine, oatmeal, Cream of Wheat, hamburger and beef, spaghetti and sauce, Nestlé powdered milk, flour, canned meats, and corn oil—although we also used palm oil. I made sure to pick up bug spray and bar laundry soap.

Cold, pure drinking water, our most precious commodity, required quite a process. Miriam was vital in boiling water from the swamp well for 5 minutes. After cooling it, she poured it through a ceramic water filter and stored it in the fridge. I used chlorine disinfecting tablets only in a pinch since I didn't like the taste.

Every week or so, I used the oven at the mission house to bake loaves of whole-wheat bread and sometimes a coffee cake—what balm to the soul! I made banana bread and corn bread in a Dutch oven over our stove, although it burned a little on the bottom. My breakfast pancakes were a favorite with the boys.

One day, a Gbandi nephew visited, bringing us 6 dozen eggs he had purchased at a Lebanese store in Kolahun. I was excited. Despite the roaming chickens, eggs were hard to come by. I cracked one and was overpowered by the rotten smell of sulfur—they had never been refrigerated. I said nothing about my disappointment. Another time, he brought me 30 small cans of delicious Dutch cheese.

I was surrounded by people, and yet I was desperately lonely at times. I wanted to be alone with my thoughts when I felt nostalgic—something no Mende could understand. One afternoon, I followed the road leading to Sierra Leone, where the new homes were under construction. Two men walking by saw me stop at one of the houses, and I heard them talking as I went inside. I looked out the back window, which opened to a valley below with a majestic mountain in the distance. The women in the swamp were stooped over, weeding rice, serenaded by loud frogs. Such an idyllic setting made me wistful in my isolation.

On the way back, I met up with some women coming from the farm, and we walked together. I saw a group of men on our front porch talking to Ben as I approached, smiling and waving good-bye to the women. The men quickly dispersed, shaking their heads. I was puzzled about it until Ben walked in the living room with me and said, "You really got me in big trouble."

The two men who had seen me on the road reported to Patrick, "We saw Ma Baindu all by herself just looking, not saying anything." Patrick reported it to Brima, who gathered a few elders, and they all went to see Ben. Brima began by saying, "What's happened between you two? Is she dissatisfied with our people?"

Ben said, "I can't think of any problem we have. She probably just wanted to be by herself for a while."

Brima countered, "We know Vahun is hers, but she doesn't speak our language. She should always have some of our women with her. It's strange for her to walk off by herself. Something must be wrong. You've got to find out what it is."

When they saw me walking up with the women, Brima scratched his head and said, "White people have *strange* ways."

I thought it was funny because I often had the same thought about them.

Living in such a different culture, there were times when I became excruciatingly homesick. On some Sunday afternoons, which were always quiet, I lay in the hammock in our palava hut playing my tape player, missing Flint and my life in America. People listening to my classical music later told Ben, "Your music is strange. We don't understand it, but we like it."

It wasn't the only thing strange.

CHAPTER 21

Wonders of God's Creation

◇◇◇◇◇◇◇◇◇◇◇◇◇◇

When I consider your heavens,
the work of your fingers,
the moon and the stars,
which you have set in place ...
Psalm 8:3

Our house, Vahun, May 1984

I walked into the bedroom, and in the bright light from the hallway, I saw every inch of the windows covered with insects. The hum of their wings beating against the screens terrified me. In panic, I slammed the door. When I rushed back to the living room, I saw that those windows were covered as well.

Steeling myself, I said to the Mende man sitting there, "What's with all these bugs?"

#

Ben and I shared a love of nature. While I was living on the farm in the great outdoors, Earth's beauties and complexities led me to worship God, the Creator. Ben's face glowed when he told me about his boyhood trips upcountry in Liberia after a winter in Berlin.

180

The dry and rainy seasons in Vahun each had their benefits and challenges. In that mountainous area, temperatures varied during dry season, with mornings foggy and cool. From 10 o'clock on, it was *hot*. Joe's and Peter's jeans quickly became cutoffs. At night, the thermometer dipped into the 50s. Since we kept the windows open, I was thankful that Allen and Mary Lou had left their sleeping bags.

The dry season, from November to May, had low humidity but a scarce water supply. The only thing hardy enough to grow then was cassava, which sprouted even if the stalks were tucked into a thatched roof. The other downside was the red dust from the Harmattan wind over the Sahara Desert, which covered the mountains with a haze. It settled on everything, including our jalousie window slats, parching our throats and lungs. Nights were stunningly clear. I stood in our backyard and marveled at the pristine sky filled with myriad dots of white light. It reminded me of Psalm 8:3— "When I consider your heavens, the work of your fingers ..."

Cyclone coming

That year, the rainy season arrived with a bang. I had just finished cleaning the fridge when dark clouds rolled in around 5 p.m. As I walked into the kitchen to wash the dishes, a strong rush of air from the open window pushed me backward. I stared in disbelief as I saw a cyclone heading straight at me; I watched it disintegrate the shed holding our gasoline barrels. It then ripped the metal cover off of our generator and veered into the valley behind our house, sweeping away our palava hut as if a giant broom sent it flying.

I ran into the living room to see water pouring in under the front door. The porch was full of water, and a piece of our roof had blown off. I grabbed a broom and swept the water out the front door. Checking the closet, I looked up and there was sky.

Two women screamed as they approached our house. Ben and I rushed outside and asked, "What's going on?"

Momo, who joined them, said, "A house fell down."

The cyclone not only damaged our house, but it also ruined 3 others, blew the roofs off of 3 more, and swept away 2 kitchens and 2 other palava huts. Our neighbor suffered the worst destruction; his house was demolished, except for the walls. Thankfully, he and his family were unharmed. In Vahun, relatives and the church community served as homeowner's insurance and the Red Cross. Ben gave him $50 to buy corrugated sheet metal to replace his roof. We knew the townspeople would help him reconstruct his home.

Ben Jr. was so weak with malaria that he never budged from his bed during the entire ordeal. Everywhere, people ran around shocked and crying. A man brought us a frantic 6-year-old boy with a gash in his head who was screaming because he couldn't find his mother. We bathed him and dressed the wound, trying to comfort him. He didn't fully calm down until his mother ran in and wrapped her arms around him.

A wall fell on a woman, breaking her thigh and her baby's foot. Momo offered to take them to Yandohun to visit the man who set bones. Ben had seen the man earlier demonstrate his ability by breaking a chicken's leg, immobilizing it, and then snapping it back in place, with the chicken running off as if nothing had happened.

The woman was in such pain, I don't know how she remained conscious as she bounced in the vehicle over Kamboi. On top of that, the clouds rolled in again. We prayed for the rain to let up, for their sake. Kamboi was treacherous, and night was approaching. When we heard the rain had stopped and they had made it safely, I breathed, "Thank You, Lord."

Things gradually returned to normal. Two days later, 4 men arrived to repair our roof; and a week later, they rebuilt our palava hut. I showed my gratitude by preparing my Western specialty—spaghetti. I was puzzled when the men smiled and tasted it but said they were full. I found out later that my spaghetti looked like long worms to them! I was embarrassed, wishing I'd asked Nancy to prepare something.

Rainy Season

During the rainy season, from May to October, water was abundant, but with it came high humidity. The rainfall was so plentiful that fences made from tree branches grew shoots, tendrils, and leaves. You could almost watch the lush foliage growing as it baked in the morning sun and soaked up the afternoon rains. Nancy did our laundry early in the morning, so it had time to dry on the grass.

Everyone planted gardens. Plots had already been marked out for the new rice farms—the land cleared and the fields burned for planting. People were puzzled when they saw me running outside with my camera to capture ominous, but magnificent, cloud formations, or snap pictures of glorious rainbows. Showers were warm, unlike Michigan's cold spring rain; the air was fresh and sweet after a downpour. Seeing the white mist rising from the lush green valleys was to watch the exquisite hand of God.

The beauty of nature made me ache for the peace, safety, and familiarity of my home in Michigan. One night, I awoke and the village was lit by a full moon, as bright as day. The absence of sound, except for the insects, was something one can only experience in such a remote place. My family was sound asleep, as was everyone else. I walked out the back kitchen door and stared at the moon. Such beauty; such longing for home.

My previous familiarity with animals stemmed from life on the farm. I grew up with dogs and cats, like other farm kids. When a feral tomcat mauled a litter of kittens and maggots had set in, Mom said, "You girls go in the house. Jim, get a bucket of water. We'll have to put them to sleep."

One spring, 50 baby chicks peeped under a warming light for Jim's 4-H project.

Dad barely broke even when our 7 Angus steers broke though the electric fence and feasted in a field of corn. That night, they looked ready to give birth as they lay there panting for air, their eyes wide with fear and their wet pink nostrils flared. I went out with Dad when the vet came. Under the barn's single light bulb in the corral, the vet punctured their bloated bellies and, after a long hiss, pulled them to their feet. They went to the slaughterhouse the next morning.

In Vahun, we were gifted with a spindly black-and-white sheep with thin hair, a frisky gray, black, and white goat, a baby anteater, and a number of roosters. We tied each rooster to the shed where we stored gas for the generator. They crowed loudly at various times during the day and squawked so much, when hens with chicks came around or other roosters picked fights with them, that they soon ended up on the dinner table.

We picked up 2 black-and-white kittens on the way up to Vahun, naming the survivor Fruilop. Each time I fed him, I used our cat call from the farm: "Here, kitty, kitty, kitty!" Pretty soon, boys in the village had fun imitating me.

According to Mende tradition, Patrick was to give his nephew, Ben Jr., the head of any animal or fish he caught; heads were considered a delicacy. Ben Jr. took one look at the fish head Patrick brought over, and graciously declined. "But Uncle Patrick, I can't eat anything with the eye looking at me." Everyone laughed good-naturedly.

In February, Ben received permission from the Liberian authorities and paid a master game hunter $100 to go in search of elephant. Two weeks later, in the middle of the night, someone rapped on our front door. I peeked out of my pile of blankets wondering who it could be. Ben reached for the kerosene lantern on the floor. I grabbed my robe as the insects resumed their night cry.

A man we had never seen before said in Mende, "We've arrived with your elephant meat."

Behind him was a row of men with rattan carriers on their backs, the sweat glistening on their faces in the lantern light. They looked tired, as if they had walked a long way. We later found out it was 30 miles.

The man asked, "Where shall we put it?"

Ben looked at me and said, "I guess in the extra bedroom."

The porters filed in, stacking the containers of partially dried elephant meat along the wall. The man handed Ben a dirty, old piece of country cloth and said, "These are your tusks and the tails." Ben thanked them and they left.

We crawled back into bed, relieved that their visit hadn't awakened the boys. I snuggled up to Ben, trying to get back to sleep, and noticed a strange, piercing odor filling our bedroom.

I nudged Ben. "Honey, what's that awful smell? It's keeping me awake."

"It must be the elephant meat."

"Please close the windows in the extra room and our bedroom. That should take care of it."

It didn't. I spent the rest of the night choking on the pungent odor of elephant blood. We learned the scent is so potent that it draws nearby villagers, who receive a share of the elephant meat for helping cut it up and smoke it on rattan platforms.

The next morning, Vahun buzzed with the news that the hunter had bagged 2 baby elephants. I, on the other hand, inspected the containers and found nothing appetizing in chunks of rock-hard meat covered with wrinkled elephant hide—wiry hairs poking out of it. I figured it would take 2 days of boiling to soften it.

Some men arrived to finish smoking the meat. Ben Jr. helped them build 6 platforms in our backyard, laying the meat on top and lighting fires underneath. I quickly closed our jalousie windows. It did no good. The house was then full of smoke blended with the scent of funky elephant blood.

Thoroughly disgusted, I asked Ben, "Honey, what are we going to do with this stuff?"

He said, "The people consider it good meat."

"Well then, let's give it to them."

"You'll win the hearts of the people with your generosity."

It was definitely a win-win situation.

Nancy stopped over for her share, telling me, "You must at least taste some elephant! I'll prepare the best part—the trunk."

Later that afternoon, Miriam brought over a pot of rice and a stew of vegetables and elephant meat. The gristly trunk was easy chewing, and I must admit it was one of the tastiest Liberian dishes I ate.

There was only one meat that topped it. One afternoon, as Ben and I were walking in town, we passed an open kitchen with several women drying meat over the fire. Ben asked them what it was, and one of them said, "Monkey meat. Would Bendu like to try some?"

Putting on my best face, I said, "Sure."

She handed me a small strip. It was absolutely delicious, with a smoky, sweet taste. I could have eaten monkey every day of the week.

That year, we were given 2 turtles. We ate the first, but the boys wanted to keep the second as a pet. It was always fun to discover in the morning where she had ended up. One day, I heard the fridge rattling. She was trapped by the kerosene tank underneath, and I pulled her out and pointed her in another direction.

What bothered me was her claws clicking on our bedroom linoleum floor, waking me up repeatedly. I gave her a chance to escape one moonlit night, putting her outside the back kitchen door. By the next morning, she was trapped in the corner of the carport at the front of the house. I had to bring her back inside since Joe and Peter had discovered her.

The Sunday after Easter, Peter ran into our bedroom, excited. "Mommy! The Easter bunny came after all! Look what I found under the living room chair!"

In his arms he carried 5 round, translucent white balls—turtle eggs. Soon he found another one our blanket on the floor.

Patrick was delighted when we presented him with the turtle eggs since they were considered a great delicacy. Impulsively, I offered, "Would you like the turtle too?"

He said, "I'll have Nancy prepare it for you."

That evening, she brought us a delicious turtle stew flavored with tomatoes and onions. I told the boys their pet turtle had disappeared. I didn't say how.

I wasn't frightened of American bugs. On the farm, Mom had provided us kids with nature lessons by bringing in all kinds of insect homes and tucking them into the organdy curtains. One morning, I walked into the living room to see 1,000s of newly hatched tiny praying mantises in the curtain folds. Sometimes I came into the dining room to watch a monarch butterfly spreading its wings to dry. In the backyard, Mom put a female cecropia moth in a cardboard box with a screen on top. Several hours later there were four males on the screen.

On summer evenings, fireflies dotted the skies. We fell asleep watching them twinkle under the covers in jars with perforated lids so they could breathe. The summer of 1955 brought an invasion of cicadas with a deafening whir each evening and into the night that made it hard to sleep. Joanna, then 5, and I picked off 100s of cicada outer shells from the tree trunks.

However, in Vahun, we lived in a world of *unfamiliar* insects—the ferocious-looking ones harmless at times, and vice versa. For that reason, I refrained from taking walks in the bush by myself. I stayed on the forest paths, not daring to wander in the foliage. I had respect for the driver ants and the large-winged insect that had laid its eggs under Joe's skin. The huge mud cones made by the termites were impressive and daunting. On top of that, the Mende boys told me about a pest they were really scared of, saying, "That bug can suck your belly button until you die."

Mosquito bites were toxic, swelling up and causing terrible itching. Joe and I had a number of sores from scratching them. Joe's were the worst since he could never leave them alone.

On a March night, I looked out of our dining room window and noticed dots of light scattered over the surrounding countryside and hills. Numerous bonfires were going in the village as well, and I wondered what all the excitement was about. We used our small lanterns until a Mende man arrived with his kerosene pump lantern, which illuminated every corner of our living room, dining room, and hall with its bright light.

The door to our bedroom was open, and I went to find out what was making a buzzing sound. Terrified, I ran back to the living room and asked what was going on. He said, "The bug-a-bugs [termites] have sprouted wings, and they're drawn to light."

I whispered to Ben, "Can you get him to take that lantern outside? This is giving me the creeps. I've never seen so many bugs in my life!"

Another man came by later and explained, "The people build fires to draw the bug-a-bugs. When they fall as they hit the heat, the women catch them in basins of water. After the wings are pulled off, the kids stuff them in their mouths raw. Adults like them after they're roasted in iron pots over the fire."

As usual, Peter was out and about. When he came home with a crowd of boys following him, I asked, "Did you eat any bug-a-bugs?"

He said, "Yep. A boy gave me one, and I ate it."

"Was it good?"

"Yeah, it was crunchy."

I had no idea those charming little millipedes crawling across the hallway floor left a poisonous residue on everything they touched, until I asked Ben why he was killing them with a match. One day, when Peter spotted one, I asked if it was a baby.

He said, "Nope, it's a teenager."

It appeared that an army of millipedes was making our hallway their home, so I asked Patrick, "Why are they congregating here?"

He said, "It's the pineapples you have stacked in the corner. They eat fruit, and they're drawn by the scent." We quickly devoured those pineapples, and that took care of the millipede infestation.

At the other end of the insect spectrum were black rhinoceros beetles the size of a small dinner roll. Despite their huge horn, they were harmless. Boys walked around with them hanging on their T-shirts. On a previous visit, I had brought 2 of them back to Michigan alive. One escaped from a heavy corrugated cardboard box on our front porch, having used its horn to shred a hole. I recaptured it that afternoon when I heard the neighborhood kids yelling, "Hey! Look at this enormous bug on the sidewalk!"

One afternoon in Vahun, 3 boys came to our house very excited, carrying a little piece of folded cloth. They opened it, displaying a large jellylike white blob about the size of half a hot dog.

I asked, "What's that?"

One boy smiled and said, "It's a queen termite. We'll sell it to you for a quarter."

I said, "Why would I want to pay you for that?"

"To eat! It's a great delicacy!"

I shuddered. Even if I were starving, I don't think I could have eaten it. I said, "I'm sorry, but no thanks."

They went away with their treasure, disappointed.

One night, we were sitting at the dining room table talking, and as usual, bugs were flitting around the lantern. Ben smacked a small beetle on his arm, and we heard a loud popping noise. Instantly the air was filled with an extremely foul odor.

I wrinkled my nose, "What's that awful smell?"

Ben Jr. said, "Hey, Dad. Maybe that's one of those bombardier beetles Grandma told us about."

Ben smelled so bad that he had to immediately heat water and scrub himself. It was disgusting, but we laughed about it later. After that he was leery about smacking anything. I marveled that such a strong, unbearable scent could come from such a tiny insect.

Bugs inspired my hinterland humor:

"People laugh when I carry a brilliant red beetle on a leaf to show the kids."

"It's funny to spray a room with bug bomb when it's full of lightning bugs. We watch as their little lights slow down in flight and spiral down on the bed."

"Spider, spider on the wall, who's the most frightened one of all? You or me?"

"Mommy, please spray the bugs. I'm *scared*."

"A truly zealous bug collector would go completely wacko here. He couldn't keep up the pace."

However, there was always more than nature to challenge me.

CHAPTER 22

Mother and Chief's Wife

◇◇◇◇◇◇◇◇◇◇◇◇◇◇

*Although the lessons of trust that Jesus sends us
come wrapped in difficulties, the benefit outweighs the cost.*
—Sarah Young, *Jesus Calling*

Our house in Vahun, spring 1984

O ne morning, as we were eating breakfast, the local medic brought
in a woman who was having difficulty with her treatment. She told
him she had run out of medicine and her husband wouldn't give her money
for more.

Ben had the husband summoned and asked him, "Did you know your
wife's medicine was finished?"

"Yes," the man admitted.

Ben said, "She told me she's still sick and needs more medicine."

Chagrined, the man said, "She never told me that. Oh, Papa, I beg
you. No problem. I'll give her the money."

Ben told the woman, "You should have explained to your husband."

She said, "You are right, my father." Bowing to her husband, she asked
his forgiveness.

Ben concluded, "Go and get your medicine. Case dismissed."

They both thanked him and left together in peace, saying, "May God bless you."

I thought, *If only all marital difficulties could be resolved so simply!*

#

Ben and I never discussed it, but I was very aware that he was a big fish in Vahun's small pond, as well as the surrounding villages in Guma District. He couldn't walk through town without spending much of a morning or afternoon doing so, since everyone had to greet and speak with him. His authority was supreme in matters of judgment and solving problems. People came by for him to settle family matters, deal with unfair treatment, or fulfill special requests. My roles as chief's wife and mother were to support him in order to facilitate the spread of the gospel. His legacy as chief applied to our oldest son as well. People called Ben Jr. "Old Man," a sign of deep respect.

Some came for medical advice despite the new clinic. One afternoon, a man walked into the living room and showed Ben a huge machete gash in his palm that was so infected the inner tissue was bulging out.

Ben took one look and said, "Heat water and put lots of salt in it. Soak your hand in the hottest water you can stand. Do it 3 times a day for a half hour. Come and see me in 2 days."

A week later, the man stopped by, beaming with gratitude. "You see my hand? It's well! Thank you, Old Man. You are good to us."

Patrick was our local customs expert. He arrived at our house nearly every day to chide Ben about doing things "the correct way." Some mornings, he walked over in his Western pajamas—a sign of status in Vahun. One day after lunch, I walked over to make an arrangement with Nancy and found him on his front porch as the local magistrate holding court—in his pajamas. After that, I called him "the pajama judge" when we were alone.

Ben held great sway in local political affairs. There were countless community meetings in Vahun that year, with elaborate discussions and plans. In every meeting, Ben stressed the importance of God's blessing and guidance in all affairs.

We soon discovered that both the paramount chief and the commissioner of Guma District—which included Vahun and other nearby villages—were corrupt, dishonest men who ruthlessly exploited the people and caused much hardship. In early May, Ben wielded his influence and replaced the top man.

The new district commissioner was a young, honest Christian man who told us we really encouraged him in his faith. In fact, as 2nd in command, he had already been doing most of the work since the former commissioner traveled most of the time. We were impressed when he ordered an intercessory prayer service at the church during his induction into office.

One afternoon, Ben said, "I want you come with me. This young man's going to show me Tolbert's house." We walked to a hill outside of town and would never have found the place on our own. Dense underbrush covered the crumbled mud-block foundation, which was half washed away by rain. I put my arm around him as he stood there weeping—not only for his friend but also for his own shattered dreams for Liberia. Tolbert had been the kingpin in Ben's aspiration to one day become president. Ben channeled his enormous disappointment into focusing on God's kingdom and doing for Vahun what he couldn't do for Liberia.

His popularity was hard on me and the kids since he spent so little time with us. On top of that, we had no privacy during the day to talk things over; we were able to do this only at night, when we were in bed. Ben had to fulfill his responsibility to the mission board to explore mission opportunities in the area, which meant frequent trips, leaving me alone to cope.

I kept busy focusing much of my attention on the boys. There wasn't an hour or a day during which I wasn't concerned about them. Tropical Africa could be a dangerous place, and I felt they were literally babes in the woods. Our 1st week in Vahun, Ben Jr. returned from a fishing trip with the boys and reported, "My glasses fell in the Mawa River. The water was swift, and my pals were afraid to dive in to look for them because of the crocodiles." I shuddered to myself. Ben Jr. squinted for a month until the bush plane arrived with a new pair, mailed from our optometrist in Flint.

One day, we heard the women wailing in town and learned that a Muslim teenager had been bitten by the deadly green mamba snake while cutting palm nuts. He fell from the tree and was dead by the time he hit the ground. Ben Jr. said soberly, "I tried to kill a poisonous snake the other day, but the boys stopped me."

I said, "It's a good thing! You should *listen* to them!" We visited the parents' hut, which was crowded with villagers. We greeted each one and stayed a while to share their grief in silence. As I watched the mother weeping, I knew it could have been my son.

Joe suffered the most. He couldn't stop scratching his mosquito bites and developed sores on his legs and arms, which took some time to heal. He had 2 serious bouts of malaria and was the most homesick of the boys.

From the time we arrived in Vahun, Peter began wetting the bed. I had to drag the mattress out each morning to dry in the sun and change the bottom sheet. The kids loved him, and he was a real runabout and talk of the town. They took him all over the place and made him cute little rattan trucks and cars. As a result, he was so wound up that I had to lie down with him to get him to take a nap. He had malaria only once, and except for occasional diarrhea, he was fine.

Peter and Joe

In March Ben Jr. told Ben that he wanted to join Poro, the men's traditional school, which had been in session for 2 months in the nearby village of Gbongoma and was soon to finish. Ben was overjoyed, knowing it would take his oldest son into the heart and soul of the Mende and Gbandi tribes. Poro was more than training. It was the essence of male identity, bonding, and shared responsibility, which were so well developed in those cultures. Poro men were blood brothers who would do anything for each other. When they graduated, it meant they had all the rights and privileges of mature men and were ready to marry.

Chiefs were summoned from nearby villages to determine whether or not to grant Ben Jr. permission to participate. After debating at length if he was black or white, the issue was finally settled by his name—Ngombu Tejjeh. He would attend the final 10 days and participate in the graduation. Word quickly spread to the other villages. In Vahun, the women danced and rejoiced all over town.

I had mixed feelings. I was happy to see Ben Jr. willingly embrace the Mende tribe and for them to reciprocate, but I worried about possible dangers. I knew Ben wouldn't knowingly risk Ben Jr.'s life. Still, I was apprehensive knowing my son was in a place I knew nothing about, doing things I'd never discover, initiated into a secret male society surrounded by a wall of silence no woman could breach. My son would have the same scars on his back as my husband, but I wouldn't be able to ask about them.

Patrick saw the concerned look on my face and said, "Don't worry. I'm sponsoring Ngombu. I'll stay in Gbongoma in case anything happens." He sent word the 1st day that Ben Jr. was okay, but there were 9 days to go. It didn't help that Ben was gone for 3 of them, traveling to Kolahun to explore mission opportunities among the Loma tribe with another missionary.

Each morning, I packed food and water to be taken to Ben Jr. since he wasn't able to drink the local water or eat hot pepper. I was glad when Ben returned, but the days crawled without end.

On graduation day, it took us an hour and a half to walk the trail to Gbongoma. Everyone warned me before we left that I must "dance with the women." The minute we arrived, Ben disappeared with the men. A crowd of women mobbed Miriam and me. I struggled to keep Joe and Peter with us as we were swept along, circling the village with clouds of dust raised by our shuffling feet. I struggled to breathe but became caught up in their joy and excitement over their sons' "college" graduation.

We heard a horrible growling, howling noise, and it looked as if lightning had struck; women and children suddenly and frantically ran into the huts. Landai, the masked being of Poro, had arrived. Miriam called for Peter, who had run off, and found him in the nick of time. We were quickly sequestered in the town chief's bedroom with the wooden shutters closed and were guarded by a man so we wouldn't open them. While we waited, I glanced around in the dim light. The room was orderly and pleasant by local standards: clean country cloth on the bed, a swept dirt floor. I wondered as I noticed cobwebs on the mud-block walls and a layer of dust on the old wooden storage boxes, *What would it be like to grow up here—to live in a place like this?*

In the meantime, Ben accompanied the elders to the school site where he addressed the boys: "You know your responsibilities according to what you've learned. From now on, you must answer for your actions. Always remember, the tribe is counting on you."

The shutters opened, and I saw Landai stride into town with authority, his raffia skirt raising dust, and his machete sticking out in front.

Landai in Gbongoma

The graduates followed, their clothes dirty and their bodies smeared with white chalk from being symbolically swallowed by Landai at the beginning of training and excreted at graduation. Men rushed up to meet him. Women and children gradually emerged from the huts, watching in fear from afar.

Everyone gathered in the center of the village, the graduates sitting on the ground, their country-cloth skullcaps pulled down over their eyes so they couldn't look at their mothers. To redeem their sons, the elders and parents presented gifts to Landai, who was squatting at one end of the village square: baskets of rice, goats, country cloth, and money. Landai's interpreter responded, "Here are your children. They have been reborn."

I will never forget the special honor paid to my son as "Ngombu Tejjeh"; in a significant gesture, he was allowed to sit on Landai's raffia skirt. Ben told me later, "It was one of the happiest days of my life."

Ben Jr. sitting on the skirt of Landai

Landai stood after a few moments, escorting the boys back into the forest to bathe in the river and put on their best clothes. They emerged wearing sunglasses, their shaved heads covered by scarves pulled behind their ears, making them look like Egyptian pharaohs.

As our family and other graduates from Vahun rode home in the co-op truck, a man blew the historic ivory horn of Ngombu Tejjeh as we approached, just as in olden days. Each graduate went to his hut so family members and others could come by and congratulate him with gifts. There was great rejoicing at our house. Nancy covered our 2 vinyl living room chairs with country cloth, making them look like thrones—one for Ben Jr. and the other for Bubba, her son by her 1st marriage. As our families celebrated together, a large group of women arrived, singing, "Father, you did well to let your son go to Poro. It made us all feel good. He's a real Ngombu Tejjeh. Nothing of his people must be hidden from him because he's a real Poro man."

I danced, trying my best to imitate the other women, as we moved through the entire village, accompanied by *sassas*, singing and visiting each graduate's hut. Everyone applauded when Nancy and I linked arms in joy. It was tiring, but I was happy to act in solidarity with the women. The vice commissioner told me, "Because you let your son go into Poro, you are truly one of us. We are very happy for this day."

Dancing with the women

However, my relief in having my son home was short-lived. The next day, he complained of a severe headache and sore neck. Our treatment for malaria didn't help, and we were concerned because a man had recently died in Gbongoma from spinal meningitis. Ben took Ben Jr. to see a doctor in Kolahun, 40 miles away over Kamboi, riding in the co-op truck, which was hauling bags of cocoa. The doctor couldn't do a spinal tap, but he gave Ben Jr. the medicine for meningitis anyway since he displayed the symptoms. No sooner did Ben Jr. recover than he popped the cap off of his front tooth, the day before we were to leave for Monrovia. I paid Miriam her weekly wages and gave her an extra $20 to clean the fridge and prop it open while we were gone, and also to supervise the boys in washing the windows and cleaning the floors, the day before our return.

Momo came with us; it was his first ride in an airplane. After we landed at Spriggs-Payne Airport in Monrovia, he said, "I'd much rather go over Kamboi a 1,000 times than go in that plane again. I thought we were high enough, and the houses looked so small, and then the plane kept going higher and higher. All I could see were trees, no ground. I didn't even know where I would jump if the plane crashed. I looked around—sky up, sky down. The pilot didn't look frightened, but me, I was scared too much."

When he returned by vehicle to Vahun, he reported on his stay with us at the mission apartment. "We all slept in the same place and used the same bathroom. I had a real good shower with hot water. I ate all kinds of food. I watched the children. They didn't complain, so I ate it. I didn't feel hungry, but I never ate rice the whole time."

Our family arrived in Monrovia thin and run-down since local food donations had tapered off and my Western food supplies weren't adequate. Ben and I had picked up a fungus infection that caused unbearable itching. Ben Jr. had sores at the corners of his mouth and diarrhea, caused by the meningitis medication. Joe walked bent over, complaining of a sharp pain in his stomach.

Our first stop was the Cooper Clinic, where the doctor gave Joe a shot of time-release penicillin for his pneumonia, which was good, since he couldn't keep any antibiotic or Tylenol down for several days. He was miserable with labored breathing, chest pain, nausea, fever, and a constant headache. I finally got him to drink fruit juices, one small glass at a time. It was beastly hot, and he actually smelled because of the drugs and dehydration.

Ben Jr. had worms. After the medication, he saw dead ones in his stools. We all ended up taking the same drug as a precaution and were told to repeat the treatment every 3 months. Our funds from the church were running low, but no matter the cost, I bought juices, fresh vegetables, and meat, determined to fatten everyone up. I also made the decision to take more food upcountry.

I wrote home, "We've really seen God's provision these last 2 weeks. Guinea is hostile to foreigners and only 1 percent Christian. Ben tried twice to fly there to survey mission possibilities. First, Nigeria Airlines went on strike. Then, 2 days later, Ghanaian Airways had mechanical difficulties. Both times, the boys and I were shocked to hear Ben rattling the gates at the mission house late at night. It reminded me of the story in Acts about Peter being released from prison and banging on the front door.

"The next morning, we heard that President Sekou Toure died in surgery in the States, and all flights in and out of Guinea were grounded. I got goose bumps when we heard about the military coup and the killings and imprisonments. The Lord had kept Ben from going there because he would have been stranded in a very dangerous situation. We are wondering if he will go at all."

At a beach in Monrovia, I stayed under an umbrella but stuck my legs out to get some sun. The result? The worst sunburn of my life. My red, swollen legs were so painful I could barely walk. They were still sore after the skin peeled.

Ben Jr. completed most of his correspondence courses before entering Poro. However, he struggled with Algebra II. I hated to have him lose a year of math and have to double up his senior year. Ben found a math tutor at the University of Liberia who came over every evening and helped him. During that time, Ben Jr. enjoyed attending the youth meetings at St. Peter Lutheran Church. When our 2 weeks were up, he still needed help, so Bible translators living in Monrovia offered to let him stay with them. Before leaving, we took him to the dentist, who gave him a temporary plastic cap for his front tooth until we returned to Michigan. When he eventually got back to Vahun, the boys asked him, "Ngombu, did your tooth grow back?"

Our stay in the city had failed to rejuvenate me, the stress of everything taking its toll. I reached a low point when Ben flew to the Ivory Coast for several days, exploring mission possibilities. Cooped up in the apartment with the electricity off half the day, I nursed Joe while still suffering from my fungus infection.

On our flight to Vahun, the bush plane carried our food supplies, but we had to leave behind Joe's and Peter's new birthday gifts. I forgot the boys' schoolbooks in the apartment, delaying their classes. Tears ran down my cheeks as I sat looking out the plane window.

Storm clouds gathered, and the pilot said, "We'll have to turn back if I don't see a clearing ahead. I don't want to fly into a mountain like that other pilot did."

I held my breath, dreading the thought of unpacking and repacking. I prayed, "Lord, please let us get through."

A few minutes later, he said, "I think we'll make it after all." I breathed, "Thank You, Lord."

I plodded to our house from the airstrip, my houseboys lugging boxes of groceries. As I walked into the living room, I immediately noticed that the window slats were still covered with red dust and the floors were dirty. The boys looked down, saying nothing as they meekly followed me into the kitchen. I opened the fridge door, backing away from the smell of rotten food; black mold covered everything. I looked at the box containing 25 pounds of frozen meat and broke down, sobbing. The boys quietly stacked the boxes before they scattered, promising to do the floors the next morning. I stood there devastated and heartsick. "What happened? How could Miriam *do* this to me? I thought we were family. Better yet, friends. Everything's against me. How will I survive?"

There was no time to feel sorry for myself. Swiping my cheeks with the back of my hand, I heated water and began emptying the fridge and scrubbing it with bleach. Just then, Ben walked in and said, "Come on out for just a minute. The people are eager to welcome you back."

With hands on my hips, I said in disgust, "Don't you *see* this mess? I *can't* go out right now!"

A few minutes later, Carol walked in the front door and offered to help me fill the kerosene tank and light the wick. While all this was going on, people rushed in to greet me. I had no privacy when I wanted and needed it most.

I found out Miriam had skipped off to Sierra Leone as soon as we left, to "do market" with her earnings and the extra $20 I had given her. She returned a week after we did. When she stopped by, I simply asked her how her market went. She said, "I lost everything."

I discovered we could survive without her. I wrote home, "I have no one helping me with the cooking since I'm afraid to trust anyone else. I'm trying to learn to prepare local food myself. Ben helps, and with rainy season coming, we'll just filter the rainwater. We won't have to boil it. I still have the boys filling the water barrels and doing the floors. The fridge is ice cold every day now, which is good."

As life in Vahun went on, our purpose wasn't simply to survive, but also to serve the Lord.

Chapter 23

Feet of Clay

◇◇◇◇◇◇◇◇◇◇◇◇◇◇

Only as far as we can live Christ before the eyes of others
can we help them to understand His message.
—Andrew Murray, Missionary to South Africa, 1848–1891

Gbongoma, December 1983

Everyone stood watching as Carol pulled up in a Ford Bronco to take Ben and me back to Vahun after the funeral of Elder Freeman, a Christian leader in that village known to be "strong in God business." By late afternoon, everybody was spent with grief and fatigue, the others from Vahun having walked to Gbongoma that morning.

When she stopped, 6 women and 2 men quickly piled into the back for a ride home. With the entire village watching, she stood with her hands on her hips, demanding, "I'm not budging until you all get out! We can't have our vehicle constantly overloaded. It's too hard on the shock absorbers."

In the dead silence, everyone was stone-faced, stunned. No one moved. I watched, speechless in disbelief at what was transpiring. After a pause, she yelled, "If you won't get out, I'm going to get you out!" With that, she grabbed a man and 2 women, pulling them out.

She turned to me and ordered, "You'd better get in right now, or you and Ben can walk back to Vahun." I meekly climbed in since our kids were waiting for us at our house. It was a quiet ride back.

#

When we had initially stayed at the mission house, Carol appeared to be in charge. A registered nurse, she was concerned about George's health since he was diabetic. Some nights, George sat up reading, and he would nap during the day. Each morning, he spent time on the short-wave radio, and at meals, there were no prayers. I didn't see him read the Bible or have family devotions.

He showed me his astronomy guides, telling me they were useless in the African sky. As a veterinarian, he had offered to help the people with their animals, but he complained, "They never asked." He said, "I tried to gain favor with them by painting the walls of the new town hall, but there was no response."

He explained the church's lack of a woven rattan ceiling, saying, "I want the people to initiate it." When we asked why the Lutheran liturgy hadn't been translated into Mende and wasn't being recited, he replied, "I don't want to influence. Liturgy must come from the people. I want them to figure out ways to worship God on their own terms—to design their own service."

A quiet man with a gentle bearded face, he considered himself an overseer rather than a preacher, primarily teaching classes once a week for the 6 young evangelists in training. Patrick Danielson, a Mende lay pastor, conducted the church services, preaching in Mende with a Sierra Leonean accent since he had come from there. During our stay, I heard George pray twice and tell 2 simple Bible stories. He didn't sing during the services.

Ben and I quickly became concerned about the way Carol treated the villagers. I was puzzled when she told me, "I've stopped letting the Vahun kids play with our kids' toys because they steal them." There was no doubt she was a hard worker, but she was aloof and could be quite rude at times. The people were wary about taking her medical advice because they found it hard to trust her. She even teased Old Man Brima about not being able to satisfy his wives!

One evening, at the mission house, Carol told me about Elder Freeman while we did the dishes. "He's one of our most devoted men. He pretty much runs the Gbongoma mission station by himself. A while back he borrowed money to fix his house, and he's never paid us back."

In December, George and Carol returned from Monrovia, a week before Christmas. The next day, she stopped by and told me, "Before we left, I drove Freeman to the clinic in Kolahun. The doctor said he has spinal meningitis. The family expects us to airlift him to a hospital in Monrovia, like we did for Old Man Brima, but it's very expensive and it comes out of our budget. I gave his family the medicine, and now they've brought him to Vahun for me to take care of. I can't do it, and besides, it's really their responsibility. I'm going over to check on him. Would you like to come along?"

I said, "Sure."

We stepped into a dark hut, the hot, still air smacking me in the face. A withered 40-year-old man lay in front of us on a woven mat on the dirt floor, so still, he looked dead. As my eyes adjusted, I saw men and women sitting quietly around him. No one spoke as we entered, their tired focus completely on Freeman. Carol perfunctorily greeted them. Taking his hand, she ordered, "Squeeze it as hard as you can." He barely grasped it.

She instructed the family, "Make sure you give him the medicine on time. Is he drinking water?"

His weary wife said, "No, we can't get him to drink."

Carol said, "You've *got* to make him do it! I'll check in again." She led me out and I thought, *That's it? No words of comfort, no prayers?*

As we walked back to my place, she said, "It's the family's fault. They're just waiting for him to die."

The next day, she told me, "The family insisted I take Freeman home to die. How could they possibly subject him to that bumpy ride in his condition?"

Two days later, Ben and I received the news that Freeman had died. Nothing unites a community like grief. We went to Gbongoma the next morning with Pastor Danielson to show our support for the family and the Christians there. As I hugged Freeman's wife, I felt her sadness seeping through her skin.

Freeman was buried that day without a coffin since he had died of spinal meningitis; the chief assured us that everyone knew his soul was in heaven. Villagers came by expressing sympathy and donating money for the funeral. Several men began digging Freeman's grave next to the tiny mud-block church he loved so much.

Freeman's male relatives would ordinarily have washed and prepared his body. In this case, Pastor Danielson perfumed and wrapped it in a white piece of country cloth. It was then lifted onto on a simple wooden bed also covered with white country cloth. As a sign of respect, the bed was carried on men's shoulders around the village three times, a small procession of Christians following. The scene reminded me of Jesus wrapped in a burial shroud and the time in Nain when he raised the widow's son who was being carried on a bier.

At the tiny church, the body was placed in front and people gathered. The women played *sassas* and sang Christian hymns, with others joining in. People walked up the center aisle, putting money into a plate next to the body. Freeman's mother swayed, "dancing" in grief, her hair disheveled. The woman next to me said, "No one willingly enters the final house of death. We must enter it alone, just as we are born. Even his loved ones will not join him now. We know that Freeman was always working for the Lord, encouraging people to come to church. We'll see him in heaven."

In late afternoon, everyone drifted out to watch the men finish digging the grave, the sun's rays softened in the clear sky and trees shading us. His body was once again carried around the village, with us following along singing. A small boy solemnly "rang the church bell" by striking a rusty Caterpillar crankcase with an iron rod. At the gravesite, Pastor Danielson read the 23rd Psalm and Scripture verses, including, "Oh grave, where is thy victory?" Freeman's mother "danced" among us.

Before his body was lowered into the grave with his tools and possessions next to him, his youngest child cut off a piece of white cloth as a remembrance. Wooden planks were laid on top, and people threw handfuls of dirt, the clods softly thudding on the wood. A Vahun elder fashioned a cross out of folded palm leaves and stuck it at the head of the grave, which was then heaped with soil. That symbolic poignant gesture brought tears to my eyes, and I wept for the family. Freeman's mother stood forlornly by the grave, a woman telling her, "When the Lord summons us, who will say no? Who will say no when God Almighty calls us?"

I was extremely disappointed with Carol after she pulled people from the Bronco, but I tried to put it behind me. After all, she had been very good to us and we were supposed to work together.

We attended church the 1st Sunday we were there and every Sunday thereafter, in Vahun or at one of the mission stations. Before the service, we welcomed people. Ben, Ben Jr., and I occasionally read the Scriptures. Ben helped with communion. I sang in the choir with Carol.

The wooden benches were usually ¾ full, with men on one side, women on the other, and children in front. The congregation's favorite hymn went as follows: "Sav-ya, Sa-av-ya, heah my humble cry. While on others Thou art pa-i-ssing, do not pass me by." After the hymn, one of the elders read the Scripture lesson in Mende. Much to our director's confusion, someone in the choir would simply begin singing another song, with the congregation joining in. Fussy babies were quieted as mothers pulled down the neckline of their polyester top and nursed them. Outside the open windows, village life went on.

The week before Christmas, Ben left for 5 days to investigate mission opportunities among the Gbandis living near Somalahun. Things were bleak as Joe and I came down with our 2nd bout of malaria while he was gone. The monthly bush plane brought us 8 Christmas cards, including one from Doe. The color photo showed him in military fatigues, sitting next to a small Liberian flag, a vacant expression on his face; he was no longer the scrawny master sergeant. The caption said, "Let us continue our search for World Peace and an Economic World Order that will bring prosperity to mankind everywhere."

I hung Joe's and Peter's construction-paper chains decorated with bells, stars, and trees in the living room. Carol gave us a small cardboard manger scene, and we put it on the buffet, surrounded by fresh palm leaves. Our houseboys tied palm branches on our porch posts—a typical sign of celebration.

The familiar Christmas songs on my cassette tapes made me cry at first, but my spirit revived as I sang along with them. We faced a Christmas with no gifts under the tree, no familiar church program, and no smell of Christmas cookies in the oven. Our only "snow" was "I'm Dreaming of a White Christmas" on the tape player.

Santa was a masked being with raffia arms and legs, his brightly colored headdress mask adorned with tiny mirrors. Instead of giving gifts, he asked for them. Peter brought him to our porch, and I took a picture of Santa hugging him with a crowd of boys standing around, grinning.

On Christmas Eve, we paused for a quick picture in front of our house before walking up to the mission house for dinner.

Christmas Eve in front of our house

Carol went all out with a branch of twinkling Christmas lights, red flowers on the table, and Frosty the Snowman napkins by our plates. We rode down the hill in their Ford Bronco, singing, "Dashing through the snow, in a one-horse open sleigh ..."

The church window shutters were open, letting in the cool night breeze. Two large kerosene pump lanterns sat on the simple wooden altar, illuminating the colorful felt banners, donated by American churches, on both sides of the mud-block wall. Everything glistened, including the palm leaves.

People reverently filed in, filling the benches, the children hushed and still. Our choir of 8, wearing robes for the first time, marched in carrying candles and singing "O Come All Ye Faithful" with an African lilt. After placing our candles in the windows, we sat down. As I listened to the Christmas story, read in English and translated into Mende—"And there were in the same country, shepherds abiding in the fields ..."—I realized this humble village was more like the setting of Christ's birth than any place I'd ever known.

On Christmas Eve, that night of nights, I was hit with an avalanche of homesickness. I looked outside the church window and saw a full moon rising, imagining it shining on my Michigan home. After the service, everyone walked home through the village, our family singing Christmas carols.

That year, everything was stripped away except the true meaning of Christmas—that the Lord came to His people. I sat there hearing afresh the message, "Unto us a child is born, unto us a Son is given …" I thought of Christians celebrating all over the world. As I watched the kingdom of God in Mende faces, Christmas became universal; its meaning and joy applied to people in every country and climate. We all had a Savior, our bond of faith overcoming cultural differences.

We had the essentials: God's love, His Gift for all time, and our faith. My family wasn't there, but we had Ben's "relatives" and our brothers and sisters in Christ. I was moved when the choir dropped by to sing Christmas carols on our porch. We gave them roasted peanuts and fried plantain chips.

The fog was lifting the next morning as we walked to church. Ben and I welcomed everyone, saying "Merry Christmas!" On this holiest of days, the wooden benches were crammed. Communion was served. From the back of the church, I quickly took a picture of the crowd.

Vahun Lutheran Church, Christmas Day

A big dance had been planned that night, with Ben and me as patron guests. However, Patrick canceled it, telling me, "Knowing you, it would probably be over by 9 p.m. since you go to bed so early."

Ben had purchased a cow for the feast that afternoon, and soon after we arrived home, Pastor Danielson's wife arrived at the door with a large enamel bowl holding the cow's liver and a choice piece of beef—the best of the animal, according to the Mendes. My kerosene fridge wasn't reliable at the time, so I urged her to keep them as a gift from me. She was thrilled.

Vahun was popping with visitors, who were all housed and fed. Santa, along with other masked beings, drifted around town followed by crowds of kids. Musicians wandered by, singing, the women playing sassas and the men accompanying on the drums.

At noon there were games for the kids at the school grounds and a hearty soccer match between the Vahun boys and the visitors. Ben Jr. had just recovered from a bout of malaria, probably brought on by training so hard for the races. Even so, he won 1st place in the sack race and 2nd in the meter race with people on the sidelines, obviously pleased, yelling, "Ngombu!"

In Vahun's "feeding of the 5,000," there was plenty of stew and rice for all, with 2 cows, 3 goats, and a sheep slaughtered. Unfortunately I missed it. After I watched the races, I limped back to our house to nurse my ankle, which was swollen from a bug bite. That day, I had put on a cheerful face, despite my homesickness, for my kids, who remained at the festivities. However, in the privacy of my home, my facade didn't hold up. I no sooner propped up my leg than Carol's daughter arrived with a small box of Christmas cookies—colored sugars, sprinkles and all, just the way my mother made them. After she left, I sat there crying at that touch of home.

I used George's typewriter to write my monthly *Mende People Newsletter.* In January, "praise" items included 8 people having been baptized in Vahun and 5 in Gbongoma over the Christmas holiday, our neighbor having asked us for a Bible, and finally, our carpenter and his son having come forward to be baptized because Ben had impressed the carpenter that "this church thing" was serious business.

Life in Vahun made Bible stories come alive for me. It was easy to imagine the agricultural lifestyle and small-town atmosphere—simple home construction and travel on foot. I pictured local tax collectors and fishermen, tribal elders sitting at the gate, and the traditional transfer of land. I felt empathy for multiple wives, surrogate mothers, and a childless woman feeling cursed. The congregation had no difficulty relating to the Scriptures since they lived it. The story of wheat being separated from chaff was no mystery because the women fanned rice chaff every day.

The congregation in Vahun was comprised, for the most part, of illiterate men and women who spoke Mende, as well as a small group of literate young men who also spoke English. Ben encouraged the church members to develop a Mende liturgy and sing Christian songs in the local style of music, accompanied by *sassas* and drums. He and I made plans to visit every hut in Vahun.

Ben and I revived the Friday-night Bible studies, which had petered out. The benches were full as we began with a Christian song, and then, to spark interest, we showed some of the slides we had taken in Vahun years before. Ben gave a Bible talk or lecture during the midway break, and after more slides, we closed with prayer.

Mrs. Danielson and I began visiting delinquent members of the ladies' Bible study group in order to revive it, and she asked me to lead it. We opened it to every woman in town, including nursing babies and small children. She translated as I taught the story using a flannelgraph—paper figures that adhered to a piece of flannel board. Thirteen attended the first meeting; 11, the second; and 19, the third.

Bible study in our living room

In February, three new mission stations were opened. Thirty-five people—the entire village, including the Muslims—attended the first church service in Folima, 5 miles away. The men sat in front of the thatched-roof meeting hall, and behind them sat the women with babies on their backs. George spoke briefly, and Pastor Danielson gave the sermon.

One of the mission stations

All eyes were on Ben as he told the people, "The most important thing in my life is Jesus." When he finished his testimony, an old man said, "Whatever is good for you, whatever you want for us, that's what we want."

I spoke briefly to encourage the women: "I am so happy to see you here. You have an important role to play in God's kingdom. My country and skin color are different, but in Jesus Christ, we are all one."

The next day, Ben and I rode in the Ford Bronco for a hair-raising ride over Kamboi to open a new mission station at Yandohun. I wondered if I would ever get used to being thrown around in a vehicle. We first stopped at the chief's house to pay our respects and then walked around greeting people and inviting them to gather at the new schoolhouse. Twenty men and one woman joined the instant audience of kids in one of the classrooms; there were 135 in all. George said a few words, and Pastor Danielson preached. The men watched with rapt attention as Ben gave his testimony.

I stood and said, "We are all one in Christ despite differences in race and culture. I'm disappointed to see only one woman here since you, too, are important in the family of God." Everyone applauded as I sat down. Ben later found out the woman spread my message to the others.

The new school was built by a Peace Corps volunteer we had met 2 weeks earlier on the road near Yandohun. I was startled to see our headlights shining on a blond-haired white man coming out of the trees to cross the road, and I was equally surprised when he said "What news?" a typical Liberian expression. After the church service, he showed us his simple one-room structure with a gorgeous mahogany ceiling and walls, a single bed, a small table with a few books on it, and a kerosene lantern on the concrete floor. We quickly discovered he had "gone native" when he introduced us to his 2 Gbandi wives and 5 children who lived nearby in a mud-block house; one of his wives was cooking in an open thatched-roof kitchen.

In April, the events leading up to Easter were strenuous. The previous 2 weeks, I told the passion story in stages at our Ladies' Bible Study meetings in my living room on Monday and Wednesday evenings. On Palm Sunday, the Christians assembled at our carport, listening to the *Messiah* on our tape player. We didn't order palm branches from a florist; everyone simply brought them from their backyards. Several elders wore cross necklaces fashioned out of folded palm leaves. We marched to the church, waving the branches above our heads, singing in Mende about Christ going into Jerusalem, much like Bible times.

Walking through town, we gained momentum, and we entered the church triumphantly singing. The choir progressed, waving their palms and singing a Mende hymn as people filled the pews. Ben and I were pleased to see the chief from Yandohun, who stopped by our house after the service, which joyously ushered in Holy Week.

Early on Good Friday morning, Carol took our family, Pastor Danielson and his wife, and 5 members of our choir over Kamboi to a church service in Yandohun. We practiced songs along the way, our voices leaping and cracking as we jostled and bumped along—mine especially when I went airborne at the very back of the vehicle. (I quickly understood why the front had filled up first.) However, nothing could dampen our high spirits of Christian fellowship as we passed through several villages, singing and waving.

As usual, it took a while for the service to begin, the choir adding a special lift to the occasion. Ben gave the sermon, and 7 people were baptized, their names written in the Lamb's Book of Life. Before we left, the people of Yandohun gave us "good chop."

We sang all the way home. In Vahun, there was little time before the afternoon Good Friday service to put my leg up; my ankle was swollen once again from an insect bite. The Christians met in our carport, and as we walked to church, we solemnly sang in Mende, "O Come and Mourn with Me a While." Neither George nor Pastor Danielson was there when we arrived. After the Scriptures were read, Ben rose to the occasion and preached passionately, telling the story of the crucifixion in his own words.

He confessed that in his weakness, he would have fought back instead of submitting as Christ did.

That night, I began itching all over with hives. Carol sent her daughter down with over-the-counter Benadryl. At first, it calmed things down. Then, as it wore off before the next dose was due, my frazzled nerves felt as though electricity were running through them. I decided not to take any more.

Saturday morning, I lay in bed with inflamed nerve endings, my body covered with red welts from scratching them. I looked horrible—my face swollen and covered with red blotches; my body, scalp, and neck raw from scratching. Shocked by my appearance, Ben quickly took charge of Joe and Peter, handling everything that needed to be done in the house.

That day, I took several warm baths to soothe my welts. Ironically, they dried out my skin, intensifying the itching. By Saturday night, I thought I'd go mad and woke Ben up. He comforted me but could offer no solution.

In desperation, I prayed, "Lord, what should I do? I'm going *crazy!*" A thought came to me: *Try skin lotion.* It brought enough relief for me to make it through the night.

By Easter Sunday, the palms of my hands and the soles of my feet, as well as the crevices between my fingers and toes, were especially painful. I scratched to relieve the itching. Seconds later, I felt as if I were on fire. I scratched again, and the burning intensified. I couldn't wear my nylon tricot nightgown or tolerate a sheet over my skin, so I lay there naked, each second trying to garner enough strength to keep from scratching. I remained completely still since the pain was excruciating if I moved an inch. The hours dragging by were utter agony.

I was in complete seclusion, the bedroom curtains closed except for when Ben brought me food and drink. Trying to bolster my spirits, he asked, "Nita, would you like to listen to your gospel music?" Soon Sandi Patti's voice rang through the air, and I tried to focus on it to take my mind off my misery.

I told Ben, "I look horrible! No visitors!" which presented a dilemma since it went against Mende culture. In Vahun, whenever anyone was sick or hurt, everyone had to stop by and say, "Gbei wei," which meant, "It's not significant. You'll be okay."

On Monday morning, the leader of the woman's society arrived to check on me on her way to the farm. Ben tried to explain, "When people from America get sick, they don't want anyone to see them, because they don't look good."

She said, "Well, we already know that. A lot of them must die, then, because no one can see them. You know our way, Old Man. The more people see you, the better it is. Someone may know about the sickness. It's more important to see how they're doing than how they look. Please let me see her."

Embarrassed, Ben adamantly protected me, and the news went like wildfire around Vahun. People said, "She's our wife too. What will we say to her parents if something happens to her?"

By Tuesday morning, several elders were on our porch. Brima told Ben, "This is our home. *We* make the decisions here. I don't care what people do in America."

Again Ben protected me.

That afternoon, Patrick came by and said with deepest respect, "Mada (Father), our wife is sick because her skin is white. People will think you brought her here to die. Please tell me about our wife."

Ben said, "We know what the sickness is. Hopefully, it will soon go away."

On Wednesday, I awoke and realized the itching was gone. I walked into the bathroom and looked at my face. My skin was clear. I felt tremendous relief, but I was still weak.

Patrick told us the people were assuaged when they saw me in the yard later that week. They said, "The Old Man was right. She's better."

We had missed the Easter service, but we learned that the Folima congregation had joined in and 30 people were baptized. It was a solemn Easter with me sick, Ben Jr. in Monrovia, and no Easter baskets for Joe and Peter.

Two weeks after I recovered, Carol came marching in our front door. "Why didn't you use the Benadryl I sent over for you?"

"It irritated my nerves as I came off of it."

"You never listen to me, *do you?* You know, a lot of the problems around here are *your* fault. Everything was fine until *you* came here. You're trying to turn the people against us!"

Losing my temper as well, I yelled in frustration, "It's your *own* fault! Can't you see how you treat them?"

"No one complained before *you* came!"

"Maybe they were too scared! You're so disrespectful to them. You can't treat them like that!"

A screaming match between 2 missionary women with the windows open was hardly a good example of Christian love. After she stormed out, I had to take a deep breath, trying to relax. That month, my stress level from the hives and everything else became so great that my menstrual periods stopped; they didn't return until we were back in Michigan. When we left, Nancy appreciated my gift of sanitary supplies I hadn't needed.

In February, 2 new missionaries had arrived and were working in other areas of Lofa County. One of them visited Vahun in May and took us back to his station for a visit.

That Sunday, we attended his joint monthly service in the town hall. The Kissi people heartily welcomed us. They listened attentively to the message and sang enthusiastically. I admired the missionary for using local cultural examples as he preached on the power of God's word. Ben shared his testimony, and the service closed with the Kissi evangelism team, called Fishers of Men, presenting the gospel as they did in other villages.

Both missionary teams lifted our spirits with their kindness and hospitality. At the same time, their contrast with the situation in Vahun was obvious. I envied them living in larger, more accessible towns. They had nice houses, and the men were able to cope with tropical challenges. Ben stayed on to survey mission possibilities. As the boys and I boarded the bush plane in Foya to return to Vahun, I came down with a splitting headache—another attack of malaria.

Four days later, Ben returned, suffering with severe gas and diarrhea. Peter came down with malaria the day of his birthday. His only request had been a birthday cake, but because of my argument with Carol, I couldn't bring myself to borrow her oven. Instead I became creative with the lemon cake mix Peter had chosen on our last trip to Monrovia. At breakfast he said, "Mommy, these pancakes taste lemony."

I said, "Actually, those are your birthday pancakes." In his great disappointment, he looked down, trying not to cry.

Not only was our relationship with George and Carol strained, but their relationship with the Mende people had also degraded to the point where they were primarily dispensers of favors and loaners of money. In fact, by the time we arrived, interest in the church had dwindled.

In my view, they had failed to relate to and identify with the people. As a result, the church trainees that preached at the mission stations had adopted a "give me, do for me" attitude. Naturally George and Carol resented such manipulation, but they had no alternative since they depended on them to carry out the work. In time, I think Carol's dissatisfaction led her to see the Mende people as the enemy. She once told me, "The people don't care. They just want things from us." And to a good extent, she was right.

I'm sure she began with good intentions, but her blunt talk didn't mesh with Mende sensibilities. She once told me, "I don't take any guff from these people. If they don't do what I want, I let them have it when I have to. Then they know I mean business." After the church library was built, she said, "They must return the book they borrowed before I'll give them another. If they're late, they pay a fine. Otherwise, they'll never value these books. We can't just give them away."

In retrospect, I realize Carol didn't have the advantage I had in being the wife of a descendant of Ngombu Tejjeh. Still, in my mind, there was no excuse for treating the villagers rudely. The new missionary teams in Lofa were close to their communities and well respected by their parishioners. However, they didn't live in such a remote area. I regret that Ben and I didn't sit down with George and Carol and talk things out. After all, we both could have used some understanding and encouragement.

The final straw came in May, when the area secretary of missions made his usual 6-month visit and stayed with us for 3 days. The people of Vahun had been hesitant to speak out because the missionaries were serving them. However, the opportunity to talk privately with the secretary in our palava hut emboldened them. As a result, he called a meeting so the people could openly state their case.

That night, the only light in the church came from the 2 pump lanterns on the altar. The place was packed, including the paramount chief, the town elders, and the Muslims. As the people took turns speaking, George didn't answer the charge that he didn't preach and did very little teaching. Towns that had asked for a church 2 years prior were just being visited. George openly argued with the chief in front of his people—an absolute no-no in Mende culture. I couldn't believe what I was seeing and hearing. George stalked out in anger, and as the people were leaving, he returned to apologize. It was too late. His connection with the people was missing, and any goodwill he and Carol had was gone.

They were frequently absent after that meeting, spending time in Monrovia. Ben supervised the 2 wells sponsored by the church, which hadn't been finished. The work resumed with the new district commissioner in place, and Ben went over to check the progress each day until they were completed.

Near the end of May, we traveled by vehicle to Monrovia for 2 weeks—a rough trip since the roads were getting bad. While there, Ben finally made his trip to Guinea during the 1st week of June, but it was fruitless. He could find no openings for mission work.

That July, we weren't in Vahun when George and Carol left quietly on the bush plane. We had gone to Sierra Leone for a week to visit the Mende relatives we saw in 1977. The people there remained interested in having missionaries come, and we reported it to the church. When we came back, the mission house was empty and strangely silent. Pastor Danielson kept up the services.

I wrote Mom and Dad, "My faith was weak for a while, but I'm praying a lot more. I need more quiet time with the Lord. I'm realizing that even when the circumstances in life are shifting, sometimes dramatically, God remains the same. That's been very meaningful to me in this year of tremendous change. God's always there, and He's always faithful. I have to commit much more to Him in prayer, and I intend to pray more fervently for the problems in this place. The Lord has been so faithful to me in the past. How can I doubt Him now?

"He must be testing our patience and resolve. Will we endure or not? Surely others have faced greater trials in the kingdom. In our devotion this morning, I read about the saints who have gone on before—how we are part of that great company that endured and is cheering us on from the sidelines in heaven. Whatever we may suffer, it's not worth comparing to the joy that shall be ours—*everlasting* joy.

"The Lord knows the whole situation, and we must leave it to Him. God will help us do what we can. I know I can't solve the problems of the church in this place; only God can. Without His help, I can't be effective in anything I do.

"I'm learning to rely on God more and more. My faith has really been stretched this year. It's been frustrating and traumatic, but it's been one of the most growing experiences I've had in my life. I've done things and endured things I never thought possible, and I must keep relying on the Lord."

In my own assessment, I was no great missionary. Despite my good intentions, I had barely managed to hang on by my fingertips, surviving each daily crisis. It was difficult to live the lifestyle, and we were always coming and going. We were there 8 months. Missionaries serve a much longer term. I wondered whether we would have been more effective in our church work if we had stayed longer.

I identified with the people but never managed to learn the language, which is crucial. At times, I thought I could serve God with my own strength and fell flat on my face. That year, I never needed God more or failed Him in so many ways.

I was sure the women came to the Bible studies out of politeness. The truth is, I never knew what they thought. I was no great Bible teacher, and the cultural contrast was so great.

Ben hadn't accurately assessed the needs of his people. We had shipped a ton of books to a remote community in which few people could speak or read English! What we really needed were simple picture gospel tracts, Good News Bibles, and Scripture portions. Ben couldn't preach in Mende. He had to have translators. That year I learned that missionaries are human and that God's work goes on—at times in spite of them.

The Mende Christian leaders had feet of clay as well. One of them preached eloquently and was a man of great faith, but he struggled with alcoholism during the sugar cane harvest. Another was also articulate in English and had great influence in the congregation, but he was having affairs with several young girls, one of them the wife of a Muslim we tried to witness to.

Ben lived and modeled his faith among his people, but there were mixed motives and deviousness in the village. Muslims and Christians believed they prayed to the same God and all would go to heaven. Christian men had Muslim wives who exerted the greatest influence over their children. It was hard to keep people coming regularly to church services and Bible study because their lives were full of daily work. Christian leaders with more than one wife posed a dilemma. The truth is, people are sinful wherever they are. We all need God's forgiveness and help in living for God.

My greatest frustration was my inability to speak directly with the women.

CHAPTER 24

Proud to Wear a Lappa

◇◇◇◇◇◇◇◇◇◇◇◇◇◇

One thing is clear to me.
We as human beings must be willing to accept people
who are different from ourselves.
—Barbara Jordan

Bunubu, July 1984

As we arrived to begin church services, we found the people preparing for the funeral of a powerful Muslim chief. I was glad I had worn my lappa. Ben went with the men, and I walked over to watch the women beating and fanning rice.

Women fanning rice

They smiled and invited me to join them. I struggled to get the rhythm of the pestle in the mortar. Still, they appreciated my effort, laughing good-naturedly. I smiled back. I so wanted to be a part of them. Ben told me later they were pleased with my effort and said I wasn't like most white women. Happy inside, I was glad to hear it.

#

It took me a while to appreciate how important I was, as Ben's wife, to the people of the village. Everyone called me "Ma Bendu" as a term of respect and affection. Still, it seemed strange to hear a 40-year-old man call me Ma.

One day, an old man asked Ben, "You wife has given you 3 sons, and yet she looks so young—how is this?"

Ben said, "Well, she is younger than me."

I remained quite a curiosity, with small children continuing to stare at me open-mouthed when I passed by. I imagine my strange ways were often the centerpiece of conversation. Still, I was pleased when Ben wrote in his church report, "The Mende people acclaimed her as a person concerned for their welfare."

Modesty in Vahun took a different form. It was nothing to see a woman nude from the waist up at times, but the only part of her leg that you ever saw was her ankle. As a general rule, women working or walking around the village wore clothing—sometimes a Western bra while cooking in outdoor kitchens.

I tried to fit in by dressing discretely, never wearing slacks or shorts. After several months in Vahun, I wore a cotton knit top and lappa; one of the women taught me to tie the lappa at the waist. In Monrovia, at St. Peter Lutheran Church, I wore a lappa to the service as a gesture of identity with the tribal women.

My biggest predicament was that I couldn't overcome the great cultural divide between me and the Mende people—in particular, the women—since I couldn't talk to them. I realized I'd never understand the nuances of their culture; nor would they comprehend mine. In fact, Ben had been away so much that he didn't understand the intricacies of the Mende language or the deep parables. Without knowing the language, I didn't understand the conversations when I participated in various family meetings. I wanted so much to talk to the women—to ask them what it was like to be a Mende woman, to have co-wives and share a husband, to speak up for the rights of their children. I barely had an inkling since I was privy only to their surface lives, as they were to mine.

At the graduation of Sande, the women's equivalent of Poro, I watched as they went around the village dancing. For the first time, I saw all of them bare-breasted in ankle-length lappas. I wondered what their songs meant as they rapidly moved their feet while playing their *sassas*. I wanted to join them but had no idea how. The only ones who spoke English in Vahun—the teenage boys and young men—couldn't tell me anything about Sande, since its customs were kept as much a secret from men as Poro's were from women.

Women playing sassas

At the same time, the Mendes in Vahun had no way to understand my background. If I described New York City, what point of reference could I provide for them? Monrovia was a small town in comparison, and most of them had never visited Monrovia. There were mostly looks and expressions of wonder and incomprehension when we showed a few slides of Michigan during the Friday-night meetings at the church.

Throughout the year, I developed relationships with Miriam and Nancy and especially with Momo's 1st wife, Kpanah, who had borne him 5 children—2 of them sons. In fact, one was Joe's friend. It was known in Vahun that Momo favored his younger wife, Quema, with whom he had a daughter. Their situation reminded me of Jacob loving Rachel more than Leah in the Bible.

My heart went out to Kpanah because, as 2nd-best, she tried harder, but to no avail. She was very industrious in her farm work, cultivating her cash crops of coffee and cocoa. Each time I looked out my bedroom window, she was busy. She loved her children. She came to church regularly.

I admired her and sought out a closer relationship with her. I visited her in the afternoon several times, trying to learn more about her. She understood some basic English phrases and knew a few simple responses. I comprehended only a few Mende expressions. As a result, our communication was primarily limited to smiles and animated gestures, which managed to convey our love and respect for each other.

When Miriam had disappointed me, I was touched that Kpanah offered to wash my windows. I turned her down, knowing she was very busy with her own work, and embarrassed to have a friend serve me. In retrospect, I could have provided her some extra cash for her efforts. When we left, I gave her all my pots and pans since she was special to me.

I hoped the women sensed my solidarity even though we couldn't converse. I never hesitated to hug them, even when they tried to decline because they were sweaty. Many times, they offered their moist forearm in greeting since their hands were dirty from cooking or other chores. One afternoon, I was snuggling with Peter, and Ben later told me, "The women were commenting, 'Look how lovingly she holds him and pats his head.'"

The men in Vahun ruled the roost, but in many ways the women were the backbone of the society. Ben told me the women's organization was very powerful. Wives were always respectful to their husbands, so I made sure to show deference to Ben. At the same time, they knew how to get their way behind the scenes, I suppose, as does every woman!

There was so much to do that wives wanted co-wives to help with the chores. A rich or prominent man was expected to link himself with as many families as possible. Many of the women were envious that I had the most eligible man in town to myself, and disappointed that he showed no interest in taking a second and third wife.

Whatever our successes and failures that year, it was time to go home. Before we left, I'm ashamed to say I sold our household goods to get whatever I could out of the situation. I wasn't tired of the people. I was exhausted by the uncertainty, the temporary housing, the discouragement with the missionaries, and especially having no control over absolutely anything.

When Ben and I said our farewells, the benches were packed at the town hall. Ben thanked them for their hospitality and said he was glad to have been able to spend some time with them. At my turn to speak, I said, "I've come to love you all, and you'll always be in my heart," choking up when they clapped. How good they were to us!

At our last church service in Vahun, I gave away empty cans and glass containers I had saved. Patrick called the children's names, and as they went up to get one, I thought, *What kind of farewell gift is that? What genuine sacrifice have I made for these people? Simply living here? What have I really given them? What long-term impact have I made?* I was a sinner when I went there, a sinner while there, and a sinner when I returned to Michigan. It wasn't a comforting thought.

At the same time, I realized that never before had I risked so much and been forced to trust the Lord as much. My time among the Mende people challenged my perceptions and spiritual courage. God had helped me overcome my culture shock, my faith in Christ making it possible to transcend many cultural barriers.

The night before we left, there was quite a downpour. A group of men filled our living room, talking with Ben. They brought bags of roasted peanuts, and as they ate, they threw the shells on the floor, as was the custom. I played the dutiful Mende wife, saying nothing.

I folded clothes, trying to get everything together. As I hung the damp clothes on the hallway clothesline, I told myself, "I'll soon be home." The next morning, the boys were excited that we were going to spend our last 2 weeks in Monrovia.

Up at the mission house, I listened to the short-wave radio to find out if the plane would be able to come; I was aware that the flight might be canceled because of the heavy rain. The business manager told us he'd let us know by 11 a.m.

I was utterly desperate to leave—to get out of there and go home! We were completely packed; we had given away our things and stripped our beds. The houseboys had swept and washed the floors. The fridge was empty and clean. I looked at the clock, whispering a prayer: "Lord, I know You won't take me farther than what I'm able to bear. *Please* let the plane come."

Eleven a.m. arrived with no word from Monrovia. Hoping for the best, I walked back into town. Ben and the boys were all over the place as people said good-bye. I put on a smile and checked the house one more time. Then, to my great relief, I heard the buzz of the plane engine overhead.

Many people had given us gifts that year. In reciprocity, we heard all over town, "What will you leave me, Ma Bendu? What did you bring me, Old Man?" Earlier I had given away different household items. Ben handed out money in small bills.

The entire village proceeded to the airstrip, where we said our good-byes in accelerated fashion. Patrick and Brima were there, of course, and my faithful Nancy. There was Kpanah and my boys—Moses, Timbeh, and Salia—who had served me so well. Pastor Danielson and his wife were there as well. As I hugged each one, the tears came. I longed to go home, but I hated to leave these people I had come to love.

As we flew over Vahun for the last time, I was sure of one thing: God had preserved us in the zigzag of that year. He brought us through. I wondered if I'd ever see the people on the airstrip again. I pondered, *What will our separate lives be from this point on?* There would be no more trips over Kamboi for a while, no kerosene fridge, and no more of the best of Mende life. I settled back in my seat, drying my tears, watching, one last time, the "broccoli" trees covering the countryside. In Monrovia, we visited the Sunday schools at WestPoint on Bushrod Island. Ben traveled to the Ivory Coast for 5 days, exploring mission prospects among unchurched peoples.

On our flight to Amsterdam, the pilot pointed out the Rock of Gibraltar from the air. Europe presented a pristine world with its well-maintained buildings and clean streets. In Zurich, we felt like royal guests as we slept under down comforters in our bed-and-breakfast.

Back in Amsterdam for our KLM flight to New York City, the customs officials waved us through. I blurted out, "Aren't you going to check our bags?" Ben glared at me because of the carved ivory tusks in our luggage.

At JFK, I went to get change with a crumpled, dirty 5-dollar US bill I brought from Liberia. The woman said, "Where'd you get *that* from? That money's *filthy!* I hate to even touch it." I had forgotten what new US currency looked like.

Mom and Dad, with my sister, Sandy, and her husband, were waiting at Detroit Metro Airport—Dad videoing our arrival. Everyone hugged each other, talking at the same time in our euphoria. Mom smothered her grandsons with hugs. My folks drove us to Flint that night, and I was relieved to see the house in good order. I kept waking up that night, each time telling myself, "I'm home! I'm home! I'm in my own bed!" Mom and Dad left the next morning, aware that we needed time to resettle.

CHAPTER 25

Mission Zeal and a New World Perspective

◇◇◇◇◇◇◇◇◇◇◇◇◇◇

Hark, the voice of Jesus calling,
"Who will go and work today?" ...
Who will answer, gladly saying,
"Here am I. Send me, send me"?
—Daniel March

St. Paul Lutheran Church's Mission Festival, Flint, Michigan, November 1984

B en gave a mission talk from the pulpit. I stood in front of the congregation, reiterating his points since his accent was difficult to understand by those who didn't know him well. He was warm and charming, as usual. Even so, church members felt more comfortable asking me questions at the reception afterward.

Our slides gave the impression our year in Vahun had been wildly successful. I knew better. I didn't mention our disappointments and problems because I didn't want to discourage the congregation from supporting the spread of the gospel. I hoped to compensate for my few accomplishments in Vahun by encouraging others to advance mission efforts.

#

In the fall of 1984, our family had a new appreciation for clean drinking water, a reliable refrigerator, hot running water, and, most of all, electricity! Our return to the good ole USA was reinforced when we watched *Star Wars: The Return of the Jedi* at a Flint movie theatre and listened to John Williams' magnificent closing theme, which brimmed with American exuberance.

Life returned to normal. Ben was back at the university teaching, and the boys in school—Ben Jr. in his senior year at Flint Central High School, Joe in 5th grade in the gifted program at Walker School, and Peter in 1st grade at Pierce Elementary near our home. The house was basically in good shape. Still, I was eager to spruce things up.

I was relieved to be home, but I was never the same. That year in Liberia had a profound effect on all of us in different ways. It had been an amazing adventure, and yet I felt that I had done little more than survive. Ben and I both wished we had done more, but we didn't reflect on it. We simply rushed joyfully into our old life, eager to catch up on things.

My new world perspective, coupled with Ben's faithfulness to his people, made us eager to serve as ambassadors for the Mende people— liaisons between them and the Lutheran church in America. It was therapeutic for me to become their advocate. After all, they were no longer simply Ben's tribe; they were my family.

At our speaking engagements, we identified with the Mende people, wearing Liberian dress: We displayed our African artifacts: wood carvings, elephant tails and teeth, ivory sculptures, tie-dyed fabric, country cloth, weaving and rice harvesting tools, and iron money from the 1800s.

Display table, St. Paul Lutheran Church Mission Festival

We first reported to the dear people of Our Savior who had read our newsletters and prayed for us. At the Sunday service, Ben, Ben Jr., and I spoke to the congregation after the sermon, sharing our various perspectives on our year there. I felt guilty during these presentations because they made us and the overall mission effort appear more successful than it was. The picture of the women's Bible study in my living room suggested it had been a regular occurrence that year rather than 8 or 9 meetings. The photo of a packed church on Christmas Day displayed a much greater attendance than our usual services. Ben's talk with the Muslims at the town hall happened only once, and just before we left for home. The image of Pastor Danielson baptizing an infant gave the impression the mission stations were thriving, when they were in their initial growing stages.

At the same time, these events were unifying for our family. The boys sitting in the audience had been a part of our life in Africa. We experienced together our 15 minutes of Lutheran fame, when we were treated as celebrities by being given the first place in line at the potluck table. In accord with our mission goals, we collected Christian materials and shipped them to Vahun.

During the spring of 1985, the Lutheran Women's Missionary League invited me to speak at their 10 spring rallies across the state of Kansas. The boys were in school, so Ben volunteered to carry on at home while I was gone for 2 weeks. I wore my lappa and showed our slides. I enjoyed being a speaker and connecting with the women. I stayed in their homes and remained friends with one of my hosts for many years. I felt I was I was doing something for Liberia. The Monrovia Sunday school project wasn't adopted, but I remained encouraged in sharing mission fervor.

In June 1985, Dennis and Chris, the 3rd missionary team, visited us in Flint. We once again shared our knowledge of the Mende people, assuring them they would be welcome in Vahun with their 3 teenage children. They arrived later that year.

Chris kept us informed about the developments there with her captivating reports. In one, she told us they received a package of used eyeglasses from the States. One by one, people arrived at the mission house to see if a pair of glasses could help, including Old Man Brima. He tried on every pair, saying, "I still can't read." It wasn't until later that Chris discovered he thought the glasses would give him the ability to read!

Our boys listened to their father witness as Ben gave sermons and talks in white and black churches in Flint. He was so busy with his classes that he once asked me to make a presentation for an in-service program for Flint public schoolteachers. It felt good that he trusted me to become a spokesman for Liberia in my own right. After I showed our slides and explained Mende culture and life in Vahun, one of the teachers asked, "Are you a teacher as well?"

I said, "No, but I want people to know about my adopted country."

The mission talks gradually tapered off over the years, but Ben's interest in Africa and Africans continued to reinforce my broader view. Similar to his involvement with the African Student Association at OU, he reached out to the few African students on campus and a number of African professionals in Flint. Together, with the newly formed African Association of Greater Flint, we worked to educate the community about Africa.

Each fall for several years, we sponsored Africa Nite, an event with a dinner, a speaker, and a dance. One year, at the International Institute in Flint, drums boomed as ecstatic dancers performed in tribal costumes. Hundreds of people sat watching at round tables, the flags of the nations of the world hanging above them. Everyone feasted on jollof rice, sweet ripe plantain, fried chicken, and greens. I wore my favorite gown I had purchased in Monrovia, and the members of the association added color to the occasion in their African dress.

Ben, in his chief's gown, sat on the dais, and next to him, the speaker for the evening—Dr. James Jonah from Sierra Leone, the undersecretary general for Political Affairs at the United Nations. Ben and I were delighted to have him stay in our home as our guest. We took him with us to church that Sunday, where he sang the hymns in harmony, flying out later that day for New York.

Ben speaking at Africa Nite

Our most famous speaker attended Africa Nite in 1986, when we featured Dr. Ali Mazrui, who wrote and hosted the PBS TV series *The Africans: A Triple Heritage.* Mazrui, at the peak of his fame and popularity, was teaching that year at the University of Michigan in Ann Arbor. Ben regaled me by telling the story of how he and Pobi, the interim director for the Afro-American Studies Center, secured such a renowned figure for our little group.

They sent a letter to Mazrui, and several days later, Ben's secretary buzzed him. "Bad news, Dr. Dennis. You ought to see this."

Ben said, "Okay, bring it in." He told Pobi, "Let's face the bad news together."

The form letter from Mazrui's business manager said that Mazrui's schedule was tight and his fee was $7,000. Pobi said, "We can't possibly get Mazrui at that price."

Ben called Mazrui and said with his usual charm, "My friend! I'm bringing another African with me to see you tomorrow. It will be 2 Africans coming to see one African."

Mazrui laughed and said, "Shall I prepare for peace or war?"

Ben said, "A little of both."

In Mazrui's office, Ben said, "Everyone's talking about your series. Our African Association in Flint doesn't have much money, but we still want you. That's the peace part of it. Your answer will determine if war follows."

Pobi and Mazrui laughed, and Pobi told Ben, "But you don't have any spear!"

Mazrui said, in the style of an African parable, "In the absence of literature, the old people must bring an answer for all catastrophes. In the same way, we Africans must take the lead in talking about Africa to foreigners who are misinformed children. Therefore, my friends, I'll come!"

Ben said, "Now, how much will you charge?"

Mazrui said, "Nothing! I'm glad to do this. I'm sure you will have African food there. I'll eat that and be satisfied. Others will pay for this, but not you."

Ben said, "Ali Mazrui, you are a *true* son of Africa. You didn't let us down. I'll spread the word all over the campus and Flint that you're coming."

Our most successful event ever was held in a banquet room at the University of Michigan–Flint, with pictures in the *Flint Journal* the next day. One of my prized photos is of Mazrui and Ben at the head table. Another is of Ben in his chief's gown, introducing Mazrui, a large Liberian flag hanging in the background.

Ben reveled in his role as a world citizen. He talked to his students about freedom in South Africa. He began a student letter-writing campaign to the president of Sierra Leone to keep other countries from dumping toxic waste there. Over the years, he and I were associated with many Liberians—countless relatives and friends—as well as numerous Africans. It would take another book to recount all of the times and projects we shared together. Needless to say, that connection was a vital, ongoing part of our marriage. As Africans shared their lives with me, I came to love many of them, all the while learning about their life experiences and what motivated them.

We were deeply in love, closer than ever. And I suppose, when all is said and done, that every marriage is unique because we're all individuals with our peculiarities and quirks.

Ben and I were no different. He was a neat sleeper. When he traveled and slept by himself, the motel maid simply flipped the turned-over corner of his blanket. I was a messy one. In the morning, our bed looked like a tornado had struck. Someone else might have found his soft snore irritating. When I got used to it, I found it comforting because it assured me he was right beside me.

I had cold feet, and he offered, "You can put yours on mine to warm them up. I don't mind. Maybe you should sleep closer to me to keep warm. How can you pile this bed with so many covers? One of these days, you'll wake up and find me *smothered*."

I laughed as I snuggled up to him.

We were both morning people and took an afternoon nap if we could. Ben showered every morning. In the evening, he reveled in his bubble bath, explaining, "The Mende people bathe twice a day, every day." When he brushed his teeth, he used so much toothpaste that they would have floated away in the foam if they hadn't been attached.

He was well-groomed, wearing a suit and tie each day. Sometimes early in the morning, I lay in bed watching as he meticulously put his belt in the loops before he put on his pants, just as his uncle, C. C. Dennis, had taught him in Liberia. He tied a Windsor knot and would never have worn a clip-on tie. I discovered he was color blind, which explained his strange suit, shirt, and tie combinations. I solved the problem by offering to lay out his clothes each morning. A friend told him, "When I see all she does for you, I know you married the right woman."

He liked expensive men's cologne, and it became my birthday and Father's Day present for him—as well as a gift to myself. He liked to be well dressed, but he wasn't ostentatious. In fact, he surprised American blacks and Liberians by driving a compact car.

I did all the shopping. When I was a child, Mom couldn't afford to buy school clothes until just before school started. By then everything was picked over. I'd find a cute blouse or skirt, only to discover my size was gone. After I married and had disposable income, I became a champion shopper. I learned to look for preseason bargains and scour the clearance racks. The boys called me "the Return Queen."

I needed peace and quiet to study or sleep. Ben read, wrote his lectures, and napped while listening to his transistor radio. We both liked classical music and shared a love of Baptist and Lutheran hymns. I grew to enjoy African music, but Ben never appreciated pop Christian music, so I played it while he was at work.

Our house on Wood Lane was at the dead end of a neighborhood street. One evening, as we sat at the supper table looking out the window, I discovered he was familiar with all of the people walking by. He knew the houses they came out of, as well as the times and directions of their routes. I was amazed. I had never paid attention. He told me that, as a boy, he wanted to work for Scotland Yard. I figured his close observation stemmed from his dream of becoming a detective.

He was a saver. I was a pitcher. His desk was always messy. My stuff was organized. When he occasionally helped around the house, he was satisfied using a broom. I needed a vacuum cleaner. He bit off the browned edge of a cut banana. I sliced it off with a knife.

At work, his secretary typed his letters and filed them, along with his lectures. At home, I began keeping track of things and filing financial papers. He paid the bills (except for the credit card, which was my responsibility), but he kept receipts and records in messy piles. Each month, I sorted through his desk in the basement. As a result, whenever he couldn't find something, his mantra was, "What'd you do with ___?"

I was committed to Ben through thick and thin. "Thin" was soon to arrive on the doorstep.

CHAPTER 26

In Sickness and in Health

◇◇◇◇◇◇◇◇◇◇◇◇◇◇

Marriage may be made in heaven,
but the maintenance must be done on earth.
—Unknown

814. S. Vernon Avenue, Flint, Michigan, fall 1990

I was in our bedroom when I received a call from the nurse in the urologist's office. When she told me, "Your husband has cancer," time—and the world—stopped. She continued her instructions, but I never heard another word. Finally, I said, "What did you say? Could you repeat all of that?"

I hung up the phone, thinking, *My husband's going to die. I'll have to raise the boys alone.* Ben Jr. was 20 and off in college at the time. Joe was 15, and Peter 12. I prayed, "Lord, I know You know all about this. Please spare my husband."

#

In the fall of 1985, I was busy with the usual church and boys' school activities, as well as faculty affairs—content in my usual household responsibilities, my life wrapped around family and home. Shopping clerks at my regular stores knew and greeted me. I was involved with the women's Bible study group and prayer chain at Our Savior. Ben continued traveling to St. Louis for mission-board meetings. The boys had filled out from eating their favorite foods. They kept "Mom's taxi" busy.

I continued cutting Ben's hair and began dyeing it since he didn't like gray hair. He told me, "When your hair gets gray, I'll stop dyeing mine." However, the boys no longer appreciated my services. When, as teenagers, their soft hair got kinky, they insisted on going to the barber.

Ben had a renewed zeal for teaching. That fall, he was first runner-up in a student survey for Top Professor of the Year. He added Afro-American studies to his sociology and anthropology curricula. In his Comparative Religion class, he identified himself as a Christian and participated in a faculty Bible study.

Racism remained alive and well in Flint, even at the university, but Ben had a way of garnering his students' trust. One day, Ben Jr. and he helped push a white man's car out of a flooded area of our street. As the man sped off, he yelled a racial slur, saying, "I wouldn't do that for *you!*"

Ben mentioned the incident in his Race and Ethnic Relations class, and a white student came to his office afterward and admitted, "Dr. Dennis, that was my father. He told me about it." The following week, the student came up to him and said, "I told him you were my professor and I had told you about him. You know what he said? 'That was *stupid*. He's going to flunk you for sure.'"

One afternoon, Ben was in our yard planting flowers, as usual. The elderly woman who lived down the street walked up to him and said, "You're doing such a *good* job. Can I hire you to do my yard?" He laughed it off as he told me, but I could see that it hurt.

One incident happened on campus. Ben was getting a drink at the water fountain in the hall when 2 white businessmen walked by; one of them pointed at a piece of trash on the floor, saying, "You missed one!"

Later that afternoon, the 2 men were coming out of the registrar's office as Ben happened to walk by. The registrar said, "Oh, Ben! I'd like you to meet Mr. Jones. He's enrolling his son at the U of M–Flint. Mr. Jones, I'd like you to meet one of our *best* professors, Dr. Dennis. He teaches in both fields of sociology and anthropology."

The man's eyes dropped and he stared at the floor. Ben managed to say calmly, "Welcome to our campus. I hope your son is very happy here." When Ben related these incidents, I grieved for him. I simply listened, unable to think of any words of comfort for such continuing humiliation.

At the same time, we faced a greater threat than racism. Not long after we returned from Liberia, Ben said, "I'd better get my eyes checked. I can't read the fine print anymore."

I said, "You probably need a new prescription."

When he pursued it, we found out he was losing his eyesight from open-angle glaucoma—increased pressure in the eye. His local eye doctor recommended an eye specialist an hour's drive away. Over the next 7 years, we made trips there for laser and other surgeries. After my 1st trip to Liberia, I had wanted to study nursing to "be of help." I then had my own private patient.

I was reminded of my own racial bias when Ben's white male eye specialist was replaced by a black woman. I was dubious when she recommended "watchful waiting," assuming she wasn't aggressive enough in her treatment. I reminded her, "I'm sure you know that glaucoma is the worst in Africans. Ben's eye problems have increased so rapidly, don't you think you should monitor his eyes more often than once a month? What if something happens? Shouldn't he be having more surgery?"

She calmly and patiently answered my questions, assuring me that she was on top of things. Ironically, I had completely trusted the former eye specialist, who had botched Ben's cataract surgery and couldn't replace the lens.

After that, Ben had to wear a hard contact lens in that eye, which proved to be a major challenge. It had been difficult enough for him to learn to use eye drops. Until he adjusted to wearing the lens all day, I struggled to insert it in the morning and went to the university several hours later to take it out. He gradually mastered both the eye drops and the lens, quoting a Gbande proverb, "Hungry makes monkey eat pepper."

As Ben struggled with his sight, the specter of vision loss loomed in the background; his sister, Angie, was then blind from glaucoma. In November of 1985, we visited her in New York City for a dinner in her honor at the UN to raise scholarship money for young women studying international relations. I felt a pang in my heart as we pulled up in the taxi and she told me, "Here I am back at the UN, and I can't even *see* it."

During our devotions at night, I listened as Ben prayed, "Lord, You made my eyes. You can preserve them." The battle to keep his pressures down was never ending. At one point, he had a drainage tube inserted in his eye and could no longer go in the ocean or a swimming pool because of the risk of infection.

He was forced to scratch his work on a book entitled *The Bible and Africa* since it was a strain for him to read for long periods. I recorded on cassette tapes several books on Liberia for him to use when he was ready to write about the developments there.

I noticed that he began putting 3 teaspoons of sugar in his tea instead of one. Not long after, he was diagnosed with type II diabetes. He denied it until a strict German nurse told him, "Dr. Dennis, you are a diabetic, and you will always *be* a diabetic." From then on, he was the ideal patient, following doctor's orders to a T. We all benefitted as I learned a healthier way of cooking—low fat, whole grains, and no sweets.

Ben's greatest challenge came with his diagnosis of prostate cancer that fall, in 1990. He took the news with his characteristic faith. In those days, the word "cancer" meant a death sentence, but he continued to pray, believing God was in control of the situation. The urologist recommended removing his prostate since he was 61 and prostate cancer was considered more aggressive in black men than other races. We told the boys what was happening and expected the worst.

By then we had transferred our church membership to St. Paul's in Flint, a larger congregation than our previous church with a dynamic youth program. An elder of the church sat with me while I waited for Ben to come out of surgery; it was an interminable length of time. Finally the doctor walked in and said, "I believe we got the cancer early and we got all of it."

I breathed, "Thank You, Lord, for giving me back my husband."

As Ben and I walked out of the doctor's office after a good PSA report, I told him, "This is not a sickness leading to death, but to God's glory," like the story of Lazarus in the Bible. I could tell it encouraged him.

While the cancer scare was over, Ben kept losing eyesight. I helped in any way I could. We explored numerous reading devices, none of which were the ideal solution. I purchased the Bible on cassette tape so we could listen to it at night for our devotions.

The good news, while all this was going on, was that Ben was promoted to executive assistant to the chancellor for minority programs, with a new office and secretary. I brought one of our large African paintings to hang on the back wall of his office. Black students, in particular, had always flocked to Ben. In his new position, they came with so many difficulties that he said his title should have been "executive assistant to the chancellor for minority *problems.*"

I had no inkling of our most serious dilemma on the horizon.

CHAPTER 27

Forced Retirement

◇◇◇◇◇◇◇◇◇◇◇◇◇◇◇

Never be afraid to trust an unknown future to a known God.
—Corrie ten Boom

814 South Vernon Avenue, Flint, Michigan, fall 1991

One morning, we were lying in bed when the phone rang. It was the university chancellor. After Ben answered, his responses were terse.

When he hung up, I asked, "What was that all about?"

With a grim expression, he said, "The chancellor just told me my teaching career is essentially over. One of my black students has accused me of sexual harassment—to the point of saying I had sex with her in my office. Three other women on campus confirmed that I made them uncomfortable. I'm not allowed to contact any of them while the university proceeds in its case against me."

He meekly continued. "I assumed this would blow over since there's no truth in it. That's why I never told you anything before now. She's the woman I introduced you to at that banquet the other night. She's the one who came to our house after we had gone to bed that night and I went down to the living room to talk to her. I was trying to advise her in a troubled marriage to a white student."

#

My trust in Ben and our marriage was shaken. I knew he had had personal relationships with students over the years. He encouraged them, loaned them books, and invited them to our home. At times, I felt that he was overly friendly with women students, and I meant to say something but never did. The chancellor had teased, "Ben, you're always the charming one."

Despite some nagging doubts, I couldn't imagine my conservative husband having sex with anyone on campus. If he had, why had she visited our home when she knew that I and the kids were there? Why would Ben have introduced me to her?

It was essentially a case of he said, she said. Ben had little recourse but to go to court; and whatever the outcome, it would mean the end of his good name and reputation in the community. Our family would be humiliated and Ben's Christian witness rendered ineffective. Sexual harassment was a big social issue then. I could just imagine the headlines: "U of M Professor Preys on Women Students."

We decided that he should retire instead of fighting the charges. He was 62 and struggling to teach with limited eyesight, plus he had just engaged in his recent battle with cancer. I told people he retired early because of health issues. There was an element of truth in it, but it wasn't the whole story. It was a painful and traumatic way to retire—Ben paying dearly for his charm—and a very hard time for both of us.

One morning, I woke up and saw him lying there praying. When he finished, I asked, "What were you praying about?"

He said, "Jesus told us to pray for our enemies. I was praying for her." We never found out what motivated her to make such base accusations.

The African Association hosted Ben's retirement dinner on campus. Ben and I put on a good front, despite our grief over the false charges. The president of the association began the evening by saying, "Dr. Dennis was never ashamed to be an *African*. I'm president, but I felt he was the *real* president behind the scenes since he was always giving me good advice." Various people addressed the audience, recalling fond memories of Ben and his tenure.

The association gave African gowns to both of us. The Liberian woman presenting mine told me, "I grew up in Monrovia. I'd never think of living in a village. I admire you, Anita, for living in Vahun a whole year." In my turn to speak, I concluded by turning to Ben and saying, "I never dreamed marrying you would be such an adventure!" I was especially proud of Joe, then a high school senior, who spoke for his brothers, as they were unable to attend (Ben Jr. was in Harvard graduate school, and Peter was in 8th grade, performing in a play that night).

Ben intended to retire in Liberia, and I teased him that he could have his "pack of dogs" then. It was just talk—a dream—so I didn't seriously consider going. As his health problems increased, I wondered how it would be possible. On top of that, Liberia was spiraling into descent, the ongoing chaos there a continuous haunting wound, a burden that never went away.

In August of 1984, when we left the country, the People's Redemption Council was dissolved, with Doe becoming president of the National Interim Assembly. While we were staying at the mission house in Monrovia, government troops from Doe's Krahn tribe pillaged the campus of the University of Liberia to quell student demonstrations protesting his policies. I vividly remember the 2 Americo-Liberian girls who fled the campus, arriving at our door, out of breath and sobbing.

Gasping, they blurted out, "We hid in a closet, but they found us anyway. They said, 'You act like you're *different* from our Krahn women.' Then they raped us."

The day before we flew out, Ben and I attended a reception at the Ducor International Hotel on Mamba Point to honor Ben's nephew, Harry, the former Liberian ambassador in London, who had been selected to run as vice president. Needless to say, it was a difficult assignment when Doe was elected president in 1985.

In 1989, Charles Taylor, a former government minister under President Doe, led rebel troops in the countryside in an effort to oust him. Taylor recruited boy soldiers and gave them drugs and AK 47s. Some were forced to kill their relatives in front of their village to ensure their loyalty to Taylor since they could thereafter never return home. Countless women and girls were raped. In Sierra Leone to the north, where the majority of Mendes lived, another civil war raged, with combatants using terrorist tactics, including rape and chopping off their victims' arms and legs. During the fight for control of Monrovia, Taylor battled other rebel forces which slowly killed Doe; he was videotaped begging for his life as his ears were sliced off with a machete.

In 1990, we heard about the unspeakable massacre that took place at St. Peter Lutheran Church in Sinkor, where our family had worshipped many times. Krahn government troops with machetes slaughtered 700 Mano and Gio women and children who had fled to the sanctuary for safety; their bodies were piled over and between the pews.

By 1992, my parents were spending their winters in Florida, and we liked the climate when we visited them. The tropical foliage and dry and rainy seasons were the closest thing to Liberia in the United States, so we decided to go there. We sold our home and most of our furniture. We kept a small number of books from Ben's academic library, shipping the rest to Liberia. A moving van took our African artifacts, Ben's remaining books, boxes of memoirs, and a few furniture pieces to Florida.

While I was packing, Ben brought home 6 boxes full of file folders and said, "These are ideas for more books I want to write."

I opened one and saw a letter dated 1966, thanking a VW dealership for a free oil change. I thought, *This is ridiculous. I'll never be able to sort through all this. Nor do I want to. He's going blind. He'll never write any more books.*

I put the boxes on the curb for the trash, but I took other boxes of the boys' old toys and souvenirs with us. It was thoughtless—one of the biggest mistakes I ever made, and I regret it to this day. Ben was a forgiving man, but it was hard for him to get past my betrayal and the loss of his cherished dream. He reminded me about it more than once.

We celebrated Peter's confirmation and Joe's high school graduation together before we left. I was 47 when Ben retired at 62. It was a difficult transition. We knew so many people in Flint, and Ben was always running into students. It was hard to part with dear church friends in two congregations and the place where we'd lived for 22 years. Still, we managed to say our good-byes, promising to visit and stay in touch.

Before we left for Florida, Ben told me one night what my father had done to him after he took me out of school. He said, "I was walking across campus one afternoon, when I happened to meet the president along the way. He told me, 'A disgruntled father asked a congressman to contact us and have you fired and deported. During a meeting with the deans, we agreed to dismiss the complaint. Ben, you're a valued member of this faculty, a man of integrity.'"

Startled and shocked, I blurted out, "You waited *all* these years to tell me this? How come you never said this before?"

He said, "You gave up so much for me. I didn't want to turn you against your parents."

In our marriage, Ben was my teacher in more ways than one. At the same time, he was frequently away, engaged in his many pursuits. I often prayed he would spend more time with me. Now, in his retirement, God answered my wish with a turnaround in our responsibilities. I became his chauffeur since he could no longer drive, ferrying him to his doctor appointments and various meetings. I took over paying the bills. I had him all to myself, with plenty of time for morning and evening devotions together, during which we openly prayed with each other.

We moved to Ft. Myers, Florida, into a well-located neighborhood with mature trees and foliage. I believe we were the first "black" couple there. Today there is a smattering of Hispanic and black families in the area.

Once again, our new house was a renovating challenge. Move-in-ready homes were expensive, and I didn't like their décor. However, the place we finally chose should have been condemned by the health department. Fruit rats had chewed holes in the air-conditioning ductwork in the attic. There was a dead possum in the wall behind the fridge. The place was not only a cockroach palace, but it was so flea-infested that the movers made the former owners fumigate the house before they would continue packing.

In the meantime, we stayed at my folks' home in Bonita Springs. In time, our 3-bedroom, 2-bath ranch house with a 2-car garage became a pleasant place to live—after much blood, sweat, and tears on the part of us and our many helpers. We installed wood parquet flooring and replaced the heavy drapes with white vertical blinds to blend in with the white walls—an ideal backdrop for rattan furniture, animal-print rugs, African oil paintings, and shelves filled with artifacts. One bathroom featured seashells; the other, tropical fish.

After finishing the inside, we tackled the lawn and shrubs. Ben would have made our front and back yards into gardens if I had let him. Instead he planted flowers and grew trees: a mango and two avocados from seed, as well as two Liberian oil palms. Of course, there were banana clusters and cassava.

We joined a Lutheran church, and it became our primary community, along with the few Liberians in the area. Ben was active in 100 Black Men of Southwest Florida for a while, mentoring a black 8th grader whose father was in prison. Over the years, he became involved in several Bible studies in which he and the other men bonded.

I suspect he felt he was being put out to pasture as he watched the video of his retirement dinner. He became a CNN news junkie, and his favorite TV fare was reruns of *Matlock*, which recalled his boyhood dream of becoming a detective. We enjoyed our time together. One of our favorite activities was walking on Ft. Myers beach at sunset while holding hands; the Gulf of Mexico reminded him of the Atlantic Ocean in Liberia.

Attending the wedding of my stepdaughter Winona in Nashville, Tennessee, was a great joy. She had struggled over the years, and Ben was on his knees every night praying for her. In time, she returned to the Lord, turning her life around. She and her husband are active in their Baptist church. In my favorite photo from that weekend, Ben is standing in his chief's gown, serious and nervous, as he is about to lead his daughter up the aisle; she looks beautiful in her white wedding gown.

The lens in Ben's right eye was eventually replaced, but he continued to lose peripheral vision. One morning, I saw him closing one eye and then the other, back and forth. When I asked him what he was doing, he said, "I'm checking my vision by looking at the fan blades."

The shadow of cancer hung over us. In 2000, his PSA became elevated and he went through radiation treatments. His new dream became visiting Liberia, rather than living there. I convinced him to have 2 hip replacements by telling him, "Honey, how are you going to be able to walk the trails when we go back to Liberia?" He joined Gold's Gym to keep in shape.

A year after we moved to Ft. Myers, Mom and Dad sold their ranch house on the farm and moved permanently to Florida. Dad became angry when I protested a disturbing letter that he wanted to send to Jim, and we were estranged for 6 months. When we reconciled from that, he made the comment, "We thought you hadn't forgiven us."

I wanted to ask, "Forgive you for what?" but I said nothing.

Ben was patient with Dad and a great comfort to Mom. A cousin told me, "When we visited your Mom and Dad in Florida, you were all they talked about. They were so proud of you and your boys."

Mom died at the age of 83, 7 years after we moved to Florida. I sobbed as I told Ben, "I'll never hear her voice again!"

I promised her before she died that I would take care of Dad, and I did. Thinking he didn't trust me, I was hurt that he wanted to be in complete control until the very end. He moved into assisted living not far from our home. One day, he told Ben, "If you didn't visit me, no one would." He passed away a year and a half after Mom died.

CHAPTER 28

Race

◇◇◇◇◇◇◇◇◇◇◇◇◇◇

Racism is ... not a thing of the past ...
—William Deane

Gold's Gym, Ft. Myers, Florida 2006

Ben came home from the gym one day and told me, "Some elderly white men were staring at me as I lifted weights. Chris, the assistant manager, walked by and told them, 'That man's from Africa, and he's a professor. I can't even tell you all his degrees.'

"They gathered around me, pummeling me with questions: 'Where'd you get all those degrees? Here or in Africa?'

"I told them, 'I attended a number of American universities and eventually received 2 doctorates from Michigan State University.'

"I could tell they didn't believe me as they persisted. 'How'd you pay for all that?'

"I said, 'I earned scholarships and worked my way.' I glanced back as I left, and they were still staring."

#

Racism in Florida, in its blunt and subtle forms, was more discouraging after all those years since the civil rights movement. In 1992, when we moved there, the University of Michigan designated Ft. Myers as the 11th-most-segregated city in America. The few African-Americans who lived outside the segregated black neighborhood of Dunbar were local professionals or retirees from up north. Dunbar residents had poor schools and little economic opportunity. Drugs, prostitution, and drive-by shootings were common.

One day, 2 young black men at Gold's Gym told Ben, "Pop, you look okay. If I look as good as you at your age, I'll be thankful to God. The way things are goin' in Dunbar, I don't think I'll see 30."

At one of Ben's doctor appointments, he happened to stand behind me at the receptionist window. The woman looked at me and said sweetly, "May I help you?"

After I stated my case, she looked at Ben and said curtly, "What do *you* want?"

She said nothing when I explained, "We're together"; she simply looked down at her work.

Ben was never respected unless people heard his strong accent, which made him an exception—a foreigner. Even then, in every social situation, he had to identify and distinguish himself as someone who didn't fit the usual expectation of a black man. I suppose it was why he proudly wore his University of Michigan and MSU shirts, as well as his ball caps from schools he or our boys attended (his collection of caps hung on a pegboard in the garage).

One Saturday, our pastor took Ben, as his token black, with him to a community forum of white and black pastors. The idea was to discuss issues of race outside the realm of their own congregations. Ben waited until the pastors said their piece and then volunteered, "We're not addressing the real problem. The best thing you white pastors can do is preach against racism in your own congregations." There was dead silence. After a long pause, a white pastor said, 'If I did that, they'd crucify me. I'd end up being both the preacher *and* the congregation.'"

One morning, we walked out of our Sunday service, and Ben tapped the shoulder of a little white boy to show him his African finger trick. He would put a piece of paper on one finger and flip his two fingers, making it look as if the paper jumped. The boy didn't respond, so Ben tapped him again. Suddenly, the boy turned and yelled, "Don't *touch* me!" His startled parents stared in shock at Ben but said nothing.

We attended our Lutheran church for a while when the parochial school instituted Grandparents Day, one year opening the event to any grandparent who volunteered to adopt a school child for the special occasion. For the first 2 years, Ben served as an honorary grandfather for 2 white girls we knew. The 3rd year, he was matched with 2 other white girls in the 3rd grade.

He called me at home and said, "You'll have to come and pick me up. I'll be out front."

When he got in the car, he told me, "The 1st girl was receptive, but the 2nd refused to walk with me and the other girl into the gym. The youth director spoke with her and told me, 'I'm sorry, Ben. I'll have to put those girls with someone else.'"

Several days later, we received a letter of apology from the girl's mother, saying her daughter hadn't been raised that way. Ben wrote the mother a note inviting them to visit us, but we never received a response.

In public, people never assumed we were a married couple. White retirees stared with frowns on their faces when they saw us walking the beach, holding hands. We were a novelty to those who didn't know us. Once, when we were sitting together with a short Haitian woman, people thought she was Ben's wife. At the Montessori school, several times people assumed I was the mother of my white daughter-in-law.

In 2001, at a wedding reception at our church, Ben was standing in line at the buffet table while I was farther back visiting with a friend. He struck up a conversation, while waiting in line, with the white woman ahead of him—a family counselor from Marco Island. He mentioned that he and I were writing a book together, and she asked where I was.

He pointed to me and said, "She's back there in line talking."

The woman said, "I don't see your wife anywhere."

Ben pointed at me again and said, "She's right there."

She said, "I can't see her."

Finally he called me up to meet the woman. The first thing she said was, "You're a brave woman."

At the other end of the spectrum, local blacks appreciated Ben's African heritage. One day, he was exercising on a machine at a fitness center when a black girl came up to use it. He demonstrated it for her with the weights he was using, and she teased, "I bet I can do as well as you." When she couldn't budge the machine, she said, "Wow."

He was sitting on a bench outside, waiting for me to pick him up, when she walked out with her friend. He overhead them talking: "You see that guy over there? He may be small, but he's strong as a bull. He says he's from Africa."

The other girl nodded and said, "Girl, that's where our strength comes from."

A year later, Ben was being prepped for surgery when the black nurse noticed his tribal marks. She told the white nurse, "You see those scars on his cheeks? Those are tribal marks. He's real. He's from Africa."

The white nurse said, "What's that again?"

The black nurse repeated, "Tribal marks! I don't have any, because I come from Jamaica. I don't even know my tribe or where I came from. Slavery took all that away from us. White people put tattoos on their arms and legs, but it's meaningless. This is the real thing. It means something."

She asked Ben, "What tribe do you come from?"

"The Mende and Gbandi tribes of Liberia."

She nodded and said with pride, "Oh, the *Amistad*! The Mendes were that tribe that overthrew the slave ship. They took the guns and knives from the white sailors. They were real warriors."

Racism wasn't Ben's only grief. Liberia was far greater.

CHAPTER 29

Ben's Dream Shattered

◇◇◇◇◇◇◇◇◇◇◇◇◇◇◇

The tragedy of war is that it uses man's best to do man's worst.
—Harry Emerson Fosdick

8931 Crest Lane, Ft. Myers, Florida, summer 2003

Peter returned from a trip to Liberia during a law internship at New York University. Reporting on his visit to Vahun, he told Ben, "Dad, you wouldn't recognize the place. The old landmarks are gone. Everything's completely different."

He handed Ben a cassette tape he had made as the people of Vahun described what happened to them. A few minutes later, I walked into Ben's office when I heard him sobbing.

I said, "Why are you crying, honey?"

He said, "My people are telling me the names of everyone who was killed."

All I could do was put my arms around him, holding him as he cried, knowing nothing could assuage grief like that.

#

Chaos and anarchy continued in Liberia, with news of more atrocities filtering into the American news media. From 1989 to 2003, Liberia suffered 2 civil wars with an interim peace of 3 years between 1996 and 1999. In the process, 200,000 people were killed and half of Liberia's 2.5 million population was uprooted.

It was one anguish after another for the people of Lofa County. We heard that government troops had burned Somalahun to the ground, setting fire to huts with people trapped inside. We received the news that Ben's brother, Morlu, had died of malaria, but Ben suspected it was ultimately due to heartbreak.

Vahun's blessing as an easy route to Sierra Leone became its curse, as marauding troops were fighting civil wars in both countries. By God's grace, Dennis and Chris were on furlough when the first war broke out in Liberia, the mission house being quickly looted by rebels in the area. In 1993, Ben Jr. called from Harvard. "Dad, have you seen the latest *New York Times*? There's a picture on the front page of refugees in Vahun. There's supposed to be 50,000 of them in the area." The mission house, with its adjacent airstrip, became the headquarters of the UN relief agency, with refugee tents lining the airfield.

We received a letter from the Peace Corps volunteer in Yandohun who had gone native, which read, "We always prayed to just be left alone. The worst sound was a car arriving in town or a couple of gunshots because that meant soldiers. A sick feeling came in our stomach all the way up to our throat.

"The rebel commander, called Death Squad Morris, walked up to me pointing a gun. He made me sit on the ground with my hands on my head and told me, 'Your own (life) finish today. What do you have to say for yourself?'

"I replied with all the faith I could muster, 'If God says it's my time, then it's my time.'

"My youngest wife broke down and screamed, 'Oh, Selle! (his Gbande name) Don't talk like that!'

"Death Squad Morris ordered me and my son, Kenny, to go with him. When he shot twice at a chicken and missed, my wife thought he had shot us both, but God spared our lives.

"Every morning, there were at least 3 dead children on the road. They had spent months hiding in the bush, eating wild yams and sleeping in the wet and cold. I know a lot of people died from starvation because so much food was looted by rebel troops."

Everyone in Liberia had a war story from those civil conflicts. At a dinner in a Liberian home in Ft. Myers, Ben and I met a dean at the University of Liberia who told us what happened to him. One Sunday, as he was coming out of church, a soldier recognized him and said, "Arrest him! He was Doe's teacher!" He was taken to the home of an Americo-Liberian who had been murdered and his body dumped in the nearby well. Along with 4 others, he was locked in the bathroom, where he prayed and tried to give them courage.

One of the men, who had served as a policeman under Doe, had his elbows tied tightly behind his back. He was delirious with pain, the thin twine cutting through his flesh. Although the dean was handcuffed, he managed to give the man a cup of water from the toilet tank. After drinking it, the man cocked his head and threw his body into the tub headfirst, trying to break his neck. Unable to succeed, he yelled in agony, "Kill me *now!* Don't wait! I can't *stand* anymore!" A rebel soldier strode in and dragged him away. After several gunshots, it was quiet.

The next day, someone saw the dean and told the soldiers, "Why'd you arrest *him?* He's a big man. Let him go!" Immediately he was lifted up, unshackled, taken to the bathhouse to wash, and given food. He said, "In the course of one day, I went from impending death to respect and honor. I can never forget the horror or my rescue."

He concluded by saying, "The losses of the war have been staggering for the university. All of the microscopes used in the science labs are gone. The natural history museum on campus is no more. The academic records were scattered. Everything's destroyed. There's nothing left."

In 1996, a peace agreement ended the first civil war, and Charles Taylor was elected president in 1997. Two years later, the 2nd civil war—a horrible free-for-all—broke out to topple him. Monrovia swelled to twice its size as 500,000 people fled there for safety. Ben and I watched on television as Navy SEALs and Army Green Berets evacuated 26 Americans in helicopters from the US Embassy to Freetown, Sierra Leone. A crowd of Liberians had laid the bodies of their loved ones outside the embassy, begging the United States to intervene.

In 1999, Ben received a phone call from a woman in Sierra Leone who said she was Patrick's granddaughter. She told him, "Doc, your brother Patrick is sick and needs an operation that costs $300." We wired $500. Patrick wrote us later that he traveled to Monrovia with the little money he received. He died there a year later. Any time there was word from Liberia, Ben said, "They call when they want something."

Finally, in 2003, American marines aided West African peacekeeping troops in liberating Monrovia. Taylor was forced to resign. After being convicted of war crimes at The Hague tribunal several years later, he was found guilty and sentenced to 50 years in prison.

The peace accord in 2003 ushered in the election of Ellen Johnson-Sirleaf, who began serving as president in 2006, with re-election in 2011. Despite her efforts, great challenges remain. Progress is slow; corruption is still a big issue.

The people in Vahun who fled to the refugee camps in Sierra Leone were desperate. In 2003, the year of the peace accord, Peter spent his internship in international law in Sierra Leone, where he and his law partner held workshops to make refugees aware of their civil rights.

At one of the sessions, a Mende man approached Peter's partner and said, "You are from America. We're looking for our relative from there—Dr. Dennis in Michigan."

Peter overheard and said, "I'm the son of the man you're looking for."

From that moment on, day and night, refugees from Vahun traveled from the different camps to see Peter, overwhelming him with a barrage of requests. Our local church as well as our national church body, along with our family, donated funds for the refugees since Peter was there to personally distribute them. Pastor Danielson told the people, "God has not forgotten us."

In all of this, Ben was consumed by his desire to explain the causes of the conflict.

CHAPTER 30

Writing His Story

◇◇◇◇◇◇◇◇◇◇◇◇◇

Great stories happen to those who can tell them well.
—David Rakoff

Route 281, Malinta, Ohio, spring 1962

In my junior year of high school, Dad called me into his office and said, "Well, what do you want to do with your life?"

I said, "I'd like to be a writer, only I haven't much to write about. I read that Ohio University has a great school of journalism. I guess the next best thing is to be a news reporter."

\#

A few early successes had fueled my aspiration of becoming a writer. As a high school freshman, I won a short essay contest. When I was a junior, I was featured as a guest columnist in the *Toledo Blade*. My childhood dream was about to come true, but not without a cost.

Liberia's tragedies compelled Ben to explain their underlying causes. Since he was going blind, I had to help him write his book. We began in 1994, during the first civil war. That epic task ended up taking 14 years to complete. In fact, I could write a book about writing that book.

We began our long and arduous task with me sitting at our electric typewriter, taking dictation from Ben. I was extremely reluctant. You might say I went into it kicking and screaming. I didn't want to spend our retirement years sitting at a desk. I initially expected Ben to simply recite it to me. Gradually I came to realize to my horror that it was his ideas, but I'd have to essentially write the book myself. It became another journey of faith since I was woefully unprepared. I had longed to be a writer, but I was hardly up to the task of researching, organizing, and writing a nonfiction book. During our 26 years of marriage, I hadn't penned anything other than letters and newsletters. I understood what Ben was talking about from my experiences in Liberia, but there was much more about the country I didn't know. And yet, isn't that how God works? He gives you a challenging, seemingly impossible task, and your faith grows as He helps you accomplish it.

Ben was adamant that the book be written, so there was no turning back. In time, we purchased a Smith Corona word processor, which could save and print what I typed. From then on, I no longer freely enjoyed visits with our kids or family trips, because the project weighed on my mind. Each time we were away or Ben had medical treatments, I knew I had to return to that seemingly impossible task as soon as I could.

Early on in my doubts about the book, I asked for a sign. One day, I lost our beginning material. I knelt by our bed and prayed, "Lord, if You want us to write this book, please help me recover what we wrote." To my amazement, He did. In all the twists and turns that followed, with no guarantee of success, I looked back to that sign.

Ben was retired, but my life was far from carefree. I was taking care of him and my parents, with the book always in the background. He helped around the house as much as he was able, willing to do whatever needed to be done. He loaded and unloaded the dishwasher. Each week, he scrubbed both bathrooms so well we could have eaten off of the floor. He was faithful with the yard work. He swept the driveway and mopped the garage.

At times, I resented his involvement in his 2 men's Bible study groups. I was jealous because work on the book kept me from participating in any church activity other than Sunday services. On top of that, he wanted me to host dinners in our home. I had to tell him I couldn't take on anything else.

After several years on the Smith Corona Word processor, Ben Jr. insisted we buy a computer. I fought it. Writing the book was hard enough without having to learn new technology. However, I'm glad I finally agreed since it sped up the work considerably.

Still, there were times when I simply collapsed from the stress. Ben had to arrange for someone to take us to the hospital emergency room, where I received a sedative to calm my nerves and end my vomiting. The 4th time, the doctor quizzed me, suspecting that Ben was abusing me. I wondered if it was because Ben was black.

Our boys refused to get involved in the project even though it consumed all of our time and energy. Ben Jr. encouraged me to find a writer's group, so I joined the Florida Gulf Coast Writer's Association when the manuscript was in its early stages. I met interesting people and attended symposiums and workshops on various aspects of writing and marketing. Sometimes the speakers were successful authors in various genres, such as romance writing, technical writing, humor, and poetry. However, the group itself comprised amateurs. We were all in the same boat, learning what we could and encouraging each other.

I wanted a published author who would work with me one-on-one. It was impossible to find since successful authors didn't belong to writer's groups. Early on, I paid $600 to a woman who had written a crime biography, to review my work and make suggestions—with little to show for it. After that, I took advice from a woman who had self-published a short novella.

I learned along the way that it's not easy to learn how to write. I was given books on the subject and instructed to read good writing, but there was no simple class to take, no straightforward rules to follow. In the end, I learned to write by doing it—writing and rewriting, reorganizing and revising, tightening and polishing.

In the meantime, life interrupted. Ben Jr. finished graduate school, and my other 2 sons graduated from college. I took care of Ben during his 2 hip replacements, numerous eye surgeries, and radiation for cancer. We told our kids about the book so often that it became a family legend. I'm sure they wondered if it would ever come to fruition.

This might sound strange, but after 26 years of marriage and travels to Africa, I learned more about Ben and Liberia than ever before. The truth is that I knew little about his childhood summers in Vahun and Somalahun and about his time in America before we met. The book became his memoir when we decided to use his life as an example to illustrate his points. I spent a year writing down his stories, really beginning to understand his life in an African context, as well as the challenges of racism he faced in America. It drew us closer together than ever before.

On top of that, I had to bone up on Liberia and its history. The library was my 2nd home as I ordered books on slavery, Liberia, and the social psychology of racism. I discovered that racism reproduces itself among people, often unconsciously, since it's embedded in the culture of a nation. Ben's unique perspective on the subject made me believe in what we were doing. His insights deserved to be shared; his message spread to the world.

At first the book was a labor of love for him. Then it became "obedience to the Lord." I began to enjoy the process. Life whirled by, with writing softening the effect of menopause and the empty-nest syndrome when Joe and Peter left home.

Still, it was hard work. Thomas Edison said, "Genius is 1% inspiration and 99% perspiration." That was very true for us. We were a real team—talking about ideas *constantly* and rejoicing each time something came together. Every time I wrote copy, Ben reviewed it, offering suggestions.

What's it like being a writer? It's taking notes—millions of them—in the car or at home. It's having a notepad on the couch and on the nightstand to write down ideas as they come. It's sitting in front of the computer for hours on end, oblivious to the world outside. It's following your editor's advice even when you don't want to.

My computer was simultaneously my greatest blessing and my greatest curse. At one point, I got the Blue Screen of Death, losing *everything*. I was grateful that Ben Jr. had insisted I save everything on floppy disks, which were then downloaded onto computer #2.

The second walk of faith was publishing our book after it was completed in a short and long version. We soon discovered it's one thing to write a book—quite another to get it published. It was grueling to search the latest edition of *Writer's Market* for possible publishers, write that all-important query letter, and try to find a literary agent. Fourteen turned us down. I finally decided to contact publishers who didn't require an agent.

In the meantime, Ben and I prayed for success. When 3 publishers expressed interest, we felt the Lord honoring our faith. One morning, I couldn't believe my eyes as I sat down at my computer. There was an e-mail from Algora Publishing in New York, which said, "Enclosed is a contract to publish your book. Please let us hear from you soon."

I ran to the sun porch and yelled, "Honey! We have a publisher!"

He calmly replied, "Isn't that what we've been praying for? God is working everything out."

That spring, we celebrated our 40th wedding anniversary, just before signing with Algora Publishing. Our 3 sons, 2 with their wives and children, came down. There were historic family photos taken by a professional at Bowditch Point on Ft. Myers Beach. That evening, the adults enjoyed a memorable dinner at a steakhouse on Sanibel Island. I cherish that photograph of us sitting around the table, smiling. Our joy, in conjunction with a contract from our publisher, made life wonderful.

Our idyllic situation didn't last long.

CHAPTER 31

Left Behind

◇◇◇◇◇◇◇◇◇◇◇◇◇◇◇

The more life has been shared, the more indescribable the sorrow.
—*Beyond This Day*

8931 Crest Lane, Ft. Myers, Florida, June 2008

One afternoon, the nurse called from Ben's doctor's office after routine blood work. She said, "The lab must have contaminated Ben's blood sample. His liver enzymes are extremely high. The doctor wants him to retake the test."

While I was gripped with a nagging fear, Ben said, "God made every part of me. He knows how to fix it."

#

The lab results came back the same. After more medical tests in July, I talked at length with the gastroenterologist, who told me, "Ben has a fatal liver disease. If you want to visit your children, I would do it right away." Death, that inevitable intruder, was making a visit, and I was about to face my greatest challenge and crisis—life without him.

I tried to collect my thoughts and calm my racing heart before I walked into his office, where he was lying in his recliner, weak and thin. I thought, *I've got to be brave for him.* I said, "Honey, the doctor said we can continue testing at the Moffitt Cancer Center in Tampa, but he's sure from your latest test results that your liver disease will give you only 3 to 5 months to live."

He looked at me and said, "Should we do the testing in Tampa?"

I said, "I don't think so. The doctor said the testing would be very hard on you, and it wouldn't extend your life. I want you to live as long as possible. Let's talk with the people at Hope Hospice."

He said, "This means I'll never return to Vahun or Somalahun."

I said, "I'm so sorry. I know how much it means for you to return." I was in shock—beyond tears—as if I were on auto-pilot. I prayed silently, *Lord, what can I say? You've given me 17 more years with him since his prostate cancer.*

We signed up for Hope Hospice and a nurse came to our house to check Ben each week. I never admired my husband more than when I observed the noble way he dealt with dying. We had a year and a half to say good-bye. Our love for each other and our faith in God were the only things that mattered, the trivialities of life instantly fading in the presence of death.

That August, we visited Joe in Chicago and Ben Jr. and his family in Washington DC. After those trips, Peter, who lived in Ft. Myers, arranged for a local Liberian woman to deliver Liberian chop to our home each week. Ben rested every afternoon and gained weight.

A great joy that October was the birth of Peter's son, Morlu, and his baptism at St. Michael. In one of my favorite snapshots, Ben is holding his newborn grandson, wearing an "Elect Obama" hat.

Several weeks later, our church hosted a dinner to honor Ben. The tables in the gym were crowded, and he wore his chief's gown. Peter spoke for the family: "You always told us boys how proud you were of us. I don't know if we've ever told you how proud we are of you."

Ben was dying, but I refused to let his dream go. I wanted him to see his book in print. After Algora accepted our shortened version of the book, I told them I'd like to show them the longer edition as well. In the end, we compromised on a combination of the two. By September of 2008, the publisher had edited the manuscript and I reviewed it online for mistakes. I skipped the final review so I wouldn't delay publication in November.

In the meantime, Ben beamed with pride when Barack Obama was elected president. He told me that Rev. Martin Luther King Jr. had predicted that a black man would one day be president of the United States. We spent hours each evening watching the news coverage.

After the book came out, I managed several small efforts at marketing, while also caring for Ben. I sent books to reviewers such as the *Journal of African Studies* and other key periodicals. I was interviewed on *Lee Pitts Live*, a local black TV show. Ben autographed copies of our book for people at church. The *News-Press* interviewed us by phone, which led to a book review in the paper. I shared with him the positive online feedback from Liberians.

We celebrated Thanksgiving at Peter's house, and Ben had to leave right after dinner. As we drove home, I was filled with grief, knowing that these family times with all of us there wouldn't continue. I held back my tears. It was a sadness beyond crying.

During Ben's retirement, he wrote loving notes to friends at church for their birthdays and anniversaries, and many of them had saved them. Before he died, he wrote love letters to me and all of his children. He dictated farewell letters to Vahun and Somalahun. He witnessed to visitors: "Jesus said, 'In my Father's house are many mansions.' He's prepared a room for me."

Peter contacted people at the University of Michigan–Flint, as well as former pastors and missionaries who had served in Liberia. Many called and wrote. Peter had a classmate make a video of Ben in his chief's gown, telling some of his famous stories.

God gave me strength moment by moment during that time. We continued our devotions morning and night, playing chapters of the Bible on CD. I read Christian books about death. In the morning, I prayed, "Lord, thank You that we can get out of this bed today and do something." At night, I played gospel hymns and would soon hear Ben snoring.

One night, during our evening devotions, I prayed, "Father, when Ben stands before you, he won't tell you about his PhDs, his years of teaching, or even his work in Africa. He'll just say your Son, Jesus, died for his sins." While I was expressing this, Ben said yes at each phrase, which assured me that he was trusting in God's grace alone. It was a great comfort knowing I would see him in heaven.

Our life together continued in a quiet routine. We attended church until the month before he died. While he took long afternoon naps, I watched the Turner Classic Movies network. I never saw the endings of the movies, because the minute he awoke, he wanted to watch something else. He remained a CNN news junkie, and we also watched *The Newshour with Jim Lehrer*. In the late afternoons, he enjoyed sitting on the sun porch, watching the squirrels play in our tree-shaded backyard.

In the morning, he listened to gospel radio; in the afternoon, the BBC World Service. He spent long hours reading the Bible with his remaining good eye. Before he died, he had read the entire New Testament and one fourth of the Old Testament.

In January of 2009, as we watched the inauguration of President Obama, Ben told me how proud it made him feel. Peter stopped by many mornings to check on us, and there were numerous visits from Joe, Ben Jr. and his family, and Winona and her husband. In June, everyone came to our home to celebrate Ben's 80th birthday. We had a picture taken of the entire Dennis clan in our backyard. However, by that time, Ben's heath was declining and he had a serious look on his face. During that visit, I distributed the African artifacts since we felt it was time for our children to have them in remembrance of their father.

One of Ben's last labors of love for me was collecting the fallen mangoes in our backyard. He knew I was severely allergic to them and insisted on doing it. I was deeply moved when I saw him walking tiredly, hauling the bags filled with mangoes. How much he loved me!

Each morning, I scrubbed his back in the shower, and after drying him, I rubbed Pond's cold cream on his ashy legs and Ben Gay arthritis cream on his back. I helped him get into clean pajamas and slipped his watch on his wrist. He then used his walker to go into his office for his morning nap. One day, as he was lathering up his washcloth, I said, "You are the only person in the world who uses so much soap when they bathe."

He looked at me and said, "How many people have you watched bathing themselves?" He never lost his humorous perspective.

He loved his evening bubble baths almost to the end. When I became nervous about him falling, I sat in the bathroom, watching as he bathed. As he stood in the bathtub and scooped water in his hand to rinse the sides of the tub, it was as though he were in a river on the outskirts of Somalahun. He methodically rinsed his washcloth, wrung it out, and dried himself with it before using his towel.

One day, as we were watching TV, he said, "My work is finished." He knew the end was coming.

While most of my attention was focused on him, I wondered how I would get on with my life after he was gone. I distracted myself with one of my favorite pastimes—decorating. While he napped, I sometimes ran errands. I bought modern white faux-leather living-room chairs and told him I wanted the memory of him sitting in them. I rearranged the living room furniture several times.

One afternoon, I heard that Men's Wearhouse was collecting suits for people who were out of work. I knew he would never wear those suits hanging in our closet, so I asked, "Honey, may I donate them? It's a worthy cause. After you die, it will be so painful for me to give them away."

He said, "If I recover, I'll have nothing to wear."

I said, "My darling, if you recover, I'll gladly buy you *500* suits!"

He had 3 pairs of white tennis shoes that were like new. One day, I put 2 pairs of them in the trunk to take to Goodwill. Later that day, he asked me where they were. When I told him, he said, "Wait until I'm *gone!*" Shame pierced my heart. I certainly never wanted him to think I was rushing him to die.

One day, when our pastor was visiting with Ben on the sun porch, Ben began to cry, expressing his gratitude for all God had done for him in his life. He said, "I was afraid if I took Anita to my village, she'd divorce me, but she loved my people. God spared us when I wanted to take my family to Liberia before the coup. He's been so merciful to me." As he wept, I realized he was reviewing his life before his death.

That December, he said, "If I'm going to live through the celebration of Christ's birth, I want a Christmas tree." I put up our little tree next to his hospital bed on the sun porch.

In time, he became bedridden and could no longer eat. Ben Jr. and Joe arrived and stayed with us. Peter and his family visited often. We took turns sitting with him, reading the Bible or playing Christmas music. One afternoon, I played his favorite, Handel's *Messiah,* and he was soon snoring. I was comforted knowing it brought peace to his soul.

One day when he was already blind, he thanked the hospice nurse for all her care. I said, "Do you know who this is?"

He said, "Yes, Pretty Girl." Those were his last words to me.

My final statement to him was, "I love you. You opened a whole new world to me. I will never forget you."

It was past midnight on December 17, 2009. Ben had been dying throughout the day and could no longer speak. His breathing was labored. I periodically squirted a dropper of pain medication into his mouth, placing it in his cheek so he wouldn't choke. Sitting next to him, I felt his cold legs.

Peter was standing beside me. Ben Jr. was resting on the couch nearby, and Joe was lying down in my office.

I said, "Peter, wait with your dad. I'm going to lie down for a minute. Call me if there's any change."

I no sooner felt my body touch the bed and start to relax in our bedroom next to the sun porch than Peter said, "Mom, I think Dad just took his last breath."

I jumped up and ran to his side. Ben Jr. and Joe came in. We watched as the pulsing of the artery in his neck stopped. In that instant, my life as I knew it ended as well. The love of my life had just left this earth.

Ben Jr. closed his father's eyes and then put his hand on my shoulder as I sat there sobbing. Joe stood watching. Peter walked over to the kitchen phone to call our pastor and the funeral home.

I asked the funeral home attendants to unzip the body bag so I could see Ben's face one more time. As they wheeled him out of the house on a gurney, I said, "That's the last time he'll ever be in this house."

The most painful thing was viewing his body at the funeral home before they cremated him. He looked wonderful, as if he could climb out of the coffin at any minute. I reached out and touched his cheek. It was ice cold.

The memorial service was held the night before Christmas Eve, but I was hardly present, feeling as if I were on a faraway cloud. The church was full with many friends from the past 17 years. Each of our children told special memories of him giving testimony to his faith, his pride in being an African, and his personal touch with students. Everyone walked out listening to a recording of the "Hallelujah" chorus from Handel's *Messiah*.

I saved a few special mementos: his worn Bible, one of his favorite sociology books, his watch, his tuxedo bow tie, and *The Prophet*, by Kahlil Gilbran, which he had given me when we fell in love.

One Sunday, as I walked out of church, a friend put her arm around me and said, "You're now in the widows' club. It's not one you'd ever want to join, but it's a *good* club!"

Although I had known for a year and a half that it would happen, nothing prepared me for the finality of death when it came. Nothing could alter it or lessen its pain. I would never again speak to him, hear him laugh, feel his embrace, or share my life with him. I knew that when we meet in heaven one day, we'd no longer share the human bond of marriage. My life with him was irrevocably over. I wished over and over that I had held his hand at the moment he died. In my mind, I told him, *It's true, my darling. I'll never forget you. You'll always be in my heart.*

For months I felt utterly helpless and didn't know how I could go on. I entered that long tunnel of grief, with vivid memories of his death playing over and over in my mind. When he was dying, my heart developed an abnormal rhythm called premature ventricle contractions (PVCs). When I first noticed them, I thought, *Maybe I'll die soon after him.*

Each time I walked into my solitary house, I felt a stab of sorrow. There were good days and bad days. In the battles of the night hours— those dark moments of the soul that petty pursuits can't dissolve—I was overwhelmed with loneliness, silence ringing in my ears. In the middle of the night, I listened to my Bible CDs or watched TV to get my mind off of things. I lived on the verge of fear, wondering what would happen next. I experienced my 1st birthday without Ben, and later our wedding anniversary, which had been so uniquely special to us. I sobbed those daily cleansing tears in the silence of my empty house, with God as my only comfort.

I missed him—the familiar way he parted and brushed his hair, how he tucked his hankie into his back pocket, his charming smile, his infectious laugh. I loved the scent of his sport coat, which was permeated with cologne. I'd watched him scratch his head when he was relaxed or fidget with the back of his neck when trying to think of what to say. I remembered how he bit his tongue when he was concentrating and how he fluffed and positioned his pillow each time he got into bed.

Everything African reminded me of him. Impulsively, I tried to give away my African music, but Peter stopped me, saying, "Mom, it's too soon." He helped me buy a new computer and set it up. He arranged a checking account in my name only and set up online bill paying.

I checked the mail, hoping something good would arrive. Instead, there was junk mail—solicitations addressed to "Dr. & Mrs. Dennis." I thought, *Don't they know he's dead?* I kept writing, "Deceased, Return to Sender" on them, but they kept coming.

The TV became my lunch and dinner companion. In the myopic fog of grief, I escaped into the Turner Classic Movies network, catching up on the endings of all the movies I'd seen while Ben was dying. For a long time, I couldn't bear watching CNN, because it reminded me of him.

I was frantic to sell the house and move into a condo. I didn't want to think or reflect as I struggled to survive. Crazy with grief, I filled my days with frantic action, doing numbing chores, oblivious to the larger world. With Peter's help, I repainted the entire house, including all of the woodwork. I waxed the floors and washed the windows. I shopped for furniture and rearranged every room. I cleared out closets and drawers and had a giant garage sale. I made photo albums of pictures of Liberia for my grandchildren.

Sitting in my garage were boxes of books and school supplies that the church had donated for Liberia. I arranged to have them shipped. That summer, I sent the blankets made at Vacation Bible School. I choked up when thanking the children as I remembered all the times we had done that together.

That 1st year, I traveled to visit Sandy in Ohio; Ben Jr. and his family in Washington, DC; Joe in Chicago; and a dear friend in Minnesota. Each time the plane took off, I thought, *I don't mind dying in an airliner crash. I'll only go to Jesus and my beloved.*

After all those years of writing Ben's book and caring for him, I suddenly had all the time and freedom in the world. My parents were gone, and the boys were grown, pursuing their own lives. The clock was my enemy, as I had time to reflect. Days moved slowly. I struggled to be present in the moment when I didn't like the moment. I stopped wearing a watch for a year and a half because it didn't matter what day or what time it was. For me, everything was measured by how long it had been since he was gone.

Loneliness was the downside of my new independence. I had the freedom to visit my sons and babysit my grandchildren. I could shop for hours for the latest fashions, but there was no one to notice. Without someone to share my day or make demands on me, I had time for lengthy individual devotions. I studied the Scriptures. I read Christian books. I meditated. Nothing taught me to surrender to God's will more than Ben's death.

People at church did their best to comfort me. I joined the Grief Share program to learn more about what I was going through. During those early months, that shared experience was my lifeline. Although the classes gave me understanding, they didn't make the pain go away any faster.

Ben's book and his death had kept me isolated. Several years before he died, God gave me 2 precious friends at church, knowing how much I'd need them. My cousin and her husband were godsends in getting me out of the house and back into the stream of life. My friend Jan invited me over for dinner many Sundays after church—the loneliest time of the week. Peter and Amanda checked on me, and the hugs of my grandchildren, Mali and Morlu, were precious.

In the end, nothing could replace the work of grief—that long process of simply coping until healing comes. I assumed getting my house in order meant I was going on with my life. Instead, in the quietness of time, I had to gradually go through the sadness of loss.

There were moments when I was ambushed by grief. One day, I went to hang something on Ben's hook in the closet and burst into tears. When I told our Grief Share director, she said, "It's because you know he'll never hang his clothes on that hook again."

At the eye doctor's office, I entered a room for testing and smelled Ben's familiar cologne on a black man sitting there. A wave of remembrance and sadness swept over me.

I put on my pair of striped pajamas one night and remembered his comment, "Those look like Joseph's coat of many colors."

Before he died, he told me one night, "You never check to see if the doors are locked. After I'm gone, I'm afraid something will happen to you." Each time I checked the doors, I thought of his love for me.

When I read Matthew 5:16 ("In the same way, let your light shine before men that they may see your good deeds and praise your Father in heaven"), it reminded me of sermons Ben had preached. Psalm 118:24 ("This is the day the Lord has made …") brought to mind a banner we had hung in our apartment on Carriage Hill when we were newly married.

I went to one of Ben's doctors when I had trouble with my knee. To remind him of who Ben was, I said, "He was a small man."

The doctor paused and replied, "No, he was a great man." Tears came to my eyes as I drove home.

At the first noon Lenten service after he died, I stumbled out, crying. It was something he and I had always done together. It was as if he were sitting next to me in the pew—only he wasn't. After that, I went to the evening services.

When people said, "I miss Ben," I replied, "No one will ever miss him like I do." No longer could I reach over in bed and feel him beside me or hear him softly snoring. Only I knew those deep intimate moments between us. It was like the song "No, No, They Can't Take That away from Me."

In time, I realized that compulsive action couldn't make the healing happen faster. While the passage of time helped, only God could comfort. Without Him, my suffering would have been unbearable.

Alone, I entered that arena of complete dependence on God. Sorrow and helplessness led me closer to Him than ever before. I prayed, "God, You are all I have, and yet You are everything." I learned to be lonely, but never alone, since God was there. I prayed, "O Lord, my need drives me to my knees to You."

I decided to become better acquainted with a number of women at church, calling it my "lunch ministry." I joined the Stephen ministers to comfort others facing crises in their lives. I determined to bridge the gap between the socially accepted and the rejected, showing black people extra respect. As a member of the widows' club, I comforted new widows.

Once my frenetic pace slowed down, there was nothing to look forward to—just emptiness and sadness. Gradually, moments of happiness came here and there. I remember dancing with my new 2-month-old grandson to lively music in Ben Jr.'s living room. Still, at home there were times of loneliness during peaceful moments in an all-too-quiet house. Some days, I thought, *If he could just walk in that front door one last time. If he could only know how much I've grieved for him and how much I miss him.*

Reflecting on my situation, I imagined him in heaven, but I didn't know exactly what that was like. I felt as if I were missing out because I wasn't sharing it with him. He had gone on, but I couldn't join him yet. I feared going into my old age and death alone. I prayed, "What can I offer except my sorrowing spirit? I am bereft. I must wait upon You, Lord, to show me what's next—what my life will be."

Still, I was grateful for the comfort of my family.

CHAPTER 32

My Three Sons

◇◇◇◇◇◇◇◇◇◇◇◇◇◇

The fact is, there is no foundation, no secure ground,
upon which people may stand today if it isn't the family.
If you don't have the support and love and caring and concern
that you get from a family, you don't have much at all.
—Mitch Alborn, *Tuesdays with Morrie*

8931 Crest Lane, Ft. Myers, Florida, 2010

I sat in the living room, looking through a photo album of the pictures taken of the boys through the years. There were the usual elementary, high school, and college-age photos in different outfits, until finally they were grown men in suits and ties.

One of my favorites is of them standing around their dad, all in Mende chief gowns. There's an aura of pride on their faces as they honor their heritage. In the final picture with their dad, they're all in blue button-down shirts—the men of my life.

In tribal gowns, 1998

\#

My 3 sons were raised with a strong white influence because of me and my family. They were all baptized and confirmed in the Lutheran faith. They grew up loving their grandparents dearly, spending holidays and summer visits on the farm. Only when they were grown did they learn hints of what had transpired.

Even so, they moved between white and black American society while incorporating an African heritage as well. In a sense, they became world citizens with connections to a range of people and cultures. They met many Liberians in America, including 3 who lived with us for a while. Because of Ben's connections with Africans, they were familiar with those in the African Association of Greater Flint. And yet, despite our travels and their year in Liberia, the Mende and Gbande cultures were not central to their lives.

White society labeled them as black, but they were just my boys to me. Strangely, Ben and I didn't discuss race or racism with them. While they had black friends, especially in grade school, they weren't deeply attached to the black American community, since Ben was African. They might mention that someone was "mixed," as they were, but it wasn't until our book was published that they told us some of their experiences. Ben Jr. mentioned being chased during a riot in Paris, having been mistaken for a Turkish immigrant. Joe told me about white teenagers who imitated the dress and lifestyle of blacks. Peter resented any comments I made about the difficulties blacks faced since I had no "understanding" of it.

Throughout their American childhood, there were the usual birthday parties, Halloween costumes, Christmas gifts under the tree, and various school activities. They attended the integrated Flint public school system and did well academically. Like everyone else, we made our parenting mistakes. And yet, they somehow managed to survive us and become successful adults. As they grew, they each had their distinct personalities, interests, and share of accolades, awards, and scholarships, as well as their struggles and challenges.

I was determined that they learn to work and demanded they do their best in household chores. Ben said, "If you can work for your mother, you can work for *anyone*." As young teenagers, Ben Jr. and Joe had paper routes and worked at Mitchell's grocery store. When Peter was in high school in Ft. Myers, he waited tables at a yacht club. They all contributed toward paying for their clothes, as well as other expenses. When Ben Jr. was a sophomore in college, we gave him Ben's old Renault Encore. Joe inherited our Ford Tempo as a junior in high school. We helped Peter buy a Volkswagen Cabriolet convertible when he was a high school sophomore.

As the firstborn, Ben Jr. was the responsible older brother who never hesitated to look out for his siblings or tell them what to do. He had an artistic side, drawing very well from an early age. He learned oil painting from a local black artist. I have a number of his "masterpieces" hanging in my home.

He began receiving awards in junior high. I'll never forget when I heard the principal say, "And now the student who made the greatest progress this year—Benjamin Dennis!" When he was in high school, I visited the Michigan state legislature in session as part of an achievement ceremony for him. I was so proud during High School Challenge when he was the go-to guy for questions regarding the Bible.

Michigan State University offered him a full scholarship. After he left, it seemed as if part of our family was missing—and it was. Lansing was only an hour away, so we made day trips to visit. Ben really enjoyed having his son at his alma mater. Each time we drove on campus, he told stories about his days there.

At Ben Jr.'s college graduation, he was asked to stand as the recipient of the Harry Truman Scholarship for graduate school. I could hardly see him from the 3rd balcony, but I reveled in my pride and joy. When he received his doctorate in economics from Harvard, our family flew to Boston from Florida to attend the ceremony.

We sent pictures of the graduation to Patrick, who was staying in Monrovia at the time because of rebels fighting in the countryside. He wrote us, "I must go up to Vahun to share this news with our people. Even if I'm ambushed along the way, I'll die in peace." He stopped in every village and went to each hut in Vahun, spreading the word and showing the photos.

After our year in Liberia, Ben Jr. became a world citizen. He was very active in Model UN, a high school reenactment of the United Nations and the issues it faced. After earning his doctorate, he worked in Indonesia for the Harvard Institute for International Development, where he met his dark-haired wife, Susan, who was of Italian descent and a graduate of Harvard Business School. It was a great joy for Ben when Ben Jr. became a professor teaching economics at the University of the Pacific in Stockton, California. We enjoyed a number of trips there, which included sightseeing in San Francisco, driving down Route 1 along the Pacific Ocean, and touring the Hearst Castle.

Ben Jr. is currently the deputy director of the Office of Multilateral Development Banks in the Office of International Affairs in Washington, DC. Like his father, he assesses things before he speaks. I so enjoyed visiting him at his office in the US Treasury next to the White House. He and Susan have blessed me with 3 marvelous grandchildren: Luke, Julia, and Jacob.

As the middle son, Joe was the buffer between the oldest and youngest—the same position I had among my sisters. His love affair with cars began at a very early age. When he was 5, we were traveling with my parents and he called out the name and model of each car as it passed. We were astonished, and I asked him, "Where'd you learn all those cars?"

He said, "I just watch 'em."

With his photographic memory, he's the personal archive of the family. Early on, he was strong-willed and, at the same time, sensitive and caring. As a toddler, he sang very well, surprising our babysitter at Christmas when he burst out with the "Hallelujah" chorus while riding in the grocery cart.

In junior high, he excelled at playing the piano, and I attended his performances as part of the St. Cecelia Society. My heart burst with pride as our family listened to his many beautiful musical pieces; Dad videotaped some of them.

In high school, he bought a series of used cars. In his junior year, he was awarded a summer scholarship to General Motors Institute, later working for GM as an intern during his senior year. He received a full scholarship to the University of Florida just as we were moving there. He finished with a bachelor's degree in psychology at the University of South Florida in Tampa.

After graduation, he made the insurance industry his career, later moving to Chicago. He owns his own condo, which is decorated in 1950s style. As a bodybuilder, he's in the best shape of the 3 boys. In recent years, he found his true love in photography, specializing in cars and their design. He carries his camera with him everywhere he goes and has the uncanny ability of spotting a classic car and capturing it in motion in the split second in which it speeds past.

Like his Dad, he's "Mr. Charm." Another description might be "party animal." He's a great Chicago tour guide and knows every bus and subway. He's currently an insurance underwriter for CHUBB on the 62nd floor of the Willis (formerly Sears) Tower. What a view! I enjoy visiting his Presbyterian Church.

Peter, the baby, is a caring family man. He's sentimental but competitive; from a young age, he was scrambling to keep up with his brothers. Full of antics, he's "Mr. Personality Plus," his creativity displayed in his unique model clay figures. He was our pet lover and made our house a menagerie of tropical fish, a ferret, and a series of hamsters, including 6 babies at one time. Of course, there were our 2 cats as well. He collected odd things, such as California Raisins merchandise, neon beer signs, and the grill of a Peterbuilt freight truck that sat in his room.

In junior high school, he excelled in the Flint Youth Theatre, participating in a number of performances. He played the baritone musical instrument and sang in several summer chorus programs. When we moved, he enrolled in the International Baccalaureate Program at Ft. Myers High School and spent his junior year as a foreign exchange student in Spain.

He received a scholarship to the University of Florida, and in his junior year, he spent a semester in Denmark. We visited him there, and he showed us a wonderful time. A treasured picture shows him standing with his arms around us on an arched bridge in Copenhagen. One Christmas, he delighted me by driving me around our neighborhood in his VW convertible to see the lights while listening to James Brown's "Funky Christmas."

Peter followed in his Liberian grandfather's footsteps when he became a lawyer specializing in international law. His graduation from NYU Law School in Greenwich Village was a source of great pride and joy. It was interesting to be back in New York City after all those years. While he worked at the Watergate in Washington DC, he met his blonde wife, Amanda, a Michigan farm girl who was a graduate of Amherst. Ben and I danced to our love song, "Let It Be Me," at their wedding reception. Amanda is a registered nurse, and she and Peter have given me my precious Mali and Morlu.

He is currently an attorney in Ft. Myers and keeps tabs on me. He and Amanda are active in our Lutheran church, and I tear up when he gives me communion. As a conscientious "people person," he's a bulldog in defending the helpless. Of the 3 boys, he has his father's passion for the Mende people and supervised the well and latrine construction projects in Liberia after Ben's death.

A light-skinned black woman once told me, "Your sons will probably marry white women because they'll be looking for their mother." Her prediction was correct, but I'm not sure they were looking for me. My 5 grandchildren can all pass for white. One of the reasons I wrote my story is to keep alive their African heritage.

My family is now the joy of my life. I'm pleased with my sons' achievements and the women they married. As a mother, I share in their successes and struggles as if they were my own. One of my most cherished comments came from my mom when she told me, "You're a good mother." Some days I was. Some days I wasn't. Through it all, I loved them without reservation.

Ben enjoyed 4 grandchildren before he died, and I used to quote to him Psalm 128:6: "…. may you live to see your children's children." He fed Luke as a toddler by mashing green beans between his fingers like the Mende women. He waited, smiling, while Julia ran into his arms. When we babysat Mali, he always greeted her by saying, "And how are *you*, Mali?" He held Morlu in his arms many times. However, my little Jacob, with red hair and dark brown eyes, came along afterward.

EPILOGUE

A relationship changes you and yet, you are still you.
—Kate McGovern

8931 Crest Lane, Ft. Myers, Florida, 2011

In my walk-in closet is a photograph on canvas of us walking and talking on the beach. It hangs on the wall next to the urn of Ben's ashes on a shelf. Nearby is our wedding picture, and the one taken for our book jacket. There's also a memorial plate from Mount Zion Baptist church in Athens, Ohio, with a picture of the pastor who married us.

In the photo on the beach, Ben and I are going toward the water as if walking into the sunset. Each time I look at it, I'm transported to that happy day when we celebrated our 40th wedding anniversary. I will again hang it by my bed when the pain of missing him lets up.

Ben and I walking the beach on our 40th wedding anniversary

My life is forever characterized by 3 stages: before Ben, with Ben, and after Ben. His death was the end of our love story. We were married for 40 and a half years, and I thank God for every hour, day, and month of that time. We had a good marriage that got better as the years went by.

God used my husband to show me the world, and I was never the same again. He became my life—not only giving me a whole new view of things but also sharing and strengthening my faith. Despite our many differences, our walk with God was the foundation of our marriage. Over time, I became immersed in who my husband was—his love, his people, his ideas, and, most of all, his faith. After his death, I had to experience a cutting away of my identity from his. I had to find the way back to myself—discover who I was without him. In time, I've learned that God will work out His will—whatever that may be—and I've learned to accept that. I realize now that He has a plan for my life, just as He had a plan for Ben.

I've grown tremendously in my faith as I've had to seek the Lord and rely on Him as never before. God was so real to me in my pain, and I no longer have nights when I can't sleep because of grief. In His time, God ushered me out of the waiting room of grief, but I had to be still and know that He is God.

I've reached the ability to be alone and to appreciate it. I'm no longer frantic to sell my house. My extra heartbeats are still there. In some ways, it seems as though Ben died yesterday. In other ways, I'm fully aware of the passage of time and all the changes in my life since then.

For the past 3 years, I've kept 2 of my favorite pictures of Ben next to my computer. In one, taken on our 30th wedding anniversary, he's wearing a suit and tie and has a confident expression on his face. The other, taken at a Walmart photo studio, captured his charming smile. On the wall above was a photo of him in his chief's gown in Vahun. I've moved the pictures near his ashes, but he remains a part of my life and identity.

I admire my husband for not forgetting his Mende and Gbandi people. In his farewell letter to Somalahun, he wrote, "Since I've been diagnosed to die, I feel comfortable for myself but sad for all of you. I feel glad because I'm going home to Jesus Christ, my Lord and Savior, where I will live forever. I feel bad for leaving you because I've been praying for all of you, all these years, that you may have the joy of knowing Jesus Christ because He died and was resurrected for you, too. I pray that you will really come to know Him before it's too late. He's ready and willing to accept you just as you are."

Before he died, he told me, "I want my ashes spread in Vahun and Somalahun."

I said, "You never fulfilled your dreams for Liberia. Perhaps, like King David, whose son Solomon built the temple, one of your sons will carry on your work."

He said eagerly, "Will you carry on my work too?"

At the time, I couldn't say yes. I thought, *I've already given you my life. Will I have no life of my own?* I answered, "I want to serve God with the days, months, and years I have left."

Shortly before he died, he said, "I want part of my ashes mixed with yours when you die." I choked back the tears.

He had other final requests regarding Liberia. In 2011, I wrote in a church newsletter, "Money was raised at the dinner which honored Ben. There were also memorial gifts. Together, these funds were earmarked to fulfill his wish for a well and a men's and a women's latrine in Vahun as well as Somalahun. Thanks to your generosity, these projects have been completed—Ben living on through you. A special thanks to Peter, who supervised the funding, as well as the development director of the church in Liberia."

Liberia today is very different from what I knew. Unfortunately the ravages of war have exacerbated its problems. A dear friend who lived there for 30 years told me at one point, "There's no authority system in the country. The chiefs had all the power. What they said, got done. During the civil wars, boys had guns. Liberians resent being told what to do.

"There's no internal accountability, and the idea is to do as little work as you can get away with. The philosophy of Liberia is to be a big man—to get someone else to do the farm work. People live by depending on NGOs [nongovernmental charitable organizations]. The wars have made the culture of dependency and corruption even worse."

To their credit, Liberians have taken over the Lutheran spread of the gospel. The people of Vahun have returned from the refugee camps, and there's a new church, although smaller than the first. There's also a little congregation in Somalahun. The Mende and Gbandi people remain my family as Liberia continues to rebuild after massive destruction, which has taken an enormous physical and human toll. I pray for them and continue to do what I can. During my year in Vahun, my childlike trust in God was based on naïveté. Now I have witnessed God's faithfulness through the years to us and to the Mende and Gbandi people. Writing my story has been a journey of faith in itself, as it has made me reflect on and recount all that God has done for me throughout my life.

This book is a classic example of "All in God's hands. All in God's time." A year and a half after Ben died, I was depressed and lonely, wondering where my life was going—or not going. I seemed to be spinning my wheels. God brought me to a point where I had to say, "Lord, if it's Your will that nothing happens with Ben's book and I never write my own story, then I accept it."

Shortly after that, in God's perfect way, He gave writing back to me. In an article about Ryan O'Neal's book about Farrah Fawcett, Ryan said, "Maybe this was my way of trying to bring her back. At least it was a way to stay connected to her." His sentiment resonated with me. I read another article about longing to say "I love you" one more time or wishing you had held your loved one once more. It stated, "You did all those things over and over. You just need to remember them." I told a young widow about my discouragement in promoting Ben's book, and she said, "What's the sequel?" Soon after, a friend told me, "We want to hear your side of the story."

Writing a memoir is reliving the past—the good, the bad, and the ugly. This book is my tribute to God's love and our love. Writing it was a way of making peace with my memories in order to move forward. In fact, if God had not taken Ben home, I wouldn't have written my story to honor our love.

We were far from perfect. We had our sins, our struggles, our failures. And yet our relationship is a testament to God's grace. He orchestrated the events in our lives together, preserving us, using us in our own small way to fit into His big plan. God has taught me through Ben's death to rely on Him alone. I no longer have my life with Ben, but I still have my life with God and my family. I am content to be a widow since it would be impossible to recreate my marriage—to find a man like Ben and be young and fall in love again.

I'm 67, having lived in Florida 20 years—almost as long as my married life in Michigan. I can't believe it's been 3 years since I've heard Ben's voice. I'm content in my house with its memories of him. I'm in a place of peace rather than tragedy. Although he will always remain in my heart, I realize I must go on. I am enveloped by the community of my peers—single white church women—the bond of Christianity and widowhood transcending all others.

I'm active in women's Bible studies and prayer groups. I spend time with my children and grandchildren. I've learned that suffering has meaning only when we turn to our Lord in faith, trusting Him in the midst of our lack of understanding. God uses our pain to bring out the best in us. In obedience to Him, we die to self, rising to love and serve others. Through my story, I want others to know that hearing each other out is cathartic. Racial and cultural slights can be eased by sharing, which generates not only awareness but also empathy between groups. As I continue to explore what God wants me to do with the rest of my life, one thing is certain: I'll always carry Ben in my heart.

We were an example of "West meets Africa" personified. My life with him was more than a marriage. It was an education and adventure wrapped into one. He allowed me to escape my narrow cultural confines and embark on my journey from farm girl to global citizen, with plenty of missteps along the way. My world was one of extreme pendulum swings because of him. I met the president of Liberia in the Executive Mansion ... and slept in a mud hut. I visited European capitals ... and lived in a remote African village. I flew in huge airliners … and was carried through the high forest in a chief's hammock.

Through it all, what grounded me was Ben's love and faithfulness, along with seeing God's purpose in our lives. In the end, Ben gave me the greatest gift—a love for Liberia and, indeed, the people of the world. I wish he could read my book. I think he would be proud of me.

Not long before he died, he inscribed a farewell message in my copy of *Slaves to Racism: An Unbroken Chain from America to Liberia*, the book we wrote together in every sense of the word.

> My dear Nita,
>
> Our story is told in the book of Genesis 2:21–25. God made you for me and only for me. Otherwise, we would not have been able to overcome the obstacles before we married. This book is a lasting witness of your true love for me. You are a beautiful girl, and there were many men who would have fallen in love with you. But the Lord said to them, "No, not this one. She is preserved for my servant, Ben."
>
> This book would not have been possible without our lives together over 40 years, our academic training, and our travels together. All have been laboratories of observation and experience. What is more, our love and trust with true faith in our Lord Jesus Christ has truly made us one. I thank God for you and for your love. Please remember me when you read this.
>
> Sincerely yours with all my love,
> Ben.

On each wedding anniversary, we listened to "Let It Be Me." Over the years, at later stages in our marriage, I reread our love letters—a glimpse back in time. In mine to him, I was amazed at my naïveté and how little I knew of life. After 29 years of marriage, I destroyed them because they were something sacred between us. For many years, I saved the coat-and-dress ensemble he bought me at Lazarus, as well as his horrible green bathrobe and clasp briefcase—precious memories.

It's wonderful to love and be loved; to share a man's life, his hopes and dreams, his bed, his children, and, most of all, his faith. Love often comes in unexpected packages. If I had to do it over again, I'd still sign up for Anthropology 101.

ACKNOWLEDGMENTS

Writing is always a collaboration. As an author, you need other eyes to point out clarifications needed and better ways to express your thoughts.

Many thanks to my supporting audience—dear friends and relatives who read my manuscript in various forms and gave their honest opinions: Jan, Anna Lou, Kim, Reta, Sue, Gwen, Dianne, Ardith, Theresa, Mertice, Polly, Ann, Irma, Jeanette, Michelle, sisters Sandy and Joanna, cousins Diane and Jane, and finally, Barb, my brother-in-law's sister. A very special thanks to Jan, a true friend who patiently and faithfully read my story more times than she ever wanted to, each time offering valuable editing advice along the way, as well as much-needed encouragement!

My greatest gratitude goes to Jesus Christ, the hero of this story, who brought me forth on this earth in time and space, forgives my sins, and lives with me each day.